# LAND
# HEALING

Physical, Metaphysical, and Ritual Practices
for Healing the Earth

## DANA O' DRISCOLL

**RED**Feather™

MIND | BODY | SPIRIT

4880 Lower Valley Road, Atglen, PA 19310

Library of Congress Control Number: 2023941051

Cover & Book designed by Danielle D. Farmer
Cover & interior Illustrations by Dana O'Driscoll
Type set in Larken/Bressay/Articulat CF

ISBN: 978-0-7643-6770-0
Printed in China

Published by REDFeather Mind, Body, Spirit
An imprint of Schiffer Publishing, Ltd.
4880 Lower Valley Road
Atglen, PA 19310
Phone: (610) 593-1777; Fax: (610) 593-2002
Email: Info@schifferbooks.com
Web: www.redfeathermbs.com

# DEDICATION

## To Karen

# SPECIAL THANKS!

This book is dedicated to Karen Biconik, healer, permaculturist, and lover of the land. Her light shined so brightly in all whose lives she touched and her legacy lives on through green, growing things and through the soil web that she so carefully regenerated.

Special thanks to Robert Pacitti for his ongoing support, gnomish insights, and whimsy. Thank you to Catronia McDonald for her wonderful collaborations in developing the chanting magical framework explored in Chapter 4, and to the Mid-Atlantic Gathering of US Druids (MAGUS) gathering for being a conducive space for our land healing and blessing rituals to take place. Special thanks to Lillian Wolf whose teachings on animism, sovereignty of all beings, and respectful interactions helped me deepen my practices as a land healer. Thanks to my sister, Amanda Rae, who spent time with me on the palliative care rituals on our own family land. Special thanks also to Michigan Herbalist Jim McDonald for his teachings on the lightbulb and water jar, both of which I drew upon for Chapter 9. Elmdea Adams was kind enough to share her vision boarding technique with me. Finally, a very special thanks to the entire team at Shiffer/REDFeather, especially Peggy Kellar and Chris McClure, for their vision, enthusiasm, and dedication in bringing this book into the world.

And most of all, special thanks to you, the reader, for being willing to pursue this sacred and important work at a time when it is most needed.

# CONTENTS

Preface..................................................................................................7

*Chapter 1:*

TAKING UP THE PATH OF THE LAND HEALER........................ 8
    The Idea of *Healing*.......................................................................9
    Why Land Healing Critically Matters, Here and Now ...................... 11
    As Above, So Below: Understanding the Energetic, Physical,
        and Spiritual Planes................................................................ 14
    A Framework for Land Healing ................................................. 16
    Where Healing Can Happen: Understanding Ecosystems
        and Healthy Places................................................................. 20
    Being Drawn In or Seeking Out Sites for Healing............................ 25
    Frameworks and Perspectives Used in This Book ............................ 26

*Chapter 2:*

THE LAND HEALER'S CRANE BAG: TOOLS FOR HEALING........ 28
    The Crane Bag.......................................................................... 29
    Sacred Timing for Magical Crafting....................................................... 30
    Herbal Offering Blend ............................................................... 31
    Herbal Blessing Oil .................................................................. 35
    Healing Waters ......................................................................... 36
    Healing Sigil Set ....................................................................... 36
    Seed Balls................................................................................. 40
    Other Ritual Tools .................................................................... 45
    You as a Tool............................................................................. 46

*Chapter 3:*

BUILDING TRUST: LISTENING, OBSERVATION, WITNESSING,
AND APOLOGY .............................................................................47
    Deep Listening and Observation................................................. 48
    Acknowledgment and Witnessing............................................... 53
    Apology.................................................................................... 56
    Remembrance .......................................................................... 57
    Settling In................................................................................. 59

## Chapter 4:

ENERGY, RITUAL, AND LAND BLESSINGS..........................................60

The Microcosm and Macrocosm............................................ 61
The Work of Land Blessings................................................. 61
Tree Blessing Ceremony....................................................... 64
Growth Sigil Empowerment ................................................ 66
Understanding Energy: The Seven Elements....................... 66
Seven-Element Land-Blessing Ceremony............................. 71
The Sphere of Protection: Using the Seven-Element Framework ... 75
The Sphere of Protection: Invoking the Six Directions ...................... 76
Opening Up a Sacred Grove: Stepping between Matter and Spirit. 79
Raising or Lowering Energy.................................................. 81
Distance Work and Levels of Energetic Connection ............ 83

## Chapter 5:

ENERGETIC LAND HEALING ................................................86

Approach 1: Working with the Seven Elements and Visualization ... 88
Approach 2: Land Healing through Chanting Magic ......................... 89
Approach 3: Sacred Fires and Smoke Prayer Bundles...................... 96
Approach 4: Land-Healing Mandalas.................................... 100
Approach 5: Setting and Blessing Standing Stones for Long-Term
    Land Healing........................................................... 103
Approach 6: A Full Season of Rituals: Infusing with the Blessing
    of the Sun ............................................................. 105
Dealing with Large-Scale Land-Healing Issues: Fires, Floods,
    Pollution, and Climate Change........................................ 107
A Vision of a Healed and Abundant World............................ 110

## Chapter 6:

ENERGETIC PALLIATIVE CARE............................................. 113

Deepening Our Understanding of Palliative Care............................ 114
Protection and Self-Care..................................................... 116
Working with Sites That Will Be Destroyed ....................... 117
Working with Sites That Are Suffering or Damaged ........................ 123

Advanced Work: Pain Management, Energy Moving, and
    Herbal Allies..................................................................................... 126
Palliative Care for the Waterways ....................................................... 131


*Chapter 7:*

PHYSICAL LAND HEALING..................................................................... **136**
Physical-Land-Healing Primer: How Do I Know What to Do? ...... 137
Fostering Ecosystems............................................................................ 140
Putting It All Together: What Should I Do? ...................................... 146
**Approach 1:** Wild-Tending Practices ..................................................... 146
**Approach 2:** Engaging in Conservation and Replanting Work........ 149
**Approach 3:** Creating Refugia ............................................................... 152
**Approach 4:** The Grove of Renewal....................................................... 155
**Approach 5:** Reestablishing Guardianship ......................................... 160


*Chapter 8:*

WORKING WITH PLANT AND ANIMAL SPIRITS WHO PASS... **161**
Holding Space and Remembering Life That Has Passed................. 162
Honoring Those Who Have Gone Extinct........................................... 165
Helping Spirits Pass and Psychopomp Work ..................................... 170
Stories of Death and Passing................................................................ 171
Psychopomping the Anthropocene ..................................................... 173


*Chapter 9:*

SELF-CARE AND LAND HEALING ....................................................... **177**
Care for Self: The Inner Light and Healing the Land...................... 178
Developing a Spiritual Self-Care Plan ................................................ 179
Care for Our Bodies: Managing and Understanding Stress........... 182
Cultivating Self-Care Practices for the Body..................................... 184
Cultivating Self-Care Practices for the Mind .................................... 186
Cultivating Self-Care Practices for the Spirit.................................... 191
Sacred Days and Self-Care Retreats.................................................... 193
Conclusion ............................................................................................. 197

Afterword: A Vision of a Healed World ................................................199
Suggested Reading..................................................................................201
Endnotes ..................................................................................................203

# PREFACE

**This book is a gift.** It is a gift to this great Earth, the land that sustains us, a planet that is in increasing trouble and increasingly needing more of us to work to reverse this destructive course that humans in industrialized cultures have chosen to pursue. Anyone who takes up this book and decides to do any of this work is offering their own gift of land healing, of their time, of their commitment, and of their energy. It is also a gift to support the good work that numerous organizations are working toward. My own proceeds from this book will be donated to the following organizations: United Plant Savers, Western Pennsylvania Nature Conservancy, and the Rewilding Institute.

Finally, I have created a network of people who are choosing to take up the work of land healing to network and support each other. Here is a URL to learn more: www.thedruidsgarden.com/landhealing/.

# Chapter 1:

# TAKING UP THE PATH OF THE LAND HEALER

**There's a reason you picked up this book.** Perhaps you've watched as wild spaces you frequented as a child have been turned into strip malls and housing developments. Perhaps you are sick of feeling powerless when you see a tree cut down and wish you could do something. Perhaps you are worried about the larger ecological challenges that we are facing as a world: pollution, habitat loss, and extinction of species. Perhaps you want to do more for nature, to find ways of reciprocating and giving back, and see land healing as a good opportunity. Whatever your reason, this book is here to help you: to offer perspective, tools, methods, and ritual for engaging in a wide variety of physical and ceremonial land-healing work.

By land healing, I mean healing any aspects of nature that are under duress from direct and indirect human actions: landscapes, forests, waterways, species, and individuals under threat, and more. I use the term "land" to describe these broadly in this book, but the techniques can be used for nearly anything, such as rivers, forests, deserts, and urban areas. By healing, I mean this in the broadest sense—offering wholeness, repair, and blessing when the situation warrants it, but also offering relief from suffering and passage for those lost, as needed.

For those of us practicing a nature-based spiritual path, living in the twenty-first century can be both amazing and challenging. On one hand, various traditions of nature spirituality offer us a growing awareness of the earth and her many inhabitants. On the other hand, this same deep connection can make us much more sensitive to the challenges present by the age of the Anthropocene (the new global "age" we are now in, which is characterized by human-driven climate change, ecological destruction, and mass extinction of species). While human-driven concerns are planet wide, they also affect us locally in a myriad of ways. As practitioners of nature spirituality, we may feel the strong need to "do something" to help the land that surrounds us or land that is faraway and under distress. "Doing something" can include physical actions and mobilizing on the physical level—through political and personal action. But "doing something" to nature-based spiritual practitioners can also include a variety of ceremonial, ritual, and energetic work. This book focuses on the latter, with the understanding that both are necessary. This book focuses on things that individuals can do physically, and energetically, to help heal our lands and waterways and to support the earth's many inhabitants. This book also provides strategies for the harder stuff—offering practices for land that will be damaged or destroyed such as through logging, natural destruction, forest fires, and working with land spirits who pass. Thus, this first chapter explores this concept of land healing: what it is, what it isn't, who might do it, how it may be included in any nature-based spiritual perspective.

This book contains techniques that I have developed over a period of seventeen years while walking the druid path, and a lifetime of experiences with physical and spiritual land healing. For physical-land healing techniques, I bring to this work a background in permaculture, regenerative agriculture, and ten years of practice on two different homesteads, both requiring extensive physical land regeneration. For spirit techniques, these are techniques that I have developed from a synthesis of spirit teachings and frameworks from the druid tradition. They may not all work for you—the point of this book is to offer you this work as a guide to you in developing your own methods and adapting what works in this book for your own purposes and path.

# The Idea of *Healing*

Let's begin by exploring what is meant by "land healing" or "Earth healing." If we explore dictionary definitions of the word "healing," they generally fall into two categories: first, "to patch up a breach or division," and second, being "restored to health" or making something once again "sound and whole."

Both definitions are directly applicable to land healing and offer us useful perspectives. First is the larger issue of patching up a division; we have a massive division between humans and nature, which I would argue is directly perpetuated by the dominant narratives of Western civilization. The challenges we face with degraded lands in need of healing aren't individual problems; they are cultural, historical, and interconnected. With the rise of the myth of progress, consumerism, and a growth-at-all-costs model as dominant global forces, the land is largely seen and treated as an exploitable resource to extract and use, rather than something sacred to build a relationship with, care for, and protect. Author Wendell Berry[1] writes about this in his *Unsettling of America: Culture and Agriculture*: we have choices between working to engage in "nurturing" practices that support the wholeness and health of the land, or engaging in "exploitive" practices that degrade and damage the land. Even if we aren't actively exploiting the land, we are still benefiting from that exploitation. As Berry and others argue, modern humans have disregarded the need to nurture the land and instead pursue wealth. But humans have not always had this relationship with nature. As authors such as M. Kat Anderson describes beautifully in *Tending the Wilds*, Indigenous cultures had a reciprocal relationship with the land. Anderson describes how Indigenous Californians tended their lands carefully, ensuring abundant harvests and monitoring the health and vitality of the land. I believe that what land-healing work can offer those of us taking up nature-based spiritual paths, of all kinds, is helping to "patch up" that breech that many of us have culturally inherited. Thus, this work helps us overcome the "division" and engage in nurturing and healing.

The second definition is more specific: we have many lands in a damaged state and needing to be made "whole" and "restored to health." But what does "restored to health" really entail? You might think about it this way: a person who has been the victim of a violent crime requires healing on multiple levels. There are physical wounds you can see, but there are also wounds that are nonphysical. The physical wounds have to be treated in a much-different way than the nonphysical ones, and treating only physical wounds will not make the person "sound or whole." This same concept can be applied to land healing as a specific spiritual practice. Thus, when we discuss land healing, we are thinking about working on the land, physically or energetically, to help restore that land to health as well as restore and strengthen our own relationship to the land at the same time.

When it comes to physical wounds on the earth, however, the challenge is that in the current paradigm, land ownership determines all rights and responsibilities. Certainly, if you own your own land, you can prevent more damage from happening and engage in regenerative practices to support the health and healing of the land (as covered in chapter 7 of this book). However, in most cases, many of us find ourselves in the hopeless place of watching things happen to the land that you wish were not occurring. But as nature-based practitioners, ownership doesn't account for connection, nor does it account for the fact that all land—regardless of ownership—has a spirit and a right to live. Part of the reason that this book exists is to help people with this exact problem: how to do something to help the land when we do not have physical power over what is occurring. In order to "do something," then, we need to more deeply understand the different ways we might intervene as nature-based spiritual practitioners.

Thus, land healing refers to physically or energetically mitigating harm, restoring to wholeness, and rebuilding connections and facilitating passage for those who need it. Land healing is a holistic approach that includes physical, metaphysical, and personal healing work.

# Why Land Healing Critically Matters, Here and Now

Taking up the path of a healer of the land—of the earth itself, ecosystems, waterways, deserts, your own backyard—is more critical than ever because of the challenges we face in the twenty-first century. All of us can probably easily witness the call for doing land-healing work in our local areas: a forest or tree friend being cut, spraying, pollution in the skies or waterways, the loss of species that you used to see, and so on. Here are some of the many reasons that this work is important:

**Tending that which is sacred.** What is nature spirituality without nature? If we are going to hold something sacred, it is right and ethical that we tend it and work to preserve it. Right now, given the state of nature, there is a lot of healing and preservation work to do. If we begin to treat the land as sacred from a perspective of daily practice, we begin putting our practices and daily life in line with our values. Different people have different abilities and opportunities, and thus this book offers both energetic and physical ways of land healing.

**Deepening connections with the land and her spirits.** If you are interested in establishing deep connections with the land surrounding you, this is a clear path forward. It creates a relationship and reciprocity, where you are giving as much as you are taking from the land. Learning about how to tend and heal nature in multiple ways allows you to share with the spirits local to you and gain their goodwill and trust. Spiritual connections deepen when you work to heal.

**Inner and outer tools for the twenty-first century.** Land healing as a spiritual practice is good work to do, offering you the opportunity to "do something" and engage in positive change. Land healing as a framework that I'm expressing here encompasses not only physical regeneration but also energetic work and self-care. Thus, it offers several tools that work together to help you bring balance and harmony to the land—and to your own inner spiritual life. And I think, given where this world is unfortunately heading, we are all going to need these tools to bring balance, harmony, and wisdom to our own practices and the world around us.

**Offering a new path forward.** Ultimately, humanity must develop a different paradigm if we are going to survive beyond the next 100–200 years. A paradigm not based on consumption, growth at all costs, and greed but, rather, one built on building a healthy and sustaining relationship with nature, based on care rather than greed. That work starts today, now, with each of us in our own way. Learning a path forward that allows us to sustain and enrich our earth mother.

**Healing the soul.** I remember a day when I just wanted to take a quiet walk in the woods. It had been a very difficult day at work. I picked a new trail in our local forest and set off. My hike turned in an unexpected direction as I came across many fracking wells, all of which had only recently been installed. After coming upon the fourth or fifth fracking well on what would otherwise be this beautiful landscape, I broke down. I lay under a giant tulip poplar tree near the well, and I cried into the earth. I felt lost, as if the landscape of my ancestors had been turned into an extraction dystopia and I was stuck in the middle of it. The aftermath of that experience made me really start thinking about land-healing practices not just as something I did when I felt the need, but as one of my core spiritual practices. I needed a set of consistent tools to combat what I was seeing and to feel as if I could do good, rather than just cry about it and feel bad. This experience really helped me begin to form the framework of this book. I went back to those woods a few weeks later with my land healer's crane bag (seed balls, sigils, etc.) and rituals that I had developed through meditation. I walked up to the fracking well where I had cried, and I worked deep ritual for sleep and healing with the land here. I scattered seeds for plants of healing and light: St. John's Wort, Goldenrod, and Calendula. I could sense the land settle, the spirits calm. Then the spirits invited me to lie back down in the spot where I had cried a month before. And they gave back, this beautiful healing light, and I could feel my own stress and strain settling. It could only be described as a healing of the soul. Land-healing work offers this deep soul healing to those who need it.

**Connecting to the energies of life.** Tied to the healing of the soul, I think that part of the reason that practices such as organic gardening and permaculture design (an ecologically based system for designing indoor and outdoor spaces) are so powerful is that they connect us with nature's healing energies of life, the energy of regeneration and hope, rather than the broader problems with consumption and land destruction. When you plant and grow a seed and tend it, you are honoring life. You are bringing the energy of life into your world—and that has a positive impact on you and on the world.

**Protecting against and responding to biological annihilation.** The impetus for doing land-healing work also is global. For at least a decade at the time I am writing this book, scientists have been clear that the world's sixth extinction-level event is underway.[2] Scientists use the term "biological annihilation" to describe what is happening—since 1970, at least half of the world's animals are gone. That means that we had twice as many animals living on this planet in 1970 than we do today. This isn't some far-off future prediction. This is something that has already happened. It is continuing to happen as you read this. It has happened in the time that you have been present on this earth. A 2017 study[3] examined 27,600 land species and found that *all species* were showing extremes of population loss, even among species of the "lowest concern" with regard to the guidelines of the International Union for the Conservation of Nature. This 2017 study suggests that 80 percent of the traditional territories of land mammals have been eradicated, making way for cities, people, and shopping malls—this is "biological annihilation." The study also indicates that this trend will likely increase in the next two decades.

Another piece of this comes from the work of Bernie Krause, who wrote *The Great Animal Orchestra*. Krause's work focused on recording nature sounds, and he demonstrates that the sounds of nature are simply vanishing, along with the life and species. Further, these issues are also not limited to vertebrate species; a 2018 study showed a 75 percent decline in insects in *protected ecological areas* in Germany.[4] These numbers are but a small part of a larger picture, where ecosystems around the world—including right here in your backyard—are under serious decline and threat.

Now, put this in context of nature spirituality. While we enjoy nature's benefits and her healing, this is happening. When we are honoring nature, celebrating the wheel of the seasons, this is happening. This is part of our reality, as nature-honoring practitioners living in the twenty-first century. Given that this is the reality, responding to this in some capacity should also be part of our spiritual practices. Anyone can do this work in some capacity— since we all live on this beautiful planet, and since we all are connected to it, so too can we learn to heal our planet in whatever ways we are able.

**Reparations for ancestral activity.** The present certainly gives us enough impetus to engage in direct land-healing work—but for some of us who have cultural and ancestral backgrounds, it may offer an additional motivation. Certain cultures have a history of exploitation that has led to the situation at present, and thus some form of reparations may be necessary. I am certainly one of those people. I am a white person from the United States, and my ancestors have been in Pennsylvania since the start of colonialization. I can trace one family line back to landing on the Mayflower. My direct ancestors certainly took part in the mass genocide and removal of native peoples, peoples who were tenders of the land and had maintained the land in healthful balance for millennia. The Susquehannock who used to live right on the soil where I now reside are extinct, killed off primarily by disease (smallpox) and being slaughtered by white settlers (despite the fact that they had peaceful treaties in place). With the removal of the native peoples came the removal of the idea that nature was sacred and honored, replaced by the idea that nature was a thing to exploit and profit from to drive progress. Thus, my own ancestors were players in the three-century-long extraction and exploitation of the natural world and destruction of native peoples. The lands they stole were tended by Indigenous peoples and therefore were abundant with rich natural resources—in less than two centuries, those resources were almost stripped bare; in some counties in Pennsylvania, 99 percent of the forest cover was removed by the turn of the nineteenth century. Thus, I feel that I have an ancestral obligation to heal these lands and bring them back into a healthful place of abundance and life. I can do this work of repair, on behalf of my bloodline, for the good of these lands.

**Offering a core spiritual practice and personal spiritual path.** One of the ways you might think about this as a spiritual practice is that these practices help bring you much closer to nature. That is, as you engage in healing work on various levels, you are giving back to nature in a considerable way. This brings you into a reciprocal relationship with nature and allows you to honor her, work closely with her, and, ultimately, connect more deeply with her. You might see this work, then, as an extended offering that you provide to the living earth. Another concern here is that healing work can help us do our own deep healing. Connecting yourself closely with a piece of land you are working with, and seeing healing take place, allows you as a healer to take those same lessons and apply them within. Thus, the more work we are able to do out in the land for the benefit of all life, the more it benefits us and our spiritual path. Eventually we will belong to the land, rather than seeing the land as belonging to us.

For these reasons and probably many others, land healing is a necessary spiritual practice in this age. Anyone can practice land healing in some capacity—since we all live on this beautiful planet, and since we all are connected to it, so too can we learn to heal it. It is for these reasons that I believe that anyone who is taking up a path of nature spirituality should consider making land healing of some kind part of the core of their spiritual practice. Our land and spirits of the land need us. Our world needs us.

# As Above, So Below:
## Understanding the Energetic, Physical, and Spiritual Planes

To get deeper into our definition of land healing and explore how we might practice land healing as a technique, we need to have a framework that accounts for the different levels of reality, commonly referred to in the Western magical traditions as "the planes." Nearly all spiritual practice and magical practice are based on the understanding (explicit or implicit) of the fact that realities and energies exist outside what we can perceive with our five senses. However, just within the Western esoteric traditions, the idea of "the planes" is complex, with a number of different models describing different kinds of planes. For our purposes, we will work with the first three planes from John Michael Greer's model in *Circles of Power*, then the planes can include the following:

*The physical plane (outer)*: What we can experience through our five physical senses. This is the physical reality of our existence, the things we can touch, smell, hear, taste, and see. For the purposes of land healing, this is the physical nature of reality that we can see: a healed and functional ecosystem, a tree being cut, a lifeless river, or a seed sprouting.

*The etheric plane*: Often when people talk about "energy" in a room or space, they are sensing the etheric plane. The etheric is also experienced through our senses, but not the same senses that experience the physical plane. The etheric is very closely connected to life on Earth; Hindu yoga would identify this as "prana," while Asian martial arts would call this "ch'i" or "ki." From a land-healing standpoint, our senses of the etheric help us say, "Wow, there is a bad feeling here," or a "heaviness" or "stagnation." It's on the etheric that a lot of the "energy" work can be done with regard to land healing: raising energy, directing energy, and focusing it in various ways.

*The astral plane:* The level of our consciousness that transcends matter, although it manifests as imagination, emotion, memory, will, or intellectual facilities. This level, of course, also transcends what is inside our heads. Much journeying work (whether it's called astral projection, shamanic journeying, or path working) happens on this plane. This is also what offers us clear pathways for "distance" work (described in chapter 4).

Both the etheric and the astral are considered "inner" planes (for a variety of reasons), and there are planes other than those as well.

The reason I present the planes here is that they are critical to framing any kind of land-healing work. Energetic land healing works along the lines of the magical hermetic adage "As above, so below. As within, so without." The principle of this adage is the basis of many spiritual practices—and the adage is simple. What is on the outer reflects inward to the inner planes, and, likewise, what happens on the inner planes and within us reflects outward. Another way to consider this is with an analogy to a human being: we have a physical body, we have emotions and heart, and we have a spirit. These are all interlinked and part of one person, but each would need a different kind of healing energy. While we can work on one level and have benefit, working on any level supports the others.

This matters for the purposes of land healing. If you are to do physical healing of the land, that healing work can have a massive energetic effect as well (even if all you are doing is physical work). But even if you aren't able to do physical-healing work because the land isn't yours or you are powerless to stop something from happening, you can do many other kinds of energetic healing. This energetic healing can have a positive effect, manifesting on the material plane and providing one of the tools for the land to heal. Understanding this principle is the key to understanding the entire framework of land healing present in this book.

**Animism and spirit work.** The other core principle to understand here is that this book takes an animistic perspective on this work. An animist perspective recognizes that plants, animals, places (e.g., rivers, forests), and objects (e.g., stones, ritual tools) have a spirit and that spirit can be interacted with. An animistic perspective acknowledges that all spirits that have agency; that is, they are not just passive recipients of the world around us but are active, involved, and interwoven. An interaction between you and spirits can lead to positive impacts both for your nonphysical and physical being. Some of the work outlined in this book connects with individual spirits, while other work may connect with the larger spirits of place (rivers, landscapes, oceans, etc.). In many capacities, to be a land healer is to connect with the spirits of the land and of place and learn what they want you to do.

On the matter of respect for all beings and all lands, you will notice certain language conventions in this book. I have capitalized all names of trees, plants, and other beings as a sign of respect. This is done in the same way that one would capitalize a proper name of a human being. I also have used "they," "he/him/hers," and "she/her/hers" interchangably to describe the land and all inhabitants, avoiding the term "it." In English, "it" is typically tied to anything non-human, and creates a very problematic linguistic division between humans and all other beings on the planet. By making these language shifts, I am enacting that animistic philosophy not only in my land healing practices, but through my language.

**Recognizing the power of magic.** Using magic (the directing of will and energy) as a means of enacting physical changes upon the landscape has been around as long as humanity. The concept wouldn't be so widespread across different cultures and time if there wasn't something to it, something that worked.[5] Despite the challenges we are seeing ecologically, *you are not powerless*. We must shed that sense of powerlessness if we are to help the land and her spirits come through this age. An inner sense of empowerment is particularly critical for land-healing work—if you go into the work saying, "I'm not going to make a difference, but I'm going to do this anyway," then you infuse your work with "I'm not going to make a difference." If you go into it with the attitude of "I'm going to help heal and protect this land," then that is what you infuse your work with. Anyone, anywhere, can do this work. What matters here is a willingness to learn, to grow, and to engage in the work of healing. With that said, there are some techniques in this book that are very advanced and should not be attempted by new practitioners (I have indicated clearly when this is the case).

Now that we have a basic framework for what is meant by "land healing" and some possibilities for action, we can dive into the different kinds of land-healing work that those practicing nature-based spiritual paths can accomplish.

# A Framework for Land Healing

Examining the above definitions and understanding the planes has given us a road map of the kinds of healing that can be done on different levels. Thus, land healing can include the following larger categories: Physical land healing (prevention, physical land healing, and self-care) and metaphysical land healing (land blessing, energetic land healing, and palliative care).

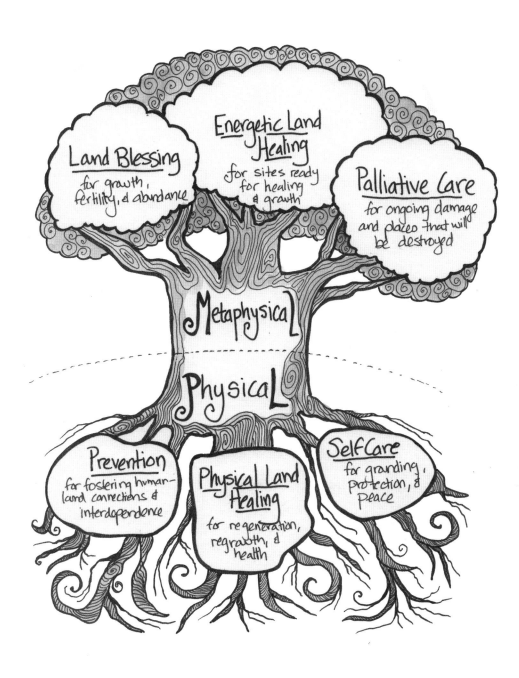

Land Blessing
for growth, fertility, & abundance

Energetic Land Healing
for sites ready for healing & growth

Palliative Care
for ongoing damage and places that will be destroyed

Metaphysical

Physical

Prevention
for fostering human-land connections & interdependence

Physical Land Healing
for regeneration, regrowth, & health

Self Care
for grounding, protection, & peace

# WORKING WITH LAND, SEA, AND SKY:
## PHYSICAL REGENERATION AND PHYSICAL LAND-HEALING PRACTICES

Physical regeneration refers to the actual physical tending and healing of the land on the material plane. Most ecosystems we live in are degraded due to human demand throughout the last few centuries, and all life is at risk. One of the most empowering things you can do is to learn how to heal ecosystems directly, whatever environment you live in: urban, rural, suburban. These practices are wide ranging and include many possibilities: conservation activities, regenerative agriculture, restoring native plants, converting lawns to gardens, scattering seeds, creating habitat, cleaning up rivers, putting in riparian zones, helping to shift land management practices of parks in your city, helping address stormwater issues, and much more. Thus, physical regeneration is work we do on the physical landscape to help the land heal and be restored to a functional and healthy ecosystem.

One of the things I want to stress here is that this work is available to everyone—we all are rooted in a local place with the earth beneath our feet. But the specifics of this work will vary widely on the basis of your own living circumstances and physical resources. We explore many of these specific practices in chapter 7.


## METAPHYSICAL LAND-HEALING PRACTICES

In this framework, metaphysical healing work refers to any work on the etheric or astral planes that is focused on bringing in healing energy, removing suffering, or helping spirits pass. There are several basic types of energetic healing you can do, depending on the state of the land and what its future holds.

### LAND-BLESSING PRACTICES
The first layer of metaphysical work with the land is land blessings. Ancient peoples engaged in many such blessing ceremonies to ensure the health and abundance of the landscape around them—both for the benefit of the land itself and for the survival of everyone who depended on the fertility of the land. This is a form of energetic work that raises positive energy for the good of all. We consider these practices in chapter 4.

### WITNESSING, HOLDING SPACE, HONORING, AND APOLOGY
Part of the larger challenge we face in today's world is humanity's collective ignorance and lack of willingness to pay attention to what is happening to the world, the ecosystems, the animals, ourselves. Thus, choosing to engage, choosing to witness and hold space, and choosing to listen to the spirits of the land are preliminary to most other land-healing work. Being present, witnessing, holding

space, and offering an apology are examples of work that each of us, regardless of where we are in our own spiritual practices and development, can offer. Chapter 3 offers entry into this work, while chapters 6 and 8 offer more-advanced practices.

## ENERGETIC HEALING: RAISING ENERGY TO HELP HEAL THE LAND

In this framework, energetic-healing work refers to any work on the etheric or astral planes that is focused on bringing in healing energy or removing suffering. There are two basic types of energetic healing you can do, depending on the state of the land: energetic healing and palliative care. Let's return back to our idea of a sick human to put these two in perspective. One sick person has recently undergone a long illness but is now in the place to recover. This person might need a lot of visits, good medicine and healing food, and positive energy—they are on a path to recovery. But you might think about another person who has been engaged in a long illness with an ongoing disease, and they are continuing to suffer, with no relief in sight. In this second case, the best you can do is try to soothe the wounds and let them rest until the worst is over. Energetic healing, as illustrated by the first case, can take place when lands are in a place to heal. Palliative care, however, should be used for places with ongoing suffering/pollution/death or for sites that will soon have serious damage. Thus, we use energy techniques in both cases, but in one case the goal is alleviating suffering, whereas in the other case the goal is active healing, and thus the intention of the work is very different.

Energetic-healing techniques, covered in chapter 5, are used when the land has been damaged but is in a position to heal. These techniques raise energy, bring blessing and protection, and work to help spirits with the healing process. These techniques include chants, rituals, and more.

## PALLIATIVE CARE: ENCOURAGING REST, SLEEP, AND DISTANCE

As just described, the opposite of energetic healing is palliative care—and unfortunately, much of our world right now needs this kind of support. To return to our sick-person metaphor, this is a person who has been engaged in a long illness with an ongoing disease, and they are continuing to suffer. The goal here is to soothe the wounds and encourage rest until the worst is over. Palliative care should be used for places with ongoing destruction or for sites that will soon have serious damage or be destroyed. It should be used for animals and species who face death. We cover these practices in chapter 6.

## HELPING SPIRITS PASS

Sometimes we can't save a forest, an animal, a tree, or even an entire species. While not everyone is called to psychopomp work and helping spirits pass, some may find it necessary to engage in this work as part of their land-healing path. Chapter 8 covers ways of working not only with individual spirits but with extinctions and other large-scale events.

## HEALING HUMAN-LAND CONNECTIONS AND FOSTERING INTERDEPENDENCE

Prevention is the best medicine, as the common saying suggests. Another consideration for land-healing work is to address that first definition of healing; that is, to "repair the divide." For generations, culturally, particularly in the West, humans have been moving further and further away from nature and deep connection. Many humans in the twenty-first century have almost no connection to the land and thus, I believe, are not willing to step in to prevent further damage. Thus, part of land-healing work can involve us building and healing human-land connections, both within ourselves and in our larger communities. All the work in this book brings light to these issues.

## SELF-CARE FOR LAND HEALERS

A final critical point involves our own self-care as land healers. Digging oneself into this work involves being faced with damaged ecosystems, places that you don't want to see, statistics that you don't want to read, and experiences you'd rather not have. It involves taking a hard look at our own behavior, the behavior of our ancestors, and engaging in self-critical reflection on "automatic behaviors" in our culture. It involves experiences that can drain you and leave you raw. This all takes its toll. Thus, a final consideration for land-healing work is our own self-care, and how we can connect with nature to form reciprocal healing relationships. Chapter 9 offers self-care practices for land healers.

# Where Healing Can Happen:
# Understanding Ecosystems and Healthy Places

The Earth, on the largest level, is an interconnected system and web of life. As we move further into climate change, we are starting to see how true this really is: what people do in New York City can have a strong effect on the melting of glaciers in the North Pole and Greenland. What acid mine drainage pollution goes into a river in western Pennsylvania makes its way to the Chesapeake River and the Atlantic Ocean. This concept—that Earth is a whole and interconnected system—is critical for understanding land healing.

Earth is made up of many smaller ecosystems. An ecosystem is a biological community of organisms that are interconnected and depend on each other for life; ecosystems include both the biological community as well as the physical environment. Many different ecosystems exist, with several major types: forests, grasslands, desert, tundra, freshwater, and marine. These can be broken down into much more specific ecosystems based on the latitude, geology, soil composition, water composition, altitude, topography, and larger climate patterns. Regardless of where you live on Earth, you will live in an ecosystem, or on the border of more than one. It's useful to learn what your dominant ecosystem is where you live, so that you know what a healthy ecosystem looks like. For example, here in western Pennsylvania, we live in a forest-dominant ecosystem that has

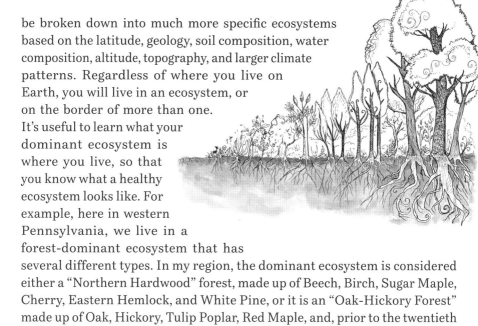

several different types. In my region, the dominant ecosystem is considered either a "Northern Hardwood" forest, made up of Beech, Birch, Sugar Maple, Cherry, Eastern Hemlock, and White Pine, or it is an "Oak-Hickory Forest" made up of Oak, Hickory, Tulip Poplar, Red Maple, and, prior to the twentieth century, American Chestnut.[6]

All of nature works toward "ecological succession," a process by which an entire ecosystem changes and grows, eventually reaching something called a climax community. Climax communities are stable ecosystems that have a diversity of species and nutritional and energy balance, are tolerant of environmental conditions, and have the kinds of species that are stable and do not change. This ecosystem thus is diverse, tolerant, and abundant. We can understand this concept better simply by considering what would happen if a person stopped mowing their lawn. If they lived along most of the northeastern part of the US, ecological succession would eventually move that lawn to a Northern Forest. Immediately, the grasses would grow tall, along with any other plant life currently inhabiting the lawn, such as ground ivy, docks, plantain, dandelion—most of these "pioneer" species are well adapted for growing in disrupted ecosystems. Within the first few years, we'd see seedlings from shrubs and trees take root, spread by the wind, birds, and animals. For a long time, this lawn would be a field populated by sun-loving annual and perennial plants, but with each year, the trees and shrubs would get taller. As these plants started producing seeds, berries, and foliage, animals—including larger animals—would return, since there would be food for them to eat. Eventually, those small tree seedlings would start to grow tall, discouraging full-sun perennials and grasses and shifting to part shade as the trees filled out their crowns. These first short-lived trees (birches, perhaps) would dominate. Within fifty years, depending on local conditions, the tree canopy would cover the entire area, allowing the soil to retain water and cooling the temperature on the ground. Woodland, shade-adapted species would then dominate the forest floor.

Within about 150 years, the canopy would change, offering more-long-lived hardwoods and reaching the end of ecological succession—the climax community. Thus, it is not a single species that causes ecological succession, but rather an entire community of species working together in an interconnected web of life. Where I live, the only places I see like this are ones under some kind of permanent protection: state parks, conservation areas, or other protected lands. If you enter these places, you'll of course notice the energy first: they are calm, restful, very vitalizing places to return to again and again. They are vibrant, alive, and functioning at their peak. There is ample food and habitat for wildlife. Everything in the ecosystem is cycled in perfect balance.

Of course, not all spaces are able to house a climax community. It might be that I can support a very healthy ecosystem in my garden, but I don't want a mature Northern Hardwood forest producing full shade (thus making it hard to grow lettuce and kale). But in order to support a more robust ecosystem and a diversity of life, my garden contains not only healthy vegetables for me, but various annual and perennial flowers and fruit to support insect and ecosystem diversity. Thus, we might think about healthy ecosystems not only in terms of ecological succession but also in terms of supporting life and diversity—of producing food (nectar, pollen, berries, nuts), of producing habitat, and of supporting the larger soil web. For example, a carefully tended bee and butterfly garden of wildflowers may never reach climax, but it still can support a wide diversity of life. Likewise, a community park with rain gardens and cultivated native plant meadows certainly supports life—and human interaction with nature. Thus, there are lots of ways that we can have "healthy" ecosystems, and they are almost all considered in terms of the amount of diverse lives that ecosystem can support. This, then, can be one basic metric for understanding our world around us and seeing the world through the perspective of a land healer: a diverse and abundant ecosystem is a healthy one.

And this "supporting life" is critical in the age of the Anthropocene. In the last few centuries, we've seen the growing dominance of humans at the expense of other life. Modern notions of land ownership in the Western world suggest that an "owner" of the land has the right to do anything they like to that land; none of the other life on that land has any rights. Thus, the owner can cut down trees, put up buildings, pave soil, or do anything else they deem fit. Because there is never acknowledgment of the fact that other life currently lives there or an honoring of spirit, it is a particularly challenging situation. Thinking about nature as something we own and can do what we want with, of course, has gotten us into the current predicament and has caused the eradication of half of all life on Earth since 1970. Obviously, things cannot indefinitely continue as they are.

Most of the human-dominated spaces around us are, unfortunately, not spaces set up for honoring and supporting other life. The typical lawn is one such suppression zone: the lawn was created by removing whatever life was growing there (or artificially maintained by draining aquifers of resources, as in the case of the desert areas). The lawn is regularly mowed (consuming fossil fuel resources and polluting). The lawn is often regularly sprayed to prevent any nongrass life-forms and offers nothing for most life in terms of food or habitat. The same can be said about many human-dominated spaces: a strip mall parking lot, a conventional cornfield, a suburban community, a local bank. All human-dominated spaces, without exception, were once healthy ecosystems and likely in a balanced state as part of a climax community. This isn't to say that cohabitation and the supporting of diversity and life can't happen even in human-dominated spaces: all over the world, people are converting lawns to gardens and wildlife sanctuaries, planting more trees in cities and parks that support diversity, creating ecovillages, setting up nature preserves, and generally working to develop and support more-healthy ecosystems. Still, this more ecologically friendly habitation is more the "exception" than the norm, and so there is so much healing to be done.

In the end, the major takeaways are these: Earth as a whole is a single interconnected system, and as land healers, we can work with any part of that system energetically or physically and help offer healing. We will always be working at a local level, within one or more ecosystems, but through doing so, because Earth is all interconnected, we benefit all of the Earth through our efforts.

Given the above, we might think about the many places where healing can happen. Here are just a few:

*Physical spaces*: Physical spaces are those where nature can begin to renew, growing ecosystems over time. Often, physical change happens in places where we have some control over (land we own or that others we know own), land where we have some influence (public lands, workplace lands), or spaces nobody cares about (e.g., abandoned city lots).

*Human-dominated spaces*: We can do palliative care for human-dominated spaces, particularly those functioning under "business as usual" practices, helping the spirits of the land rest and be at ease. This is particularly useful for sites whose spirits are not at rest.

*Damaged natural spaces*: Natural and wild spaces that have recently had some damage (or have had damage over a long period of time) are good places for land healing. These are spaces that may have repeated logging, forest fires, drought, or other issues. Depending on the issue, you might use a combination of physical healing and energetic healing.

*Sites of pollution or extraction*: Particularly challenging and necessary healing work can take place at sites where resources are being extracted from the earth: strip mines, conventional mines, sites for logging, factories that are polluting, etc. This is another very good place for palliative care.

*Ecosystems*: You can work on healing on the level of ecosystems, supporting them physically or energetically.

*Bodies of water*: Bodies of water are increasingly under duress in the twenty-first century. Healing work at the source of rivers and at oceans, lakes, springs, and streams is all work that can be done.

*Healing for species or specific animals, invertebrates, fish, birds, plants, trees*: Land healing isn't just about working with places and spaces, but also about working with the inhabitants of the land. This might be working with a single animal, plant, or tree or for larger work on the species-wide level.

As I was making the final revisions on this manuscript, I visited a forest that is very dear to me: a 6-acre, old-growth Eastern Hemlock grove at Laurel Hill State Park in western Pennsylvania. I was shocked when I entered the grove—a number of the ancient trees had fallen, their enormous root systems leaving huge holes in the earth, and their absence leaving large patches of light in the canopy above. I counted the rings on one of the trees that the park rangers had cut to preserve the path through the forest: at least 275 years old. I sought the spirits of the place to see what healing needed to be done and how I could be of service. They needed nothing from me and were content—the energy of the forest had been what it always was. The spirits explained it clearly: these trees had died a natural death from a microburst or small tornado that had come through. They would not be removed but would be allowed to decay naturally, Hemlock Reishi mushrooms breaking down their bodies and mosses covering their bark. After many years, they would fully return to the forest, their nutrients being endlessly cycled. The Eastern Hemlock grove needed no help because the trees died naturally, and it had taken place without any human intervention.

Thus, where land healing is usually warranted and necessary is when humans have direct or indirect negative impact on the land. While these ancient trees did not need any assistance from a land healer, the forest that was logged a mile away would need such assistance, because humanity disrupted the natural life-and-death cycle of that forest. The trees were cut, they were not allowed to return naturally to soil, and the cycle of the forest was broken. Since humans caused the damage, so could spiritual and physical healing be greatly aided by human hands. I think this is an important distinction, and much of this book rests on this premise: we provide healing and repair to help mitigate and address a host of human-caused damage to the natural world. That is where we are needed most and where we can do the most good. To be clear, even many natural disasters now (tornadoes, droughts, floods, hurricanes, etc.) are caused by human-driven climate change and large-scale changes to the ecosystem, and thus, are also important sites of healing. This isn't to say that you can't do land healing on "naturally caused" issues, but the overwhelming amount of damage that humans are currently causing to the natural world leaves us plenty of opportunity to intervene where we are most needed.

# Being Drawn In or Seeking Out Sites for Healing

I remember the first time I saw the hill overlooking the highway. I was driving to work from my new homestead, and right in that moment the clouds opened up and a ray of sunshine descended upon the hill. The experience was powerful. All that week, each time I drove past the hill, I saw some sign from nature: three hawks flying overhead, a spiral of birds flying over the hill, or simply a slight glow to the hill if you looked at it from a certain angle. The next week, I drove to the other side of the hill and found a big-box home improvement store parked there. I had found a grassy hill stuck between a busy metro highway and a home improvement store! But I knew I had been drawn to that place for land-healing work. Nature had called me to that specific spot.

Often, this is how the work of land healing goes. Just being open to experiences, paying attention to what is happening, and paying attention to messages from nature can lead you on fantastic journeys. This requires us to be open to seeing and interpreting the quiet call of nature. In the case of my hill, I ended up working with the place for a full ritual year. I was asked to take a handful of soil from the hill and place it on a bowl on my home altar. I chose to house the soil in a handmade ceramic bowl that I had made some years before, with beautiful carved vines. I was told to come back at the solstices and equinoxes and take another handful of soil. I did so, and I left offerings each time at the hill. After doing so, I returned to the hill over a year after I had originally gone there. At that point, I was asked to never return, since the hill was going to sleep until a different time, and that sleep would span my lifetime. As a last request, I was asked to take that soil to the most sacred place I knew. Eventually, I left that soil at the roots of an ancient Hemlock tree. The next day, after I finally emptied the contents of the thick ceramic bowl, it inexplicably broke into many pieces, and I knew that whatever healing I needed to do was done. When I drove past the hill after that, the hill was just an ordinary hill, the magic of the place gone into slumber. In this case, all that the hill needed was someone to take notice, to come in, and to listen. To this day, I don't exactly know why I was asked to do this work—and that's okay. The ways and reasons of spirit are not always known to us. As land healers, we are in service to spirit—that service doesn't always come with an explanation.

Often, you will feel some kind of draw to a space. The place might not be a wild space, such as a forest or quiet beach, but rather a space right there in the middle of the suburban sprawl. The place may not even be accessible, such as the soil beneath your apartment building. Pay attention to these calls and offer yourself in service.

*Feeling the need.* Other times, like in my opening story for this chapter, it is you who feels the strong need to do something—to work with a new space or to be in service. This may require you to "prove" yourself in some way through some of the other techniques here in this chapter. For example, when I was driving to a friend's house to visit, I had to go a different way than my normal path due to a road closure. As I drove along the road, there was a tall embankment on my left that I could not see beyond. As I passed the embankment, I had this horrible feeling in my stomach. I looked on an aerial map of the space when I got home, and I found out that behind this embankment was a gravel pit. Wanting to do something for the gravel pit, I approached. The gravel pit was so angry that the pit wanted nothing to do with me. I then engaged in the deep-listening techniques described in chapter 3 to see if I could build a relationship.

## Frameworks and Perspectives Used in This Book

All of us also may have a personal path into the work of a land healer. I want to close this chapter by sharing mine, so that you can understand what I draw upon and the work that is present in this book.

When I was a child, my cousins and I spent as much time as we could in the woods behind our house. We lived at the top of a mountain in the Alleghenies, and the woods stretched down into the valley and seemed to go on forever. Each day, we'd make our way deep into the woods. There, in the bottomlands, grew the mysterious Eastern Hemlocks. They were majestic, a perfect place to build a cabin or play fort. In the woods were many enormous rotting stumps. Each of the stumps was a world unto itself—insect life, lichens, and multiple kinds of moss. On the stumps also grew a particular reddish shelf mushroom with a white underside, which we called fairy mushrooms. The forest also had these old roads—we called them spirit roads. They seemed to go from nowhere and lead nowhere, but we would follow them. As children, we didn't understand what we were seeing—the remnants of the history of a forest that had been repeatedly logged. When I was fourteen, the loggers returned. For weeks, I could hear the cry of the chain saws. I would stand on the edge of the forest, looking down, wanting to go save my trees. But my parents forbade it, and I could only sit up on the top of the mountain and hear the chain saws and the machines. For many years after that, I couldn't bear to go into the forest because I didn't want to witness the destruction. Almost a decade later, after taking up the druid path, I finally dared to return to the forest. It had changed, with many of the trees I knew and loved gone. But the forest was also still the same—the smaller Hemlocks rose to take the old ones' place. The birches rose up in large thickets to help heal the land. The springs and streams were still there, the stones unchanged by time. And there were the stumps. In that moment, I realized what the "fairy" mushrooms of my childhood were—they were *Ganoderma Tsugae*, the Hemlock Reishi, one of the most medicinal mushrooms in the world. Nature's response to the logging was to grow healing mushrooms, to adapt, and to thrive. The forest was still there, and each day it was regenerating. It was a profound awakening moment for me, the first steps on the path that would turn into a lifetime of spiritual practice of land healing. I made a promise to myself that I would not look away from the suffering of the land ever again, and I would use this experience to help heal other places. These are the kinds of stories that often draw us into land healing—seeing the land and her inhabitants suffer—and wanting to do more.

My own background is varied, and this work draws from a number of traditions. The core tradition that it draws from is revival druidry and the druidry and frameworks practiced by the Ancient Order of Druids in America (aoda. org), a tradition that works in a multitude of ways at connecting with and working with nature. Specific to this tradition is a seven-element system. The seven elements, explained in more depth in chapter 4, include the four traditional elements (earth, air, fire, water) and three aspects of spirit (above, below, and within). These elements are a useful framework for land healing, since our earth is made up of a combination of these elements and their connection to spirit. It is also useful since many individuals walking pagan paths are familiar and work with some form of four-, five-, or seven-element system.

The chapter on physical land healing and some of the practices offered for developing tools for crane bags comes from my long-term study and practice of permaculture design. Permaculture is an ecologically based design system that works with nature to help build better gardens, communities, cities, and relationships with nature. Considering permaculture's role as a spiritual practice was explored extensively in my first book, *Sacred Actions: Living the Wheel of the Year for Earth-Centered Sustainable Practices* (REDFeather, 2021). To this work I bring experiences as a certified permaculture designer, certified permaculture teacher, and someone who has been actively practicing physical-regeneration techniques on two homesteads for over ten years.

Finally, this book assumes an animistic framework as described above. Animism in its most-simple terms is a belief in spirits. It's a belief that the land and the many inhabitants of the land have both physical bodies and metaphysical agency—those spirits of the land can interact and engage with you, and that work done for the land is done both for the physical side of beings as well as their metaphysical side. This framework does not require the omission of others, such as in polytheism or monotheism, but does require some basic understanding that the world is full of spirit, is alive, and is an "enchanted" place. Thank you so much for joining me on this journey!

# Chapter 2:

# THE LAND HEALER'S CRANE BAG:
# TOOLS FOR HEALING

**I remember a time** I was at a home improvement store only a few days before Christmas, and I felt myself drawn to a particular part of the store. Following the call, I rounded the corner and found myself in the aisle with all the live Christmas trees that the store was still selling. The trees were not likely going to be sold, loved, or decorated at this point in the year, only a few days before Christmas; these were the leftovers, the trees that never would leave the store and would probably end up in a dumpster by the week's end. These trees desperately wanted my help, but there were people all around the store—I could hardly perform a ceremony for them. What I sensed they needed was sleep and passage (see more on palliative care in chapter 6). So I quietly reached into my purse, where I always carry a small bag of healing sigils, blessing oil, and a tiny bag of offering blend. I tucked two of the sigils firmly into the branches of one of the trees—sleep and passage. The magic of those sigils had already been established. All that I was doing was activating them and placing them where it needed to be. The trees were thankful and the sigils did their work, long after I left the store. The sigils also connected me back to the store, so when I was at home, I could do some distance work on their behalf. Without my little healer's crane bag, I may not have been as prepared, or effective, for this work.

The term "crane bag" comes from Irish mythology.[7] Manannán mac Lir is a powerful sea god and guardian of the otherworld. One of his many treasures is a magical bag, known as a crane bag. He originally crafted the bag from the skin of a crane; hence the name. This wonderful, bottomless bag was full of many treasures, including human language and the ogham, a magical Celtic tree alphabet that is still in modern use. Today's crane bags, often used by those in the druid tradition, are bags full of sacred objects, magical objects, or ritual tools.

While a skilled land healer recognizes that skills and knowledge are the only tools they truly need to work magic, land-healing work can be enhanced with the right set of tools. Thus, this chapter focuses on how to construct your land healer's crane bag and create a number of different healing tools that you might include in your bag.

Part of what your crane bag does is prepare you for the "quiet" work of a land healer, the kind of work described in the opening story to this chapter. As we'll explore in this book, there are a lot of different kinds of work that we can do as land healers—from powerful group rituals to quiet prayers. Once you are attuned to the work of land healing, you will often find yourself getting requests for help in unexpected places, as my opening story demonstrates.

It may take you some time to gather up the supplies that end up in your crane bag, and you certainly don't need to start by creating them all. Likewise, your bag is likely to go through some changes as you deepen your practice as a land healer. See it as an evolving set of spiritual tools that help you do your land-healing work. We'll now turn to some specific things that you can make and include in your land healer's bag.

## The Crane Bag

The bag itself is an important consideration. Crane bags can be made from any material (e.g., leather, cotton, wool, canvas), can be of any size or shape, and can contain any number of things. A healer's crane bag is as unique as you are! My current healer's crane bag has two parts: a little pouch with a pinch of offering blend and healers' sigils, and then a larger bag with my ritual tools, blessing oil, healing waters, seed balls, Japanese hori hori knife / saw / digging tool, and representations of the elements.

I would suggest before picking out a bag or constructing your own bag that you might read through the rest of the chapter and plan out what you want in your bag and your goals. See the options present in this chapter, and consider what else you might want to include. You might also consider the size of the bag. Will you take your bag with you everywhere? If so, that might suggest that you keep a plain bag and keep everything compact so you can tuck it in a backpack, purse, or pocket. You can also create two bags—a large one with all your tools and a small one for carrying with you everywhere. Where will you be using your bag? Under what conditions? These kinds of questions will help you start to envision your own unique bag.

One of the things I want to stress with all the tools here in this chapter is that as part of land-healing work, you want to work to honor the earth and minimize your ecological footprint. Thus, if you want a crane bag, try finding one used rather than new. Support a local artist working with more environmentally friendly products rather than a big-box store. Learn how to make your own bag out of an old leather couch you found on the side of the road. My point here is that a good bag is not only functional but also intentionally low impact toward the land. Honor the materials you work

with for your tools and bag, recognizing that they come from the land and may have been harvested under less-than-ideal circumstances.

If you are going to be doing a lot of wild tending and seed scattering, a larger backpack or day pack that you can easily take onto the land with you is a good choice. If that seems too big, work smaller. One of the things I like for a simple healer's kit is a small toiletry travel bag. You can fit a lot into one of these bags; they are very easy to find used, and they pack well into larger bags. You can also use a fanny pack or leather belt pouch that can be easily strapped about the waist. One friend of mine made a little leather pouch for his belt, and he wears it every day, thus taking his tools with him everywhere he goes.

Even if you aren't going to carry all your tools with you all the time, do consider having something pocket sized for when you are out and about. I have a few smaller land healer's kits that go with me when I'm out. I have made a kit as small as a rectangular breath mint tin that I can stick in my pocket, full of blessing oil, healing water, and land-healing sigils. I also have a few small cloth bags that I can keep with me in a purse, suitcase, or backpack and that can travel with me.

## Sacred Timing for Magical Crafting

Before we start making anything for our crane bag, it is wise to use sacred timing to give your spiritual tools additional empowerment. The sun, moon, and turning of the stars all exert influence on our surroundings (as the practice of astrology demonstrates). A part of many of the traditional peoples across the world was an understanding that certain times were more beneficial than others for certain work.

*The path of the sun.* The path of the sun, which some in the neopagan traditions recognize as the "wheel of the year," can offer us many times of power, both on a yearly and daily basis. To raise energy or empower something, using one of the major times of power, the solstices or equinoxes or the cross-quarter days (those days that come directly between a solstice and equinox) are excellent days. Different times of the year have different energy and, depending on where you live, may not be consistent with the wheel of the year in other places. You can learn this just by looking outside your window: when the landscape is covered with snow or ice and things appear asleep or dead, that's likely a good time to make tools for sleep, remembrance, or apology. When you look out your window and you see the land full of vibrancy and life, it's probably a good time for energetic healing and raising energy. As a rule, when the sun is in the light half of the year and in the holidays in that time (Beltane, May 1; summer solstice, June 21; and Lughnassadh, August 1), this is the best time for any kind of energizing, blessing, or healing work. When the sun is at its lowest light of the year—where I live, this would be between Samhain (Nov. 1), winter solstice (Dec. 21), and Imbolc (Feb. 1)—this is the best time for palliative-care work. The two equinoxes, fall (Sept. 21) and spring (March. 21), are days of balance and transition and are thus good for any work you want to do. Daily, the same cycle of light and dark can be used—it's better to empower something and raise energy by the light of the sun at midday than it is as the sun is setting. Of course, you might not want to wait till the summer solstice in nine months to craft something for your crane bag, so we can also use other approaches.

*The path of the moon.* Just as the sun has its yearly and daily cycle, the moon has its monthly (twenty-eight day) cycle when it comes from a place of darkness (new/dark moon) and into fullness (full moon) and back to dark. As with the path of the sun, the time period between dark and full (the waning moon) is good for raising energy, with the best time being at the full moon itself. The time between full and dark (the waxing moon) is good for removing energy. This is useful to land healing, since so much depends on whether we are looking to infuse land with energy or slow that process down. Thus, it's useful to make blessing tools on a full moon, but it would be better to make sleep tools on a dark moon.

*The path of the planets.* The turning wheel of the planets and the celestial heavens provide us yet another layer of influence and require more advanced knowledge than the paths of the sun or moon. You can certainly learn to work with the planets astrologically in the same fashion as I'm suggesting above. For more on this approach to fortuitous timing, I suggest starting with learning about the astrological approach used in biodynamic farming and picking up a yearly planting calendar or farmer's almanac.

# Herbal Offering Blend

Having something you can use for offerings is an absolute cornerstone of your land healer's crane bag, and if you make nothing else from this chapter, I strongly recommend that you make an herbal offering bag. A bit of background is helpful here to know why this is the most critical tool in your bag. Traditional cultures made offerings and rituals regularly to the land to recognize the interdependency of humans on the land and to help promote abundance and vitality of the land. The making an offering, particularly of a plant blend you have crafted yourself, demonstrates that you understand and respect this cycle of reciprocation, and is a way to directly honor the land and her spirits. Thus, reestablishing these traditions is a step toward helping us rebuild our relationship with the land as those who tend and regenerate it, rather than simply take from it. Thus, I have found offerings to be a central gratitude practice that helps deepen relationships and trust with the land and her spirits.

At the same time, I also recognize that many offerings we might go out and buy are simply not acceptable for this kind of work. A bottle of wine at the store, for example, may have came from a vineyard using chemicals to grow their grapes, was transported with fossil fuels, and has been handled by many before getting to you. I believe it's thus important to create "zero impact" offerings, ones that I can forage or grow myself, so that I can eliminate the vicious cycle of consumption that is causing our lands so much harm.

I would suggest working with the herbs you have access to in abundance or those you feel drawn to, and working to create your own blend. Intuition goes a long way here. One of the best ways to make a herbal offering blend is to walk through a garden (your own or someone else's that you have permission to be at) and let your intuition draw you to certain plants. Harvest small amounts and use this as a basis for your healing blend. If you don't have access to a garden, you can gather whatever you can find that will work (such as leaves coming off the trees in the fall). You can also grow much of what you'll need in a windowsill.

In terms of meanings or what plants to use in your blend, I again encourage you to use your intuition here. While it is certainly okay to look things up in books, remember that you are working in a local ecosystem as a land healer. What is written from traditional herbals may or may not apply to your specific ecosystem or circumstance; for example, if you live in North America, many of the Old World herbs may have different energies or functions upon the landscape. I prefer to use a combination of material from other sources, such as herbal books, as well as observing the plants in their ecosystem, and deep-listening work with the plants themselves,[8] to create my blends (do research the plants you are using, however, to make sure you aren't using anything toxic or poisonous such as poison ivy or water hemlock). Here are some more specifics about how to obtain plant material for your offering blend:

*Gathering material.* At a time of power (full moon, at the solstices or equinoxes, on another day of spiritual or magical significance), go out and gather aromatic plant material. Aromatic plant material is that which has a high concentration of volatile oils. When you crush the leaves of a plant or needles of a conifer and you can smell that wonderful smell, this is an aromatic plant. You can gather your plant material from a variety of places, such as a cultivated garden, an abandoned lot, an edge space, a field, or a forest. Before you gather your material, ask for permission from the plant and use inner listening skills to see if you can gather. You can also use homegrown and dried materials from your garden that are wild crafted. Make sure you leave an offering.

*Purchasing material.* If you purchase your material, make sure it is organic and ethically sourced. You don't want any chemicals in your blend. Chemicals on the landscape are damaging to nature, and thus we don't want to create magical tools from anything that has harmed nature. There are a number of ethical online retailers that tell you not only where plant material came from, but the conditions under which it was harvested or grown. Beware that overharvesting can come from wild harvesting. You may also want to add some essential oil to your blend, but recognize the enormous amount of plant material that goes into each drop of oil and make sure the oil is ethically sourced.

*Making a locally based blend.* Part of the reason that the land is suffering is that humans have been sourcing materials from all over the world, without much attention to how and what those impacts might be on the ecosystem. Thus, many traditional spiritual supplies, including white sage, palo santo, sandalwood, frankincense, myrrh, sweetgrass, and more, are all currently at risk due to overharvesting and overconsumption. Thus, you will not find any of these kinds of ingredients in the blends I am suggesting here. Instead, what I suggest is that you make an herbal blend that is based on what you can find that grows abundantly and locally and —just as importantly—from plants that will work with you as a land healer. Your own backyard and bioregion have plenty of plants that can be used to make these kinds of blends. I'll offer a list of plants that might be good for this work that grow in bioregions both in Europe and most of North America:

- **Garden herbs that offer healing and protection:** Sage (*Salvia officinalis*), Rosemary (*Salvia rosmarinus*), Thyme (*Thymus vulgaris*), Lemon Balm (*Melissa officinalis*), Lemon Verbena (*Alysia citrodora*), Oregano (*Origanum vulgare*), Marjoram (*Origanum majorana*), Bay Laurel (*Laurus nobilis*), Catnip (*Nepeta cataria*), Mint (*Mentha* spp.), Chamomile (*Chamamelum nobile*). Most of these herbs have been working with humanity for millennia both as cooking herbs and medicinal herbs and will gladly join you in your healing work.

- **Plants and trees that produce petals that will make a wonderful oil infusion:** Rose (*Rosa* spp.), Apple blossom (*Malus* spp.), Cherry blossom (*Prunus avium*)

- **Field herbs that offer protection, vision, and direction:** Mugwort (*Artemesia vulgaris*), Yarrow (*Achillea millefolium*), St. John's Wort (*Hypericum perforatum*), Wild Bee Balm (*Monarda* spp.), Goldenrod (*Solidago* spp.), Aster (Asteraceae spp.)

- **Tree herbs that offer strength, consistency, and vitality:** Pine (*Pinus* spp.), Eastern Hemlock (*Tsugae canadensis*), Spruce (*Picea*), Black birch (*Betula lenta*)

- **Plants and trees that are not aromatic in nature but offer resiliency and strength because they are "first responders" in situations where ecosystems are trying to regrow:** Ground Ivy (*Glechoma hederacea*), Dandelion (*Taraxacum officinale*), Burdock (*Arctium* spp.), Yellow Dock (*Rumex crispus*), All Heal (*Prunella vulgaris*), Plantain (*Plantago major*), Chickweed (*Stellaria media*)

In the Americas, Tobacco is a traditional offering and one that is often responded to quite well by the spirits of the land. Unfortunately, that sacred plant has become an unwelcome addiction for many. One of the jobs I see as a land healer is to help reestablish sacred relationships, including with specific plants that have been abused. Thus, I grow my own Tobacco (a sacred strain called *Nicotiana rustica*) and use that in my offering blend. You can grow a little bit of it in a pot on a sunny windowsill or in a small patch of garden (it doesn't need much space). In colder climates, it self-seeds. I would not recommend purchasing commercial Tobacco, due to the larger Tobacco industry's environmental record. You might feel differently about Tobacco and can thus make an herbal-offering blend with any plants that you feel connected to.

The offering blend that I currently use is as follows: *Nicotiana rustica* tobacco (homegrown and harvested at a sacred time), Rose petals (wild harvested, usually from multiflora rose that grow abundantly on our land), Lavender and Sage (grown in my garden, harvested at a sacred time). Sometimes, I will add other materials to the blend.

*Making your blend.* After you have selected and obtained your herbs, make sure they are all fully dry (any dampness will likely make your blend go moldy). You will want a small bowl, a mason jar, sharp scissors, and a small bag or pouch for inside your crane bag. What I like to do is to create a larger jar of my blend and then add a small bit to my crane bag. I refill this as necessary.

Begin by opening up a sacred grove, as described in chapter 4. Next, begin to crush up your herbs with your hands and chop them up with the scissors. As you do so, sing to the herbs, thanking them and putting a bit of your own energy into the offering blend. For my blend, I would sing, "Tobacco that connects to spirit, Rose that protects and defends, Lavender that soothes and heals, Sage that empowers and blesses, thank you for your aid." Mix your blend up until you are satisfied. Thank the plant spirits for their aid. Close out your grove.

# Herbal Blessing Oil

An herbal blessing or healing oil is a simple magical tool that you can make that directly comes from the living earth and is a wonderful addition to your crane bag. The herbal-blessing oil can be used in a variety of ways, including blessing seed balls, doing candle magic, or leaving a small bit of oil in a place where other kinds of magical work are not able to be done (e.g., in an area that has a lot of people nearby). Use the herbal instructions and insights presented under "Herbal-Offering Blend" for how to gather and obtain herbs. Here are a few blends that I have used in the past for land-healing herbal blessing with great effect:

- **A healing blend for vitality and strengthening:** Black birch (inner green bark) (*Betula lenta*), Wintergreen leaf and berry (*Gaultheria procumbens*), and Mint (*Mentha* spp.)

- **A blend for healing and protection:** Lavender (*Lavendula* spp.), Lemon balm (*Melissa officinalis*), and Rosemary (*Salvia rosmarinus*)

- **A blend for connecting to and strengthening spirit connections:** Mugwort (*Artemesia vulgaris*), White Pine (*Pinus* spp.), Burdock root (*Articum* spp.), and Sage (*Salvia* spp.)

To make your oil, you will need a pint jar or other glass jar and some shelf-stable oil (a good-quality olive oil or fractionated coconut oil work well) and your herbs for the oil. Dry your herbs before moving on (even a few days on the counter should do the trick).

Open up a sacred grove, using the techniques described in chapter 4. Using a pair of scissors or a mortar and pestle, break up the large plant material / grind up the plant material. As you grind or cut, offer a chant, calling to the plants. For example: "Birch of new beginnings, Mint of soothing, Sage of awareness, please offer your healing!" Next, loosely pack the plant material into the jar. Now, take a good-quality olive oil or other shelf-stable oil and pour the oil over the plant matter until it is completely covered. Thank the plants for their assistance. You could say something like "Birch, Mint, and Sage, thank you for your healing power." At this point, you can raise additional energy for the healing oil, through drumming, singing, dancing, or even visualization work (many techniques can be found in chapter 4). Close your sacred grove.

Put your oil in a place out of direct sunlight and allow it to macerate for a full moon cycle. Then, strain the herbs, making sure to get all the herbs out of the oil (plant matter will make your oil go rancid faster). If you want, add a few drops of essential oil at this point. Give it a label. Your oil is complete and ready for your crane bag. You might keep a larger jar on the shelf and a smaller vial of oil in your bag, refilling the vial as necessary.

# Healing Waters

Because many natural springs and old wells have such strong connections both to the energy of the earth (telluric current) and the element of water, both of which are healing in nature, a vial of healing water is extremely useful for a land healer's crane bag. Sacred waters are vital to have if you live near waterways and intend on doing healing work with any bodies of water. The simplest approach to gather your water is to find a clean local spring[9] or visit a sacred spring if you are able to find one on your journeys. You can also collect clean rainwater, use snow, collect water from clean waterways, or find any other water source that you deem to be clean and pure. Collect your water on a day of power if at all possible. When you arrive at the spring, state your intention and make an offering to the spring of song, herbs, drumming, and so on. Then, in a glass jar, collect your water. Use a glass jar, because glass will retain the pure energy of the water better than plastic.

For healing waters, you want only waters that are pure and unpolluted. You can research this but also energetically sense it. Put your hand in the water, connecting to the vital life energy there. How does it feel? How does it taste when you drink it? (Obviously, you want to drink from it only if this is a spring that people drink from, and has been indicated to be safe.) Do you feel vitalized and refreshed? If so, this is probably good water to use. I live in an area with a lot of fracking, so finding springs is a challenge—but I have a few, including one that provides a lot of spring water regionally, and I use those regularly as part of my healing practice.

Storing and using your sacred water also deserves some consideration. If the spring or water source is local and you can regularly gather from it, you can just use and replace the water as needed, storing the water in a glass jar in a cool, dark place when not in use and refilling the vial in your crane bag as needed. But if you have only a small amount of sacred water and it is hard or impossible to get back to the source, you can create a "mother" water. For this, take a larger glass jar and fill it with clean water. Now, place only a few drops of the sacred water (3, 7, or 12 are good numbers) in the jar. When it runs low, just add more clean water, forever replicating your sacred water energetically. Yet a third option is to create a "mother" water of many different water sources that you have gathered, using three drops of each source, and adding to it over time. Any of these will create a wonderful sacred water that can be used as a tool in your healing practice.

# Healing Sigil Set

A healing-sigil set offers you a powerful set of healing tools, one that I suggest putting into your crane bag and also carrying with you on your person through daily life. These are sigils I developed specifically for land-healing work; they were developed primarily through meditative work and sigil creation techniques adapted from Jan Fries's *Visual Magick*. The exception to this is the protection sigil; for at least 5,000 years, the pentagram has been a protective symbol, and I adopt it here for protection. You are welcome to use these sigils or create your own. You can also use runes, ogham, hermetic sigils, or another magical system—just make sure you fully understand what energy you are drawing upon for your healing work. Part of the reason that I decided to create new sigils is that the challenges that we face right now are unprecedented, and I wanted that unique energy put into the sigils for very specific purposes. Images of the sigils are found on page 39.

The sigils described here will take some time to make. You have to decide what material you want to use, then inscribe them at a fortuitous time. Each of the sigils should be empowered with rituals, each at their own time. If you do all these steps, you will have a very potent set of tools, tools that can be used in a variety of land-healing circumstances, including quietly around people or in busy areas, for the kind of quiet magic that we often have to do as land healers. See your sigil-making practice as an initiating journey in its own right, a process to help you create the tools that can be used effectively.

Seven Land-Healing Sigils:

- **Blessing:** A sigil that offers a blessing—positive energy for an unspecified purpose. The energy in this sigil can be used for whatever purposes the spirits of the land need.

- **Growth:** A sigil that offers growth energy. This sigil can be used in areas where replanting is happening, at the base of a tree you have planted or anyplace else where that specific energy of growth is needed. I use it primarily in conjunction with physical land-healing and planting techniques.

- **Healing:** A sigil for damaged lands/animals/places that need a strong dose of healing energy. This sigil jump-starts that healing and begins the process of repair. You can use it in conjunction with growth or on its own.

- **Protection:** A sigil that helps protect a place, to preserve that place and to prevent it from coming to harm (or further harm).

- **Sleep:** A sigil that helps put the spirits of the land and the awareness of the land to sleep; a deep palliative-care technique to be used when suffering will continue in the foreseeable future. It is most appropriate for sites that are actively being damaged, repeatedly (e.g., fracking sites, mountaintop removal, logging, polluted streams).

- **Acknowledgment:** A sigil that conveys an acknowledgment of suffering or an apology, on behalf of humanity, to the spirits of the land. Can be used for preliminary work or for places that do not want to work with you, or for any situation where any suffering or death has happened. Apology also includes remembrance: that you will hold this place in your heart.

- **Passage:** A sigil of passage is for those who are dying or have recently died. This sigil helps spirits pass beyond the veil. This is used for extinction, situations where the death of animals, plants, insects, and so forth has occurred or will occur in the near future.

## SELECTING MATERIAL FOR SIGILS

You can inscribe your sigils onto anything that is natural and can be placed on the land without harm. I like to use a homemade walnut ink and paint the sigils onto small flat stones, small shells, or small pieces of bark, nuts, or sticks. You can also use simple wooden sticks, cut off an end with a saw, and then wood-burn the sigil into the end. Or you can cut wood rounds yourself by gathering up branches fallen in a storm and using a miter saw to slice them into small rounds. You can also use a recycled paper or even a handmade paper full of healing seeds, a variant on the magic seed ball approach described later in this chapter. A very portable set of sigils can be made with thick recycled paper—you can put one or two of each in a pouch and slip it into your pocket or bag easily. Then, your sigils are always ready when you need them.

Once you have your materials together, you can make a large number of the same sigil at once, enough for several years of use. The process of making sigils can take time, and thus I want to make sure that when I make them, I make enough to last.

## INSCRIBING YOUR SIGILS

I recommend selecting a fortuitous time to inscribe your sigils. Open up a sacred space with the intention of raising healing energy into your sigil, and put on some instrumental music that allows you to focus. Inscribe your sigils, directing intention into each sigil. Also as part of this work, I suggest you honor and acknowledge any bit of land (trees, stones, etc.) that offered materials for your sigils.

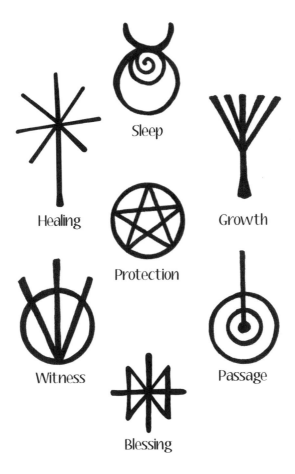

Sleep

Healing

Growth

Protection

Witness

Passage

Blessing

## EMPOWERING YOUR SIGILS

The sigils themselves hold power, but they are much more powerful if you imbue them with additional energy specific to each sigil and at a time of power. Each of the sigils can be empowered by using the rituals throughout this book. This is a list of the empowering rituals. Each of the rituals in the various chapters includes instructions on empowering your sigils.

- Acknowledgment—chapter 3, Witnessing Prayer and Chant
- Blessing—chapter 4, Land-Blessing Ceremony
- Growth—chapter 4, Tree-Blessing Ceremony
- Healing—chapter 5, Ogham Chant Healing Ritual
- Passage—chapter 7, A Blessing upon Passing Prayer

- Protection—chapter 4, Sphere of Protection Ceremony
- Sleep—chapter 5, Sleep Ceremony, Drumbeat Portion

### USING YOUR SIGILS

Throughout this book, I'll be sharing a variety of specific ways to use and incorporate your sigils into land-healing work. Here, I'll share some general ideas and suggestions for all the sigils. The first thing is to carry your sigils with you wherever you go and whenever you travel. If you make some paper-based ones as I am suggesting, you can put them in a small envelope and literally slide them into your wallet or purse. This is one of the best uses of the sigils—you can now do powerful land healing by simply placing a sigil quietly in a place. This is particularly good for areas that have a lot of people in them (tourist attractions, parks, cities, stores, etc.) where you feel called to help. The second major way of using the sigils is to build them into your existing ritual. You can place a sigil of apology after doing apology work; for example, to help "continue" the apology work beyond that moment. The sigil, buried in the earth, will slowly break down and continue its magic. A third way you might use these sigils is to offer them to friends who may need them. I am often approached by people I know who ask things like, "We have this tree being cut on our rental property. What can I do?" If they are a nature-based spiritual practitioner, I often have a lot of suggestions for them. But if they aren't following these kinds of practices, giving them the sigil (in this case, sigils of apology, sleep, and passage) and telling them to bury the sigils there and leave a little offering for the tree is an excellent way to help. This is all to say that there are many, many different ways that you can use these sigils to bring healing and light into the world. You are really limited only by your imagination as to how these can be used for healing work in the world.

# Seed Balls

Seed balls are a simple way of replanting the ecosystem and are always part of my land healer's crane bag. A seed ball is a small clay-and-compost ball that includes native seeds that can easily be given as gifts, thrown into, and spread to new areas. Seed balls were first described by Masanobu Fukuokoa in his book *One Straw Revolution*[10] and since that time have been widely used by people to spread life. Seed balls have a number of benefits over other methods for scattering seeds. First and foremost, they are easy to throw and toss into spaces you can't reach (such as an abandoned lot behind a chain-link fence). They also provide a little platform for growth, with clay to hold moisture and compost. You can tailor them to specific ecosystems. You can imbue them with some additional healing energy or blessing. Thus, your "magic" seed balls can carry the energy both of physical life through seeds as well as the spiritual energy of blessing and growth. They are easy to make, requiring very few ingredients, all of which can be foraged in your local ecosystem or purchased at very little cost.

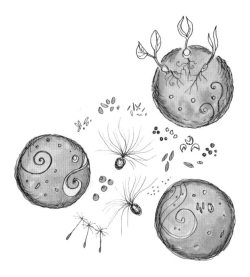

## DESIGNING SEED BALLS

One of the key considerations for seed balls is deciding what basic growing needs the seeds require, and combining those into the same ball. You don't want to put seeds that require damp shade and forest conditions with those that require full sun. So, you will want to select seeds that grow together and that require the same kinds of growing conditions. The material contained in chapter 7 will offer you extensive guidelines for how to select the right seeds, given your own bioregion. As an example, I have three primary seed balls recipes that I regularly make, which are based on my Zone 6 ecosystem here in western Pennsylvania, USA:

- **Full-sun native medicinal ball** designed for fields, roadsides, ditches, and more. It contains Common Milkweed (*Asclepias syriaca*), Butterfly Weed (*Asclepias tuberosa*), New England Aster (*Aster novae-angliae*), and Echinacea (*Echinacea purpurea*). These plants represent a range of nectary plants and also target forage and habitat for several kinds of endangered bees and butterflies in my region. Plus, they all are edible, medicinal, and native to the eastern US.

- **Forest medicinal ball** designed for damp forest conditions. This includes Ramps (*Allium tricoccum*), Black Cohosh (*Actaea racemosa*), Blue Cohosh (*Caulophyllum thalictroides*), Trillium (*Trillium* spp.), Dutchman's Breeches (*Dicentra cucullaria*), and Trout Lily (*Erythronium americanum*). I designed this seed ball by observing conditions in a local forest that had not been logged, and collected seeds there. I would also like to add American ginseng (*Panax quinquefolius*) seeds to this ball, but at present I plant them separately due to the fact that I am still building my population of seed stores for this plant.

- **Green thumb seed ball** with Daikon Radish (*Raphanus sativus*), Purple Top Turnip (*Brassica rapa*), Red Russian kale (*Brassica napus*), Lettuce (*Lactuca sativa*), Chives (*Allium schoenoprasum*), Tomato (*Solanum lycopersicum*), and Onion (*Allium cepa*) seeds. These are obviously food plants that can be eaten by people as well as animals, and they self-seed quite well, thus establishing a potential food hedge. I like to give these to enterprising gardeners who are first starting out and don't know what to plant. I also like to toss these in urban areas where recent construction has damaged the land, or toss in areas with food scarcity.

These three seed ball recipes represent three different needs: The first ball represents the need to offer more biological diversity to the local landscape for endangered and at-risk bee and butterfly populations. The second represents the need to replant the forest floor and bring in ecological diversity to replant forests in my region after extensive logging, pipelines, spraying, or other disruption. The third represents the need to help engage in "people care" and plant some food that can be harvested.

In terms of obtaining seeds, I like to harvest my seeds from as local a source as possible, since those varieties are best adapted to my area. I prefer to wild-harvest them from the local landscape or grow them in my refugium (see chapter 7). I also talk with friends with gardens to see if I can come and harvest seeds in the fall. Sometimes this is not possible. In that case, I look for a regional seed company that is growing the seeds organically, GMO free, and in a relatively same climate to my own. Bulk is better for purchasing in this case.

A final note about seeds—the best seeds that work with these balls are smaller seeds, the kinds you'd use to plant flowers, herbs, or vegetables. Large nut seeds, such as acorns, hickories, walnuts, pawpaws, and the like, should be planted individually, not added to seed balls.

# GATHERING MATERIALS

*Clay.* Most areas in the world have some source of local clay. If at all possible, this is what you want to use. You will be returning all the materials you gather (seeds, clay, compost) to the land, and the more local sources you have, the better. Look for clay when people are digging into the subsoil, look at eroding banks of rivers after flooding, look at new construction—these are easy places to find clay. Clay is easiest to collect it with a shovel and a bucket. If your clay is super wet, you might want to lay the clay out for a few days to dry out a bit before making your seed balls. If the clay is rocky, you can lay it out and pull the rocks out individually. The clay doesn't have to be particularly clean or pure for making seed balls.

*Compost.* In addition to clay and seeds, you'll need some sifted and finished compost or topsoil, ideally something that is seed free. You can easily dig this yourself, again, trying to keep your materials as local as possible. Rich soil from a garden or a compost bin will do nicely. You can often also get soil for free from a municipal facility that accepts "yard waste" many times a year. If you think you have unwanted weed seeds in the soil that you don't want to spread, you can bake the compost at 350 degrees for ten minutes (but this may kill off other microbial life, so be warned).

*Other supplies.* You will also need the following supplies to make your seed balls:

- A large plastic bucket is necessary for mixing. A 5-gallon bucket works well.

- A bucket of water for cleaning your hands and adding water to the mix. If you are making seed balls when it is cold outside, fill your bucket with hot water.

- An old towel is useful for cleaning your hands.

- A small tarp or large garbage bag. This will be for sorting out your clay and adding your seeds.

- A few friends. Good friends make seed ball making fun!

# THE PROCESS

The first thing you want to do is to make sure your compost and your clay are relatively free of large debris, woody material, leaves, or stones. You want to sort your clay and compost, removing any large sticks, stones, or leaves.

Second, you'll want to make sure your clay is at the right wetness: more on the dry side than the mucky side. Most clay you dig right out of the earth will be the perfect consistency, but if the clay had to wait awhile, it may be a little dry. If the clay is too wet, I suggest letting it sit out on a tarp for a few hours until the clay dries out a bit (it is easy to add water but hard to remove it, and if the clay is too wet, you won't be able to use it to form balls).

Next, you'll want to measure your clay and put it in your mixing bucket. You want to use a ratio of two parts clay to one part compost. This doesn't have to be exact, but close will help you make a better seed ball that is strong and will hold its shape. You may have to play around with the ratio a bit; part of this will depend on the kind of clay you have (and if it is pure or has part silt or sand). Don't fill your mixing bucket more than half full with clay.

Now, add your compost and mix well in the bucket. Test your seed balls at this point and see if your mixture sticks together. If it doesn't stick and form a ball, you can add a bit of water, mix again, and test it again. Once it forms a nice ball, you are ready to go. If you add too much water, spread the mixture out on a tarp and let it sit in the sun for an hour or two, and then you should be good to go.

Now, spread out your material on the tarp or garbage bag; this way you can monitor mixing in your seeds and give all balls a good and consistent mix. Spread it out so that the mixture is about 1"–2" high. Then add your seeds, spreading them across the top of the mixture evenly. Milkweed puff and other seed debris are fine for the balls. How many seeds you add is up to you, but I like to get at least five to ten per ball. Start mixing everything together.

Now, make your balls. One strategy to make a lot at a time is to roll out a long clay snake and then break off pieces and form into balls. Or you can roll them individually.

Let your seed balls sit out in a well-ventilated place, and they should be dry within a week or so. Once they are dry, you can store them in egg cartons or paper bags. Your seed balls will stay viable as long as your seeds are viable, usually one to three years depending on the seeds.

No magic seed ball would be complete without a blessing. While there are lots of options, I would suggest using the seven-element blessing ceremony in chapter 4. Also, you can choose to make these at a special time, as described earlier in this chapter.

## SPREADING SEED BALLS

Now that you have your seed balls, take them with you on your journeys with your other tools—or use them on their own. Remember that some seeds need a cold period (cold stratification), so tossing them even in the wintertime isn't a bad idea! I also love to make extra balls and give them away as gifts (particularly to fellow nature lovers and children) so that they too can enjoy helping wild-tend and replant the landscape. With each toss, you regenerate the land, bless the land, and scatter abundance (for more on physical land healing and this approach, see chapter 7).

In terms of uses, you can target specific areas or have them generally. I like to toss them from my car or along edges of roadsides (wildflower mix) or scatter them in forests that are regenerating after logging (forest mix). Where I live, we also have many "boney dumps," where old mine refuse was piled into mountain-sized piles and we have little life or diversity. I toss many of my wildflower ones in these areas to help replant these very damaged landscapes.

## Other Ritual Tools

If you are planning on doing ritual work in places where you take your healer's crane bag, it can be a good idea to create a mini ritual kit to use in your bag. Having these tools on hand makes a lot of sense. Ideally, these will include representations of the four classical elements and representations of spirit, particularly if you are using the grove-opening and grove-closing ceremonies offered in this book (chapter 4). You might choose to include physical representations (e.g., incense or a feather for air, a shell for water, a candle for fire, a stone for earth) or more-abstract representations, such as sacred animals: stone carvings of a hawk for air, a stag for fire, a tortoise or salmon for water, and a bear for earth. Whatever you use, it should be meaningful for you. Also in your bag, you might want a small cloth to place your tools on—an ornate handkerchief found at a thrift store works great for this purpose. You can also include any other tools you might want to work with, such as a small knife or wand. None of these are necessary for raising energy or doing the work of a land healer, but they can help.

A ritual tool that I find particularly useful in my crane bag is a musical instrument. I like to play flutes, so I often will have a small wooden flute tucked into my crane bag along with a small travel rattle. Raising energy through music or drumming is an important part of how I interact with the land and communicate with the spirits, particularly if there are other people around and I can't do more-ritual-like practices without drawing unnecessary attention.

A final tool that I put in is a pen and a small pocket-size journal. I often have deep insights and experiences when doing the work of a land healer, and I don't want to be without an ability to record those insights. Messages, songs, stories, and experiences all go into my small healer's journal.

Personalization here is key—both the bag itself and what you put into it. Each land healer's crane bag will be unique and different. Make sure you have anything you might want that helps you with your work: stones, statues, and other meaningful objects.

# You as a Tool

A final consideration for your crane bag is you, the land healer. While the crane bag can offer you a wide range of possibilities and be useful for healing and strengthen your confidence when you are starting out, the truth is that the only tool you truly need is you. You can shape symbols with your hand or visualize them on the broader landscape. You can clap a beat with your hands or raise your voice in song. You can dance, raise energy, and do anything else any tool can do. You are your ultimate tool. The way I like to see the tools is that they offer you some assistance and shortcuts. The tools are simply aids to assist you, to strengthen your work. They are not necessary, but they are certainly useful.

# Chapter 3:

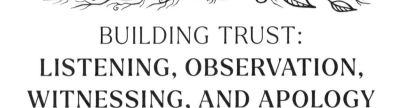

# BUILDING TRUST:
# LISTENING, OBSERVATION,
# WITNESSING, AND APOLOGY

**When I first visited my new homestead in Michigan,** I was saddened by how closed off the land was. In the center of the property, two large white pines had once grown—but one was reduced to a tall stump, oozing sap, the other standing tree in sorrow. I continued to the back of the property, where a huge pile of cut cedar trees lay. Garbage was strewn about, numerous burn piles were present, and active chemical spraying was happening. This land had been actively harmed and was unwilling to trust me. And why would the land immediately trust me? I was a stranger, a new "owner" who perhaps would come in to do more damage. That first day walking the land, the only tree that would speak to me was the white pine. In our initial conversation, he said that the land was in sorrow from the loss of the many cedars and pines, and if I wanted to live here, I would have to know this sorrow. I asked, "Are you willing to work with me to heal?," and his response was "Are you willing to work with me to build trust? Your kind are not friends here." This interchange, and the five-year period of relationship building and land healing that followed, taught me a great deal about how land healing works and the criticality of recognizing the sovereignty of nature.

Attending to human-caused damage is a place we find ourselves time and time again as land healers. It is no secret that today, humans are radically reshaping the world. Scientists even have a term for it—the age of the Anthropocene, where human disruption and change are shaping the entire globe. Given this cultural history, a new land healer can't just immediately jump in and start raising energy or slinging around seeds. Because we begin with the premise that nature has its own agency, that nature should always be treated as a sovereign being with rights and respect.

Thus, this chapter focuses on what I call "trust-building" land-healing techniques. These are not energy work, physical work, or ritual. Rather, trust-building techniques are those that we do every time we start a healing process; they are the foundation upon which everything else can be built. We need these techniques as preliminaries for two reasons, both of which are illustrated in this example: Let's say you have found a stray dog and decided to keep her as a pet. This dog has suffered long-term abuse at the hands of a previous owner. Because of this, she doesn't run right up to you and be excited to see you. Rather, she cowers, afraid that you will be yet another human causing abuse. Even if the dog isn't cowering, she may take a tentative footstep or two toward you, seeing if you could be trusted. If you immediately started reaching out to the dog to touch her or anything else, it would be too much, too soon.

The first thing to be learned from this example is that spirits of the land can be like that abused dog. Some may be in "cower and retreat" mode, and thus the first step of healing is not directing energy, planting seeds, or doing anything else—it is showing respect to the dog's boundaries and building trust. Thus, we take land healing one step at a time, building trust. Some pieces of damaged land might not require much of what is in this chapter (particularly if you already have a relationship with that land), while other pieces of damaged land may require all of it over a period of years. The second principle we learn from this example is that nature herself is made up of many sovereign beings, and nature herself is a sovereign being, in the same way that the dog is a sovereign being and communicates her wishes. Some of the more problematic thinking that has developed in Western culture is that nature is passive, that nature lacks agency, and thus we can do whatever we want to nature. Even the most well-intentioned land healer can cause more harm if the relationship is not one met directly with respect and acknowledgment. Thus, to be a compassionate and effective land healer, we must always make sure we are acting in a way that attends to the wishes and desires of the spirits of the land.

This is to say that the techniques in this chapter—deep listening, acknowledgment, apology, and remembrance—are almost always the appropriate place to start for the many kinds of land healing we might do. You can't be effective in a ritual sense if you don't do this groundwork. If you don't do this groundwork, the rituals and other practices described later in this book will not have the effect you want them to have, and may even be seen as intrusive or unwanted by the spirits of the land. Land healing is *healing work*; it must be done *slowly, intentionally, and respectfully*. You might think about these activities as being on a set of stairs: you must start with the first few stairs to reach the higher floors.

## Deep Listening and Observation

Before doing anything else, it is necessary to listen and to observe.[11] Listening takes a lot of different forms, including inner spirit communication, inner journeying, observing and interacting with the land, using your "gut" feelings to feel out a situation, or using various kinds of divination practices (Tarot, ogham, oracles, pendulums, etc.) to receive messages from spirit. Most people who have been practicing nature-based spirituality for a while find that they have a knack for one or more listening strategies and that they can cultivate others with time. If you are newer to land healing, you will want to invest considerable time in learning how to listen—because communication with the spirits of the land is one of the core skills you will use in almost every part of your practice.

This deep listening to the needs of the land is critically important for the healing work you are going to undertake—what does the land want and need? How can you best serve the land? Do you need to be engaging in physical land healing, blessing, energetic healing, or palliative care? The question of how to go about this healing is an important one. Depending on how long you've been on this path, and what your own gifts are, you may not need any advice in this area. But for those of you who are newer to this work and are still developing your gifts, there are many ways to listen, and here are a few of them:

**Directly observe with your five senses.** Pay very close attention with your physical senses. Look at what you are seeing in the land around you. What do you see? What is missing? What impacts do you see that humans have made? Are there humans on the land now? What are they doing? Understand the picture of this land with your five senses.

**Communicating with nature on the outer planes.** Nature can communicate directly with us with our five senses. The basic practice here is to allow yourself to be open to those kinds of messages—and let this happen on nature's timeline. Go to the site you are thinking about working with. Walk around the site and observe. Sit still—for at least fifteen to twenty minutes—and see what comes. The land can speak through many forms; pay attention to all that you see. What messages can you interpret from what you can hear, see, touch, smell, and, in some cases, taste? What does the wind say to you? How do the trees move? How do the blades of grass grow? Where do the tracks in the soil lead? How does the water crash upon the rocks? Just as though you were listening to a human friend telling us of their suffering, we don't just listen with our ears. We look at them, we may use our sense of touch, and we may pay attention to body language.

The silences are just as important as the sounds. This is particularly true as the silences of the natural world are descending on the landscape— what sounds should be there but are not there? We may listen for the pauses, the spaces in between what is said, and what is not said. Thus, communicating requires all of our physical senses; they are a part of this "deep listening" work. In *The Great Animal Orchestra*,[12] Bernie Krause encourages us to use sound as a way to hear the "biophony" of nature, the sounds of all life on the plant that is not human. Unfortunately, as Krause explores, the sounds of the living landscape have, in some cases, gone to silence.

This method often leads not only to a deeper understanding of place but also a "knowing" of what to do or direct messages from spirit.

**Intuition and inner knowing.** All of us have "gut feelings," although the strength of such feelings may depend on how much we've honed that intuitive gift. Sometimes, when I meet new land that is in want of that healing—I get a strong gut feeling. I just know what I am to do; it's like it unfolds from within me. I won't immediately act on it but instead check it with other methods of deep listening to ensure that it is the will of spirit. These gut feelings should always be treated as meaningful information and communication, since such feelings are often on the level of our subconscious and spirit from where these feelings flow.

**Listening on the inner planes.** Deep listening involves listening not only with our five physical senses but with our senses of spirit. Spiritual and magical traditions offer a wide range of methods for inner listening and inner communication. These may include spirit journeying, spirit conversation, paying attention to the shifts in energy or feeling, or using divination tools. Learning to listen on the level of spirit is one of the more formidable challenges for individuals early in a path of land healing, but once you practice, you will be able to listen.

One of the best strategies I use for land-healing communication is to sit still on the landscape and quiet my mind by attending to my breathing and letting thoughts of other things float away. I settle more firmly into my body, growing comfortable and allowing my awareness to center on my breath for a few moments. When I feel ready, I then open my awareness to the land around me and put out a query to the spirits of the land. "Hello, spirits of the land; I am Dana, a land healer. I felt drawn to this place. Is there anything I can do for you?" And I wait to see what response I get. You can speak this aloud or speak it internally. Usually, there will be an internal voice, not your own, that will speak in return.

This strategy takes practice—we have to quell our own thoughts enough to hear the land's quiet but powerful voice. But with practice, and time, messages will come. Messages may be in many forms, depending on your own gifts—you may hear inner messages, get visuals, get a strong feeling, or hear music. You may also not get a message right away, but it may come to you a few days later through dreams or in meditation. Be open to these, and don't doubt your intuition.

I will also say that every one of us has the capacity to listen in this way. But deep listening on the inner planes requires you to quiet your mind enough to hear the voices of spirit, and to gain focus and practice. It may come easily to you or take months or even years of practice before you can easily converse. If you are having trouble with this part of the land-healing work, there are a few techniques that might help you so that you can proceed to the later steps. Meditation is one of the very best; engaging in daily meditation will help you be able to clear and quiet your mind to the voices of spirit. Both empty-mind meditations and more-focused thinking techniques such as discursive meditation are very useful. For a simple empty-mind meditation that can build your focus and quiet your mind, use a candle and your breath. Light the candle, stare into the flame, and try to allow your own thoughts to subside—focus only on the candle and your breath. Regular practice with this technique will prime you for inner listening. Discursive meditation, which is a kind of focused thought, is another technique that will aid you with inner listening. I recommend the *Druid Magic Handbook* by John Michael Greer, in which he describes, in detail, a discursive meditation technique that will assist you with developing quietude and focus. Once our own chaotic thoughts can quiet down, the voices of spirit will be present to us.

If you are learning to practice these techniques, I suggest you start not on land that you want to actively heal (especially not damaged land) but somewhere that is healthy and vibrant, such as a garden or forest preserve. These kinds of places are easy to communicate with, since they have been well tended and protected by humans and thus are a good place to work blessing magic and other basic techniques.

**Divination.** It is a useful practice to check your understanding with some form of divination. You may already have a divination system that you are familiar with, such as Tarot, geomancy, a pendulum, I Ching, ogham, and so forth. Use that to ask questions about the nature of the messages you receive, and to confirm what you have gotten using other methods. You can also use this as a primary method to communicate, particularly if you are still developing your inner awareness and intuition.

If you don't have a method of divination, one of the easiest to learn and most direct for land-healing work is the use of a pendulum. You can make a pendulum out of almost anything: a string and a stone will work well. If you are out and about and have nothing, unlace one of your shoes and tie a stone to it. Now, ask the pendulum to "show you yes" where it will move in one direction. Then, ask it to "show you no," where it will move in a different direction. Finally, ask it to "show you no response." Thus, perhaps your pendulum goes west to east for yes, and north to south for no, and then makes small circles when it has no response. With these questions complete, you can now ask any yes/no question to the spirits of the land (e.g., "Is there something you want me to do?"). With enough yes-and-no questions, you will be able to directly answer the call of the spirits of the land.

**Timing.** Land healing is a process of unfolding; the unfolding and connecting may happen over a period of seasons or years. These cycles and seasons are how nature moves, communicates, and exists. What this means is that sometimes, this listening will take time, many visits, and intuition. You may not get a clear sense of what to do on your first visit. The land works on the seasonal cycle and moves at a different pace than you do. Nature heals slowly, but surely, and so it may take time for you to ascertain what, if anything, you are to do. Begin by taking the time, the real time, to listen to the land.

The other piece of timing that is critical here is that in most ecosystems, there are times when the land is more fully awake and times when the land is in hibernation. That is, it is unlikely that you will hear strong spirits of the land, particularly from trees and perennial plants, at the winter solstice in the northern hemisphere—this is when plants and trees are fully dormant. You are more likely to hear them just as they are budding out in spring or in their full abundance in summer or fall. With that said, some plants and spirits do not enter hibernation and may be available to communicate (e.g., conifers, birds).

**Suffering and sleep.** Another issue that you may experience is that the land has been so damaged that it does not communicate—decades or centuries of mistreatment may have encouraged any spirits or life present to go deep and hibernate. If you get the sense that a very damaged piece of land is in this state and the damage is ongoing and active, the very best thing you can do is allow the land to rest. Do not try to communicate or awaken land that has found a way to distance itself from the pain. This is damaging and, ultimately, disrespectful to the spirits of that land.


## RESPONSES FROM THE LAND

When you begin to deeply listen to the world of nature around you, you might encounter any of the following types of messages: Sometimes you get a very favorable response—the land was waiting for someone just like you to come by, and is happy that you are here. If you get this response, I still suggest doing everything in this chapter, but I also suggest that you can quickly move on to some of the other techniques in later chapters. In this case, you might be encouraged to do something very specific (such as gather stones, move soil, place a sigil in a particular spot, etc.). This may be a test, to see if you can be trusted.

You may also get a "Perhaps, let's see" response, which is like the response something similar to my initial interaction with the White Pine on my homestead when I first arrived. This response is basically saying, "We are willing to consider this, but we don't yet trust you." Many of the techniques in this chapter can help you establish trust. I have found that this is one of the most common responses from the land, especially when you are going into unfamiliar areas. And trust building can take time, so be prepared to invest it.

Rarely, you might get a strong sense to "Get out!" and an indication that you are not welcome. This often comes with lands that have been severely damaged by human hands and want nothing to do with humans. It's a very understandable response, especially after prolonged or severe trauma. When I meet spirits of the land like this, I will immediately respect that land's wishes and withdraw. However, I won't give that land up as a lost cause. At another time, perhaps some weeks or months later, I will come again to the edge of that space and leave an offering, perhaps sitting for a time, and simply be present. I will certainly offer an apology (see later this chapter). I might do this a few times over a period of months or years, and if I ever feel the energies shift, I once again inquire if I can help. Usually, after a few visits to the edge of this land, the spirits of the land will begin to open. Sometimes, though, even after several visits, the land doesn't have any interest in me or my help as a land healer. I tell the land that I will not be returning at that point, and I make sure that's what the land wants. And again, I respect the land's wishes.

In some places, nature prefers to heal on her own and does not want outside help. And if that is what your deep listening has revealed, respecting that boundary and honoring it is a tremendous healing step forward for the land. I know this seems counterintuitive, but I encourage you to think about it this way: the land has repeatedly had boundaries crossed by humans without its consent. A human who *respects and honors a boundary* is a tremendous step forward and builds trust—since too many humans simply take what they want from the land repeatedly. So, if this is the message that you receive, do as is asked, and understand that that, too, is a deep kind of healing work. It might be that you are asked to walk away permanently, or, perhaps at a later point when you return you are then invited to do healing work. Walking away can be a kind of test, or it might be the genuine desire of the land at that time. Regardless, when you are told not to engage, respect that request.

## Acknowledgment and Witnessing

Sometimes, the hidden or the unacknowledged hurts are the worst kind. These are the kind that you bury deep within yourself, or that a society pretends doesn't exist. We hear stories of these kinds of issues in human society every day—massive cover-ups of the truth only now revealed, people coming forth after decades of silence, the relief that one feels when one can finally talk about something. To have others know, to see, to understand, and to acknowledge are acts of tremendous healing power.

In land-healing work, acknowledgment and witnessing are extraordinarily powerful tools, especially in the twenty-first century, when so many ordinary people are powerless. Modern ownership laws allow for landowners to do anything they want on their land—and we are often left on the sidelines, unable to stop the tree from being cut, the sewage line from going in, the mountaintop from being removed. We aren't all powerful, we don't command sums of money or influence, and we certainly can't stop what has already occurred. This exact situation, feeling powerlessness, is why some may prefer to look away or turn their attention elsewhere. Seeing destruction is too hard, and they feel there is nothing that they can do.

But we can engage in healing work by choosing not to look away. There is deep healing power in acknowledging the suffering of another. We can choose to see, to bear witness, to acknowledge suffering, and to hold and share the memory of what has been lost. I find myself doing acknowledgment and witness work often with cut trees—remembering them and honoring them long after they are gone. You might be the only person who will do this work for the land—and it is powerful and meaningful.

Acknowledgment is where we start the actual healing work. We cannot address an issue if we fail to acknowledge that there is one. Part of the reason that acknowledgment is so powerful is that culturally, at least here in the US, there is this collective blindness, this collective unwillingness, to engage, see, or acknowledge what is happening around us. I see this a lot firsthand where I live, where fracking and energy extraction are taking a serious toll on our health and lands. People don't really talk about the oil wells, the equipment, the pollution, the spills, or anything else. If the issue is raised, the only comments are that it "produces good jobs" for the area (in a poor area, fracking jobs are well-paying jobs). In fact, after moving back to the area, I was told by environmental activists that it was best if we "didn't talk about fracking" because that is a fight we cannot win. If we fail to acknowledge that these things even exist, if we fail to talk about them or draw attention to them, we cannot begin the repair work necessary to heal. The longer that a painful issue goes unacknowledged, unseen, the more deep rooted the pain surrounding the issue can be.

Acknowledgment requires us both to *be capable of seeing* and *be willing to see*. These are important distinctions. Being capable of seeing means that we have enough knowledge and wisdom to interpret what we are seeing and to recognize that it is a problem—this is part of why we covered understanding what healthy ecosystems look like in chapter 1. In other words, some damaged spaces have become so normalized that we may not recognize them as being immediately in need of healing. The typical lawn is a good example of this: lawns are not good for ecosystems and animals, insects, or birds, but they are so pervasive that we might look at them and just see a "normal" part of being.

Being willing to see is the next step. We put aside the inner dialogues or cultural baggage that tells us these things are normal, that everything is fine, and instead choose to see the damage for what it is. It is easier to look away than to look directly at something. The will to see is a powerful moment. And to be clear, this is very hard work.

Thus, tremendous power lies in acknowledgment. All our healing work stems from this. Being ready to heal, ultimately, first means being ready to acknowledge. I have practiced being in a state of acknowledgment and openness with each day. I pay close attention to the land, in whatever state it is in, engage, and interact with it. If I see something awful, such as a forest being cut, I do not look away but instead I acknowledge.

Speaking aloud is another powerful healing act. As you are engaged in the practice of witnessing, you can say whatever comes from the heart. Such as "I see your suffering. I am here. I witness what is happening." Acknowledgment requires both bravery and a compassionate heart. Also recognize that this is really hard work. This book concludes with chapter 9 focused on self-care for this very reason.

# Witnessing Ritual:

## PRAYER AND CHANT

The following prayer is a simple prayer of witnessing and acknowledgment.

*I come in peace,*

*I come in sorrow.*

*I witness what has happened here.*

*I will not look away.*

*I share in your grief.*

*I cannot change what has happened here.*

*But I choose to stand with you now.*

*And I honor you*

After the prayer, you might do a soothing chant—more details of chanting and chanting magic can be found in chapter 5. For a simple chant, I will use three sacred trees focused on healing, protection, and new beginnings: Apple (Quert), Hawthorn (Huath), and Birch (Beith). I simply chant these three words for a time until I feel that the work is done. These three words come from the ogham, an ancient Celtic tree alphabet. More about the ogham, including pronunciation, is included in chapter 5.

## ACKNOWLEDGMENT FOR SIGIL EMPOWERMENT

You can use the above chant to empower your apology sigils (see "Healing-Sigil Set" in chapter 2). To empower your sigils with this prayer, open up a sacred grove (see chapter 4). Place your sigils in the center of your grove and surround them with candles. Then, focus on the energy of apology. Say the apology prayer three times, with your hands outstretched over the sigils. As you say the chant, imagine a gold-green light entering the sigils and making them glow. Once you are finished, close your sacred grove. Your sigils are now ready to use.

# Apology

Just as tremendous power exists in acknowledgment and witnessing, so too is there incredible power in apology. In the age of the Anthropocene, humans are driving massive changes to every part of this globe. And because humanity has directly or indirectly caused such incredible destruction, it is very helpful for an apology that must come from one of us. Apology may also be historical, recognizing the centuries of exploitation of the land at the hand of one's own ancestors.

Engaging in the work of apology is not complicated—you simply say, "On behalf of humans, I apologize for what has been done to you by my species." Speak from the heart. Recognize yourself as a spokesperson for humanity. When you say it—feel it. Let your sorrow and remorse for what has been done resonate within you. While you are apologizing on behalf of humans, it is important to recognize that what has been done is not your direct fault. Do not take on the energy of someone else's behavior—keep your apology to that which is representative of the whole of humanity. You do not have to carry the guilt of others' actions—but speaking on behalf of the species that is causing the harm is acceptable.[13]

Once you are in direct communication with the spirits of the land, sometimes as part of the work of apology you will be asked for an explanation. For example, in a town I was living in, they were cutting down all the trees on one side of the street to do sidewalk work. These were trees that I loved dearly, trees that I spoke to each day as I walked to work. I had no power to stop these trees from coming down, and every day the ring of the chain saw was so loud and painful in my ears. But I could stand with the trees on my street as they came down, bearing witness and offering apology. The tree spirits began to converse with me: "Thank you for your apology. Why is this happening to me?" We had a conversation about humanity, I invited them to follow along for a few days to understand human perspective, and they began to understand how disconnected humans are from the spirit world. They were then able to move on in peace. Thus, in situations where death has occurred (such as deforestation or oil spills), the inhabitants that have passed may need something from you.

This apology will help them pass on, to help heal. More details about this kind of work can be found in chapter 8.

The work of apology is also good for situations where another culture's sacred sites have been desecrated. Here in the US, where many Native American sacred sites have been colonized or turned into tourist attractions, there is a lot of collective pain surrounding these acts. I do not feel comfortable doing any other work on these sites, but I certainly can bear witness and honor the site with an apology. And I can work to directly support tribes that are in my region to reclaim their sites.

## Remembrance

In many pagan traditions, some form of the statement "Those who are remembered live on" is present. This statement acknowledges that even if loved ones have passed, if we keep them in our mind and hearts, they are not truly lost. This statement demonstrates the incredible power of memory.

One of the events that set me on the path of the land healer was the cutting of the Silver Maple in the neighborhood where I grew up. I had come home to visit my parents, and we were out taking a walk. Even from a distance, we could hear the ring of the chain saw. The Silver Maple they were cutting down had been a friend since my childhood and was at least a hundred years old. Another neighbor shared with us that the new homeowners "didn't like raking up the leaves." I did the work of witnessing and apology. When I still go back to the old neighborhood, I pause for a moment where that tree once stood, and take a moment to remember.

After the tree was cut, I managed to get a small piece of the wood that fell off the back of the tree service truck. From this, on the stump of the fallen tree, I created a remembrance shrine, which I called the "shrine to the fallen." My shrine had a simple stack of stones, and around that stack I placed the piece of the silver maple, and representations from other trees, plants, animals, and other places that had passed that I wanted to remember. Over the years, I added many such things to the shrine and regularly tended it, and, at Samhain, I made offerings of my homemade dandelion wine and sugar cakes. The "shrine to the fallen" was a small gesture, not taking much time, but it helped me engage in this practice regularly.

This story illustrates a few key components that can be included in the work of remembrance. I want to stress that any of these are appropriate: like much of land healing, it is setting the right intentions that matter, not the physicality of the work itself.

- *Moments of silence.* A moment of silence, at the site or elsewhere, is a simple way to practice remembrance.

- *Ringing.* Ringing the bell, gong, or bowl is a powerful and simple tribute to memory.

- *Honoring the Fallen shrine.* A shrine can be indoors or out and can include specific representations of those you wish to remember. You can use actual pieces from the land (such as my small piece of wood), write names, or use photos or anything else you'd like to develop for this work. This shrine can be an evolving place for the purpose of your work with witnessing, apology, and remembrance.

- *Remembrance rituals.* You might designate one or more times a year when you do the work of honoring those who have passed. Samhain, which takes place on November 1, or any dark moon both are good times for this kind of work. Your rituals or activities don't have to be complicated. Lighting some candles, saying some words from the heart, or visiting a site all are appropriate. See one such sample honoring ritual that follows.

- *Creative works.* You can engage in creative practices with the goal of remembrance. Create a song, poem, drawing, or painting in honor of someone who has passed or a species that has passed.

- *Remembrance garden.* Consider planting and tending a "remembrance" garden. In this garden, you might plant new seeds for those who have fallen, offer pure water for those who have died in polluted waters, and so on. This idea helps balance the energies of death with those of life and thus is ideal for this kind of work. If you are working with trees or plants that need to be remembered, and you can save their seeds to plant, this is a very powerful act of remembrance.

Practicing remembrance is a powerful act of healing for the land and her spirits. There is no right or wrong way to practice remembrance. Let your heart lead you on this journey.

## Remembrance Ritual

This simple ritual can be used for practicing remembrance. You can use a bell, gong, or singing bowl (or replace this with a moment of silence). You can also optionally leave an offering of incense or food.

Begin by taking a few moments to breathe deeply and center yourself.

Next, speak from your heart about your memory of the land, tree, animal, place, etc., allowing them to flow from you. Alternatively, you can use this:

> *I hold you in my heart*
> *I hold you in my memory.*
> *As the wheel turns, your memory remains strong.*
> *As your sun has set, it will once more rise again.*
> *What is remembered lives on.*
> *On this day, I honor you.*

Ring the bell, gong, or bowl three times (or, alternatively, hold a moment of silence). Leave an offering (I like to use a special incense for this and leave it burning after the ceremony concludes). Cross your arms and bow your head, then say, "Blessings."

## Settling In

I would suggest spending some time with the practices in this chapter before moving on. These fundamental practices will take you quite far as a land healer. It can take time to be able to listen to the land, read the broader landscape, understand the needs that the spirits convey, and figure out what to do. Nature works in cycles and seasons. There is no need to act prematurely or too quickly. Give yourself time to work with and deepen these practices.

# Chapter 4:

## ENERGY, RITUAL, AND LAND BLESSINGS

**A group of people stand on a warm winter day** with the sun shining through the bare branches of the Apple orchard. We stand, smiles on our faces and steaming mugs of hot cider in our hands, to wassail this Apple orchard for health and abundance. We offer a toast to the branches, pour cider upon the roots, and circle the tree together in song. We make noise and drum to ward off any evil spirits. After the ceremony, we retreat to the house to enjoy an apple-themed potluck and enjoy each other's company.

As we can see from the Apple Wassail, blessings for the vitality and health of the lands are an important part of the broader scope of land healing. Not all lands that we work with are necessarily damaged or in need of active work—but all lands can benefit from blessing work. Blessing the land for abundance and fertility is one of the oldest forms of rituals we have from our human ancestors all over the world. Ancient ancestors understood the relationship and interdependence of human survival and nature, and thus these kinds of rituals were done by peoples in all different cultures worldwide. In the case of blessings, a usual goal is to send out positive energy for healing, abundance, and prosperity. A blessing is a raising and directing positive energy for a specific purpose; many other kinds of advanced land healing use similar principles. Thus, these kinds of rituals are a good practice as a land healer and help you learn to raise and direct energy for specific purposes, which will be put to other uses in later chapters.

This chapter has two primary functions. First, it offers us an energetic framework in which to work for land healing. The framework is shared through a discussion of blessing rituals, such as the wassail ceremony described above. To illustrate many of the energetic framework concepts here, I will offer these in the context of basic healing, blessing, and sacred-space-opening rituals—all things we need to do as land healers before getting into some of the deeper work of palliative care or energetic healing.

# The Microcosm and Macrocosm

The first core principle for land healing and blessing is the principle of the microcosm and macrocosm. Stemming back thousands of years within hermetic philosophy, the macrocosm refers to the broader world, the larger living landscape, the principle of the whole. The microcosm, on the other hand, is a small yet representative part of that whole. Using objects or representations of the broader world to focus for healing is a basic principle found throughout the land-healing work described in later chapters.

As a more specific example in traditional lore, as described in the opening, in old wassailing rituals a group of people gather to bless an orchard. The blessing doesn't take place throughout the entire orchard, however, but rather, a single tree is selected to represent all trees in the orchard. All ritual work is done around the tree, which is then radiated outward to all the other trees. Thus, a blessing to one is a blessing to all. Here, we can see the principle of the microcosm and macrocosm tying to the basic structure of the ritual—the one receives a blessing that goes to the many. This same principle can be used extremely effectively in many land-healing practices, especially distance work or working large areas. Thus, we now consider two land-blessing ceremonies: one specific to fruit-bearing trees (Wassail) and one more general for any piece of land.

## The Work of Land Blessings

Wassail magic is a form of land and crop blessing that has long been practiced by peoples in Western cultures, particularly those in the British Isles and North America. The wassail tradition, coming from the Anglo-Saxon "waes-hael," means good health. One form of wassail was a drink placed in a large "wassail bowl" containing mulled cider, sugar, cinnamon, ginger, nutmeg, sometimes cream, sometimes baked apples, and other things.

This drink was brought around to others for their good health during the new year (it is where we get the song lyric "Here we come a-wassailing, among the leaves so green / Here we come a-wassailing / So fair to be seen"). After the wassail for the humans, this same drink and bowl made their way into the apple orchard for the wassail (in some cases, wassail was also done for pear trees with perry, fermented pear cider). Traditionally, Apple tree wassail took place on the twelfth night, either January 6 or January 17. The goal of this ceremony, as passed down in the traditional lore, is to awaken the apple trees, to drink to their health, and to scare away evil spirits that may interfere with a good harvest. As in many old customs, there are many potential parts to the ceremony and many ways of performing it. One such version of this ceremony is as follows.

# Wassail Ritual

**Group size:** Nearly any size of group can do this ritual; a good number is five to fifteen for a robust ceremony. It can be done with much larger groups and also individually. I will also note that since this tradition is not strictly "pagan" in nature, it is a ceremony that many different people can participate in. Here in the US, many orchards and cideries are now doing public wassail ceremonies for their orchards.

**Materials:**
hot mulled cider in a bowl
mugs
toast (presliced)
noisemakers/drums

Consider putting the mulled cider in a thermos or cooler to keep it warm and then pouring it into your bowl right before the ceremony.

**Selecting the tree:** One tree is selected to receive the blessing for the apple orchard. This is usually a large, old, or otherwise dominant tree with space to move about the tree, branches that people can reach, and accessible roots. This tree is the microcosm, connected to the larger macrocosm.

People gather around the tree with noisemakers. A wassail song can be sung (see the song that follows). Try to practice your wassail song in advance and put a tune to it, and you will have a very entertaining ceremony!

Cider is ceremoniously poured from the steaming wassail bowl into each participant's cup.

Participants pour an offering of cider from each of their cups on the roots of the tree and then drink to the tree's good health.

Participants bless the tree with an offering of toast, dipping toast in their mugs and then hanging the pieces of toast from the tree's branches. Alternatively, a king and queen are chosen, the king offers the queen his mug, and she dips the toast in the mug and then hangs the toast on the branches of the tree.

Participants should circle around the trees and make a great deal of noise to scare away the evil spirits that may be lurking there, using drums and noisemakers, shouting, and stomping. Usually this is done by everyone walking in a clockwise pattern around the tree and making noise.

When official ceremony is over, and people may enjoy a potluck with apple-themed ingredients.

Sample wassail song, adapted from 1906 from the United Kingdom[14]:

*Old apple tree, we'll wassail thee,*
*And hoping thou wilt bear.*
*Spirit does know where we shall be*
*To be merry another year.*
*To blow well and to bear well,*
*And so merry let us be;*
*Let ev'ry person drink up their cup*
*And health to the apple tree.*

## KEY ASPECTS OF THE WASSAIL RITUAL

There are three key aspects of this ritual that are useful to point out, since we'll see them again in the more general blessing rituals in this chapter and in other rituals later on in this book. First is the selection of a single tree that receives and radiates outward the blessing to all other trees. By selecting a single tree or other representation from a site (e.g., a stone from a polluted river), we can use that as a focus for magic and healing work. The second aspect of this ritual work is a specially prepared offering, prepared if at all possible by human hands and tied to the local landscape. The third is raising energy through sounds around the tree to drive off any evil, recognizing that negative energy or other negative influences may be present and need to be addressed.

# Tree Blessing Ceremony

The general wassail approach can be adapted to bless many other kinds of trees, forests, or the broader landscape. This blessing can again be done as a group or individually. For this, you will once again want to choose a representative of the land you are blessing (the microcosm)—a large and dominant tree is ideal. While you can certainly do this during the traditional wassail days (January 6 or 17), you can also do this at any point in the year.

**Materials:**
offering of bread and wine
optional musical instruments

**Opening:** Open a sacred space as described later in this chapter.

**Honoring:** After the space is opened, honor the trees with a simple blessing that establishes the intentions of the ceremony. You can honor the tree through your own words. Or you can use this:

*Trees of life, of bounty, of peace, and of wisdom*
*Strong in your growth, your branches shelter us*
*Deep in your roots, you anchor the soil web of life Many are your*
*leaves, to share breath with us*
*Abundant are your [fruits, sap, nuts], that remove/s our hunger*
*Full of wisdom and knowledge, your teachings guide us*
*Quiet in your growth, you bring us the sun*
*Today, we are here to honor you*

*Today, we offer you blessings and healing*
*Today, we wish you long life, health, and abundance!*
*Mighty forest and trees, may you grow and thrive!*

**Make offerings.** Offer the trees a fermented beverage and bread/cakes (ideally, homemade or locally produced). Offer a hot beverage for each of the participants, instructing them to pour half out at the roots. Offer participants pieces of bread or cake to the tree's branches.

**Radiate an energetic blessing.** Drawing upon the Three Currents framework (described later in this chapter), radiate an energetic blessing to the land.

With your dominant hand, trace a circle around the tree's trunk above you in a clockwise fashion. To do this, you can either walk around the tree, pointing above you as you walk, or you can stand in one spot and trace the circle around the tree's trunk above you. Visualize this circle in orange light. Say, "We call upon the solar current and the radiant energy of the celestial heavens. May a ray of the solar current descend and bless these trees with the fire of the sun!" All participants should envision a golden ray coming down from the celestial heavens, through the tree, and into the roots.

With your dominant hand, trace a circle around the tree's roots in a clockwise fashion. Visualize this circle in purple light. Say, "We call upon the telluric current and the healing energy of the deep earth. May a ray of the telluric current rise and bless these trees with the blessing of the heart of the earth!" All participants should envision a green/gold ray arising from the heart of the earth and filling the tree with green/gold light.

All participants should visualize the solar and telluric currents mingling within the tree. Say, "We call upon the lunar current to radiate outward and bless this land. With our blessing, may this land be abundant and full of vitality!" All participants should touch the tree and envision a glowing sphere of white light radiating outward from the tree to the whole forest.

**End in music, drumming, or song.** End your ceremony by scaring away any negative energy with drumming, blessing, or song. Tree hugging is also appropriate.

**Close.** Close out your ritual space.

# Growth Sigil Empowerment

Empower your growth sigils (chapter 2) with the Tree-Blessing Ceremony. Open up a sacred grove (as described later in this chapter). Place your growth sigils in the middle of your sacred-grove space or in front of a large tree if at all possible (you can also do this indoors if not). Speak the poem under "Honoring" or other words of honor you choose to use; share these three times. Then, bring the energetic blessing into the sigils, tracing your finger in a clockwise pattern above and below the sigils. Rather than radiating the energetic blessing out, use your hands to place the blessing within the sigils. Thank the spirits and close out your sacred grove. Your growth sigils are ready to use, and when placed, the energetic growth blessing you infused will radiate outward from them.

# Understanding Energy:
# The Seven Elements

As we see with the tree blessing above, having an energetic framework to work with is a very useful tool for land-healing purposes—a framework will always give you a go-to approach when you aren't sure what to do. Thus, this book works with a seven-element system[15] that draws upon the four classical elements (earth, air, fire, and water) as well as three aspects of spirit (spirit within, spirit above, and spirit below). These concepts are used as a foundational energy system throughout this book and thus are presented here in some detail.

### "ENERGY" AND NYWFRE

The term "energy" is used a lot with metaphysical practices, often without any clear sense of what it is or where it comes from. It's one of those words that we all think we agree on the meaning on the surface, but when you dig down into it, we don't necessarily all mean the same thing or even really understand what "energy" is. What is usually meant here is energy in the magical sense: the divine spark, the energy of life, the spirit in things, the creative inspiration flowing through all living beings—what druids call nywfre (noo-IV-ruh). As John Michael Greer describes in *The Druid Magic Handbook*, other traditions have different names for Nywfre, including qi/ch'I (Chinese), ki (Japanese), prana (Hindu yoga), ankh (ancient Egyptian) or the secret fire (alchemy). *Star Wars* fans might notice the similarity of these concepts to the "force," and the concept is largely the same. While this concept of energy is found in many cultures in the world, it's ironic that the English language *does not have a specific word.* Most cultures recognize that working with nywfre is part of being human and inhabiting the world, and they recognize the need to work with it in various ways both within and without. It's only mainstream consumerist culture that pretends such a thing doesn't exist. We can see this ignorance reflected in the dominant theories of medicine in the West (compared to, say, Chinese traditional medicine or Ayurveda, both of which recognize an energetic aspect to human healing, not just a physical one).

In every living being, the nywfre flows. Biologically, the vital energy that sustains our bodies comes from the sunlight that shines down, which plants convert into energy, which is stored. The plants grow from the rich earth with her nutrients and nourishment. The plants are the great transformers, providing us nutrition and vitality. We eat the plants, or the animals that eat them, and that sustains us. This same relationship is reflected metaphysically through the three currents: the solar, the telluric, and the lunar, and through the specific energy of the four elements.

## SPIRIT ABOVE: The Solar Current

The *solar* current is the energy—physical and metaphysical—that comes from the sun, our ultimate source of life. The solar current is magically associated with things in the sky: the heavens, and birds: hawks, eagles, and roosters. Additionally, certain plants also can draw and radiate solar energy quite effectively. In my bioregion, these include Dandelion (dominant in the spring); St. John's Wort (dominant at midsummer/Lughnassadh), and Goldenrod (dominant in the fall). As we explore in later chapters, we can use these specific solar plants when we need to light up dark places and focus the solar current's healing light.

Solar energy, being directly tied to the sun, changes on the basis of sun's position in the sky. That is, solar energy is different at noon than it is at dusk, dawn, or midnight. It also changes on the basis of where the sun is in the wheel of the year; the energy of the sun is different on June 21, the summer solstice, than it is on the winter solstice on December 21. Connected to the sun are the other solar bodies in our solar system and more broadly in the celestial heavens. In *The Druid Magic Handbook*, John Michael Greer notes that other planets in the solar system directly reflect the energy of the sun, so astrological influences can help us understand the current manifestation of the solar current at various present moments. This is all to say that the solar energy is ever powerful, and ever changing, in our lives.

We can see the solar current manifested differently in the world's religions—Christianity, for example, is a very solar-focused tradition. When you look at pictures of saints or Jesus, they are often accompanied by rays of light from heaven, god's light shining down, even the halo of light around a saint's or

Jesus's head. Buddhism, likewise, focuses on achieving "higher levels" of consciousness and being—these all are solar in nature. Anytime that you hear things about ascension, the light of the sun, and so on, that's the solar energy being connected to and being drawn upon. Part of the allure of these traditions, in some cases, is the idea of escapism—since the material earth is problematic and imperfect, we can ascend and go to more-perfect realms. The problem with some of this thinking is that it separates the living earth from all things sacred or holy—I firmly believe that part of the reason that such pillaging of the planet is happening is because of the emphasis in dominant world religions on solar energy as the only sacred and meaningful energy. The earth, then, is seen only as a resource worth taking from.

## SPIRIT BELOW: The Telluric Current

While the light of the sun comes down to Earth, the *telluric* current rises from the heat and energy of the earth itself. Ecologically, we have the molten core of the earth, which drives the earth's tectonic plates and thus shapes the land mass on the surface. Tectonic plates and land masses, along with the energy of the sun and the composition of the atmosphere, determine our climate.[16] The great soil web of life, which contains millions of organisms in a single teaspoon of rich soil,[17] is created as part of this process. Thus, we can see the importance of the biological aspects of the earth in the larger patterns of life on this planet.

The telluric current's name comes from Tellus, a name for the ancient Roman goddess of the earth. She was also known as "terra mater" or Mother Earth; later, this was a word in Latin, "telluric," meaning "land, territory, or earth." These ancient connections, then, are present in the name itself, where the earth and her energy were often personified and worshiped as divine.

Energetically, the telluric current starts at the center of the earth and rises through the layers of the stone and molten lava flows, through the groundwater and underwater aquifers, through the minerals and layers of fossils, and into the crust of the earth. It takes its shape from what is on the surface: plants, trees, roads, rivers, valleys, and so on. As Greer notes in *The Druid Magic Handbook*, it is powerfully affected by underground sources of water (aquifers); springs and wells that come up from the land have very strong concentrations of telluric energy. This helps explain why sacred wells, throughout the ages, have been such an important part of spiritual traditions in many parts of the world—and why we can use clean spring water for healing purposes. This also explains why fracking, that which taints the underground waters themselves, is so horrific.

As R. J. Stewart notes in *Earth Light*, it is from the currents of the earth that the nutrients flow from the living earth into our bodies, regenerating them. It is from the telluric that you can find the light of transformation and regeneration. The telluric represents the dark places in the world, the energy found in caves and deep in the depths of our souls. The telluric energy sometimes is about confronting the shadows within ourselves and realizing that those are part of us too, that each of us is a balance of light and dark. The telluric currents are tied to lived experience—the act of being—rather than rationalizing and talking about. In *Lines upon the Landscape*, Pennick and Devereux (1989) sum this up nicely when they write, "For us, the sense of traveling through a dark and elemental landscape, pregnant with magical and spiritual forces, is no longer experienced. We have separated ourselves from the land and live within our own abstractions" (p. 246). Take a minute to think about the word "dark"— in modern Western culture, it is immediately associated with evil (showing our strong solar bias). But darkness can be a place of rest, of quietude, of inner learning and knowing.

There are fewer traditions that work primarily with the telluric currents— the Underworld tradition (see R. J. Stewart's works) is one such tradition. Many forms of shamanism, where the practitioner is going down into the depths of the earth or their own consciousness to seek allies and assistance, is also telluric in nature. These traditions are frequently concerned with transforming the here and now, and seeing the earth as sacred, understanding the sacred soil upon which life depends.

## SPIRIT WITHIN: Lunar Current

A third current—the *lunar* current—can be created by consciously bringing the solar current and the telluric current together in balance. As Greer writes in *The Druid Magic Handbook*, "When the lunar current awakens in an individual, it awakens the inner sense and unfolds into enlightenment. When it awakens in the land, it brings healing, fertility, and plenty" (p. 30).

We can see ancient humans' deep knowledge of the three currents and their interaction reflected in the ancient ley lines upon the landscape—for example, Cuzco, Peru, which means "navel of the earth," had at its center the Inca Temple of the Sun. It was here that the *coricancha* (emperor) sat at the heart of the temple; radiating the light of the sun outward from this temple like a sunburst was a large web of straight lines reaching into the countryside (Pennick and Devereux 1989, 251). On the other side of the world, we see the same principles at play in China, where the Chinese emperor sat on his throne in the center of the Imperial Palace (the "Purple Forbidden City"), centered on the imperial road and with gates leading outward to the four directions (Pennick and Devereux 1989, 251). In these, and in other ancient civilizations, the rulers, associated with the sun or considering themselves as "sun gods" or "sons of heaven," radiated via these "transmission lines" to bring the solar energy down and radiate it outward to bless the manifestation of the telluric.

In both cases, the ruler was the person awakening that third current and sending it out for the bounty and health of the land.

The lunar current also helps us resolve the binary created by the telluric and solar currents—it shows us that unification is possible and that part of awakening the lunar current can be part of our healing arts. We unify what is above with what is below to bring the two into harmony. To return to our opening discussion of "energy," the Nywfre flows from the awakening of this third current, through the alchemical synthesis and transformation of the other two. Knowledge of the three currents and practice working with them are incredibly useful for deep land-healing work. These concepts will be used throughout this book.

## THE FOUR ELEMENTS

The final part of the energetic framework that is present in this book is working with the four classical elements. The classical elements of earth, air, fire, and water or some similar equivalent were part of many ancient cultures, including those of ancient Greece, Persia, Babylonia, and China. In ancient Persia around 600 BCE, the ancient philosopher Zarathustra (Zoroaster) seems to have originated the four-element theory in the West. Zoroaster described the four elements as "sacred" and "essential for the survival of all living beings and therefore should be venerated and kept free from any contamination."[18] The failure to keep these elements pure could anger the gods. If only the modern world had such wisdom, we wouldn't need a book about land healing! Drawing upon the earlier writings of Empedocles on the four elements, Aristotle writing between 384 and 322 BCE, added a fifth element, Aether (spirit). These elements were considered four states of matter, with the fifth being a connection to the metaphysical (that which is beyond the physical), with different ancient cultures working with them in different ways. Centuries later, the aspects of spirit were more fully explored as above, below, and within (as we just explored). The classical elements have been with humanity for a very long time, and they are very useful archetypes to draw upon.

The four elements are physical (e.g., the soil as earth, the fire as fire, water in a stream), metaphysical, and conceptual. Thus, you can see the elements at play along the landscape but also understand their metaphysical and conceptual qualities. Earth is the element tied to the north, to the dark moon, to the energy of winter and midnight. We find the earth physically in mountains, stones, and trees, all of what classical writers would call "the firmament." The energy of earth, manifesting metaphysically, offers grounding, stability, strength, and perseverance. Earth encourages us to be grounded and stable in our work.

Air is the element tied to the east, to the waxing moon, to the energy of spring and dawn. We find the air physically in the wind, the sky, the clouds, and the rustle of the leaves as they blow in the breeze. The energy of air, manifesting metaphysically, offers us clarity, knowledge, wisdom, focus, and objectivity. Air encourages us to temper our emotions with reason, evidence, and clear thinking.

Fire is the element tied to the south, to the full moon, to the energy of summer and noon. We find the fire physically as a fire itself (such as that at a campsite or in your fireplace) but also in the combustion materials to create heat and energy (in the modern word, oil or electricity). The energy of fire, manifesting metaphysically, has to do with our inspiration, transformation, creativity, passions, and will—how we direct our lives and what we want to bring into manifestation. In the classical texts, fire is often closest to the divine, since it is a transformative agent.

Water is the element tied to the west, to the waning moon, the energy of fall and the dusk. We find the water physically in rivers, lakes, oceans, springs, streams, storms, and even in our own bodies. The energy of water, manifesting metaphysically, offers us intuition, emotion, healing, wisdom, connection (particularly connection with nature and spirit), and flow.

Now, to further illustrate how the seven elements can work together for healing, we'll explore two rituals: a Seven-Element Land-Blessing Ritual and a Land Protection ritual.

## Seven-Element Land-Blessing Ceremony

Many traditional land-blessing ceremonies include using some form of energy raising to bless and protect a space. This ceremony draws upon the energy of the seven directions for blessing and healing and demonstrates one way they can be used. This ceremony is ideally done walking the perimeter of a piece of land you want to protect. If you aren't able to walk a perimeter, you can adapt it by simply calling in the elements from a central location. I would suggest that before performing this ceremony, you do deep listening (chapter 2) with the land to make sure such a ceremony would be welcome. This ceremony has individual and group variations.

# Land-Blessing Ceremony for a Solitary Practitioner

**Materials:**
smoke-cleansing (smudge) stick
bowl of lightly salted water
candle that can be carried (to relight smoke stick as necessary)
bowl of herbs, flowers, or sand for marking the circle of spirit below
wand, staff, sword, or knife for tracing the circle of spirit above (or just use your hand)
bell, rattle, or drum for sounding spirit within

You can place all materials on a central altar or lay them on the ground. I will note that if you don't have some or any of these tools, you can still do the ceremony, visualizing the elements as you work.

**Select your anchor:** Prior to the ritual, select a central stone, tree, or other natural feature to be the anchor for the energy that you will be raising.

**Declare intentions:** Start the ritual by declaring your intentions in your own words. For example: "The purpose of this ceremony is to bless and protect this landscape and allow for regeneration to happen. I am here as a healer, friend, and fellow inhabitant of this land. May peace abide in this working and throughout these lands."

**Make an offering:** See chapter 2 for appropriate offerings. You can use your own words or say, "Spirits of place, spirits of this land, I make this offering to honor and acknowledge you. Guardians of this place, of matter or spirit, be with this place." Pause and wait for any messages or feelings before continuing.

**Fire and air:** Walk the perimeter of the land or in a large circle within the land (or both) for the next part in a deosil (clockwise) pattern. As you walk, you will begin by blessing the space with the four classical elements: air, fire, water, and earth. First, bless and clear the space, using air and fire with your smoke-cleansing stick. As you walk, visualize the elements of air and fire strongly in this place (you can envision them as a yellow and red light). As you walk, chant: "Smoke of healing herbs and sacred fires that purify. Clear and bless this sacred place."

When you return to the place you began, pause as you envision the energy of air and fire.

**Earth and water:** Now, bless and clear the space with water and earth. Again, envision the elements strongly in this space (you can envision them as a blue and green light). Take your bowl of water and flick it out with your fingers as you walk. Say, "Waters of the sacred pool and salt of the earth. Clear and bless this sacred place."

When you return to the place you began, pause as envision the energy of water and earth.

**Spirit below and telluric current:** Move to the center of the space. Say, "I call upon the three aspects of spirit, those that connect the worlds. Let the spirit that flows within all living beings bless and protect this place today and always."

Draw a circle on the ground in a deosil (clockwise) pattern, as large as you would like. Alternatively, you can once again walk the perimeter of your space. Mark as you are drawing your circle, marking it with the herbs/flowers/sand. Move to the center of the circle and place your hands on the earth. Pause and envision the currents of energy deep within the earth. Say, "I call to spirit below to bless and protect this land. Great telluric current that moves through this land, great soil web of all life, I ask that you fill this land with your energy and blessing."

Pause and envision the currents deep within the heart of the earth as a green gold, rising up from the core of the earth and blessing the land around you, bathing the land in a gold-green glow.

**Spirit above and solar current:** Using a wand, staff, sword, or knife, or just using your hand, draw a circle in the air above you. Alternatively, if your space is small, you can walk the perimeter with your hand or tool in the air. Move to the center of your circle and raise your hands into the sky. Pause and envision the energy of the sun and movement of the planets, all providing energy and influence. Say, "I call to spirit above to bless and protect this land. Sun that shines above and the turning wheel of the stars that bathes this land in radiance, I ask that you fill this land with your energy and blessing."

Pause and envision the sun radiating the solar current down to you in a beautiful yellow-golden light. Envision the stars and planets each contributing their own light. This light blesses the land around you, bathing the land in a golden glow.

**Spirit within and lunar current:** Using the drum, the noisemaker, or a simple chant, begin to reach out to the spirit within all things. The spark of life, the Nywfre that flows within each thing—this is the power of spirit within. Place your hands on a living thing within the land, such as a central tree or stone, and sense the spirit within it. Say, "I call to spirit within, the enduring spirit within all things. Nywfre, Nywfre, Nywfre. Spirit that connects us all, I ask that you fill this land with your energy and blessing."

Pause and envision the spark of life and spirit of all things, rising up from within. Envision the other six energies coming to the central point where you have your anchor stone/tree and see the energy pouring into that anchor point, only then to radiate outward to the surrounding land being protected.

**Deep listening and divination:** Make space for the spirits of the land to communicate with you before finishing your ceremony. For this, I suggest either deep listening or using a divination system such as Tarot. Allow yourself to grow quiet and let the voices of the land speak to you.

**Gratitude and parting:** Close the ceremony by thanking the seven directions.

> Move to the east and say, "Spirits of the east, powers of air, thank you for your blessing this day."

> Move to the south and say, "Spirits of the south, powers of fire, thank you for your blessing this day."

> Move to the west and say, "Spirits of the west, powers of water, thank you for your blessing this day."

> Move to the north and say, "Spirits of the north, powers of earth, thank you for your blessing this day."

> Move to the center and put your hands on the earth. Say, "Spirits of the below, power of the telluric current, thank you for your blessing this day."

> Raise your hands to the heavens. Say, "Spirits of the above, power of the solar current, thank you for your blessing this day."

> Cross your arms over your chest and close your eyes. Say, "Spirit within all things, power of the lunar current, thank you for your blessing this day."

This ritual can be done in a group setting. If you have fewer than seven people, divide up the elements among you. You can also split up earth and water and air and fire into separate elements (see language that follows). If you have a larger group, multiple people can carry a representation of the element or some other energy-raising object, such as a bell, drum, or rattle. Language for all four elements is as follows:

> **Air:** "Smoke of healing herbs and sacred fires that purify. Clear and bless this sacred place."
> **Fire:** "Sacred fires that purify. Clear and bless this sacred place."
> **Water:** "Waters of the sacred pool. Clear and bless this sacred place."
> **Earth:** "Salt of the earth. Clear and bless this place."

## BLESSING-SIGIL EMPOWERMENT

Empower your blessing sigils (chapter 2) with the Land-Blessing ceremony. Open up a sacred grove and place your sigils in the middle of your sacred-grove space. Rather than walking a perimeter of the land, instead circle the sigils with each of the elements, one at a time, and speak the words of blessing into the ceremony (use your own words here). Call to the telluric, solar, and lunar currents, bringing each into the sigils. See the sigils you inscribed glow with the gold-green light of blessing. Thank the elements and close the space. Your sigils are ready to use.

# The Sphere of Protection:
# Using the Seven-Element Framework

This ritual, using the seven-element framework, was created by Dr. Juliet Ashley in the 1960s for a host of spiritual orders she was heading, including the Ancient Order of Druids in America (AODA). I was taught this ritual as part of my training in AODA, and this ritual is still used by AODA for a variety of purposes. The version presented here is an adaptation used as a land protection ceremony. It is recommended that you perform this working outside if possible. Part of the use of rituals using the seven-element framework is that they are highly adaptable. Because the elements and currents are part of every aspect of life on Earth, we can call upon them and draw upon them in a variety of circumstances.

Use this ritual to protect anything from a single tree to a large forest. To prepare, you will want something you can anchor the center of the ritual to, such as a stone or tree. Perform your ritual around that anchor point and, when you get to the last part of the ritual, tie the sphere of protection to that anchor point in your mind. You can also use this as part of a sacred-grove opening, as described in the next section.

Please also note that while this ritual may initially seem complex, the first four elements are repeated, simply with putting new information for each element. Once you have the hang of it, this ritual is quite simple! You can modify it in any way you want, using language, movement, and more. Also, what is written here is a sample of what you can say. For each of these, you can call on your own understanding of these elemental powers.

# The Sphere of Protection:

## INVOKING THE SIX DIRECTIONS

**East.** Move to the east. Trace the symbol of air (a circle with a line coming up from the top of it) in the air in a clockwise fashion. As you trace it, envision the symbol glowing with a strong yellow light. Say, "I call upon the powers of the east. Power of the hawk of dawn and the element of air, come and protect this land."

Feel the power of the air coming forth. If you are performing this when working outside, pause for a moment to attend to the physical powers of the air: the wind upon your skin, the rustle of the leaves, and so on. Say, "I thank the powers of the east."

Trace the symbol of air in a counterclockwise fashion and say, "With the help of the powers of air, I banish from this land any forces that would cause it to come to harm."

Envision the air sweeping anything away that may harm the land.

**South.** Move to the south, clockwise from the east. Trace the symbol of fire (a triangle with point facing up) in the air in a clockwise fashion. As you trace it, envision the symbol glowing with a strong red light. Say, "I call upon the powers of the south. Power of the stag of the wood and the element of fire, come and protect this land."

Feel the power of the fire coming forth. If you are performing this when working outside, pause for a moment to attend to the physical powers of the fire: the heat in the landscape, the sun warm upon your skin, and so on. Say, "I thank the powers of the south."

Trace the symbol of fire in a counterclockwise fashion. Say, "With the help of the powers of fire, I banish from this land any forces that would the cause it to come to harm." Envision the fire sweeping anything away that may harm the land.

**West.** Move to the west, clockwise from the south. Trace the symbol of water (an inverted triangle with point facing down) in the air in a clockwise fashion. As you trace it, envision the symbol glowing with a strong blue light. Say, "I call upon the powers of the west. Power of the salmon of wisdom and the element of water, come and protect this land."

Feel the power of the water coming forth. If you are performing this when working outside, pause for a moment to attend to the physical powers of the water: the moisture in the air, the singing of the brook, the dampness of the soil. Say, "I thank the powers of the west."

Trace the symbol of water in a counterclockwise fashion. Say, "With the help of the powers of water, I banish from this land any forces that would cause it to come to harm." Envision the water sweeping anything away that may harm the land.

**North.** Move to the north, clockwise from the west. Trace the symbol of earth (a circle with a stem moving toward the ground) in the air in a clockwise fashion. As you trace it, envision the symbol glowing with a strong green light. Say, "I call upon the powers of the North. Power of the great bear and the element of earth, come and protect this land."

Feel the power of the earth coming forth. If you are performing this when working outside, pause for a moment to attend to the physical powers of the earth: the stones beneath your feet, the strong trunks of the trees, the mountains in the distance. Say, "I thank the powers of the north."

Trace the symbol of earth in a counterclockwise fashion. Say, "With the help of the powers of earth, I banish from this land any forces that would cause it to come to harm." Envision the earth sweeping anything away that may harm the land.

**Spirit below.** Move to the center of your space. On the ground, trace a large circle (physically or metaphysically) and envision this circle glowing a vibrant orange. Place both of your hands on the ground in the center of the circle. Say,

"I call upon the powers of spirit below, the powers of the telluric current deep within the earth's core and the soil web of life. Telluric current, rise and bless and protect this land."

Envision a gold-green light rising from the core of the earth and coming into the space. Sit with the energy for a time. Say, "I thank the powers of spirit below."

**Spirit above.** Staying in the center of your circle, trace a large circle in the sky and envision this circle glowing a vibrant purple. Raise both of your hands into heavens and say, "I call upon the powers of spirit above, the powers of the solar current in the sun's heart and the turning wheel of the stars. Solar current, descend and bless and protect this land."

Envision a golden light descending from the sun and coming into the space. Sit with the energy for a time. Say, "I thank the powers of spirit above.

**Spirit within and sphere of protection.** Draw your awareness to each of the elements you have called. As you draw your awareness to the elements and symbols in the six directions surrounding you, breathe deeply and call them to the center of your space. Place your hands on your anchor stone or tree or the earth below you and say, "As the six powers have been called, so now do the six powers unite to protect this land from all harm. May the spirit within be awakened by these powers to bring blessing and protection to this land."

Envision each of the elements swirling into a white light around you, forming a large sphere that enlarges to protect whatever your intention is to protect. Spend as much time as you need to envision this strongly before continuing. If you want, you can do another action here, such as beating on a drum to enhance the effect.

When you have visualized this firmly, say, "As the elements here in the physical world come, so, too, this protection remains. As the sun rises and sets, so this protection will remain. As the winds blow, the rains come, and the wheel turns, so this protection will be tied to those natural forces. I ask that this place be protected from harm this day and always."

Pause, feeling the energies of the working settling into the landscape. When you are ready, cross your arms and bow your head toward the land. Say, "I thank the powers of the elements and the spirits of nature for their gifts. May the powers of nature guide my path as a land healer, now and always."

As we can see from the Land-Blessing ceremony and the Sphere of Protection ritual, the seven elements provide a very powerful framework for healing and blessing, drawn from literally millennia of human history and human spiritual work. Thus, we use these elements extensively throughout this book. I also want to say that while I'm providing many rituals and practices in this book, the seven-element framework and the sphere of protection offer you a useful framework for developing your own approaches.

## PROTECTION SIGIL EMPOWERMENT

The sphere of protection can be used to empower your protection sigils (chapter 2). Place your protection sigils in the center of your working space. As you envision a glow of light as you call each element, direct the light into the sigil itself, seeing it begin to glow with the color of the element. When you finish calling the six directions and prepare to complete the sphere, envision the sphere of protection surrounding the sigils and then going into the sigils, swirling with rainbow light. As you close the Sphere of Protection ritual, offer gratitude. Your protection sigils are now empowered.

# Opening Up a Sacred Grove:
# Stepping between Matter and Spirit

A third principle that is useful to understand for land healing is the interconnection of matter and spirit. The physical world is connected to the metaphysical world, and both influence each other. What we do on the physical world can have deep metaphysical connections, and vice versa. Many traditions recognize that transitioning between the everyday world and the world of spirit can be aided by a variety of tools: opening a sacred space, energetic cleansing of participants, attending to breath work, ringing a singing bowl, entering into meditation, or drumming, to name a few.

If you are going to engage in any energetic land-healing work, it is often necessary that you use some form of space opening and closing. A sacred-space opening and closing not only will help you, as a human land healer, come to the right frame of mind but will also help open the world of spirit to you so that you can do this the best way possible. It allows you to create a safe space in which to work, and to protect yourself and the spirits you are working with. Land healing can tie you, at times, to energy that is dark and painful, and having good practices for sacred-grove protection will benefit you tremendously. Because this is a more advanced book and most traditions teach some kind of sacred-space opening, which you may already practice regularly, I would suggest that you use what you are already familiar with for land-healing practices. However, if you do not have a method, I suggest a variant on the Sphere of Protection ritual, with some additional opening and closing pieces which is what is presented here.

1. Begin by attending to your breath. Take several deep breaths. With each breath, feel the weight of the world and things that concern you start to fade away. Optionally, do other cleansing, such as smoke cleansing.

2. State your intentions for the work you are going to do in your own words (e.g., "I am here to offer a ritual for sleep due to the impending forest cutting that is happening here").

3. Call forth the energies of the seven directions, using the Sphere of Protection ritual (*above*). Envision the sphere of protection surrounding you and the space you are working to heal (or the space you are working in).

4. Make an offering in gratitude and thanks to the spirits of the land.

A variety of ways exist to call in elements to work with them in a sacred space, not all of them verbal in nature. You can use your imagination and visualization, music or drumming (for example, having a different beat or tune for each of the elements), you can use your body and dance, you could use a hand motion, or you can simply pay attention to the element manifesting in the world at that moment. There is no right or wrong way to do this—just find something that you can do naturally and comfortably.

For example, to call in a sacred space silently, I would stand in the east and feel the wind blow upon my face. Then I would move to the south and feel the heat of the sun. I would move to the west and pay attention to the water present in the landscape, then move to the north and feel the earth and solidity around me. I would place my hands on the soil, feeling the energy of the earth and connecting to the earth's core. Then I would raise my hands in the air and draw down the energy from the heavens. I would place my hands on my altar or central space and draw these energies together to form a sphere. This could all be done silently and effectively to create the space for your work—no tools, no words, just breath, attention, and movement.

Once you are finished, it is necessary to close the sacred grove. Closing the space helps bring the energies of the space back into balance, signals that the work is over, and also helps you transition back to the physical world. A similar approach can be used to close a sacred space as above:

1. Again, attend to your breath, allowing the release of the energies you raised or your experiences during the ritual to settle into you.

2. Walk to each of the directions widdershins (counterclockwise), thanking them for their help. You can do this verbally in a silent thanks.

3. Release any excess energy from your ritual. Place your hand on the earth and say, "If there is any remaining energy from this healing ritual, let it be returned to the land for blessing." Envision this energy traveling into the earth.

4. If appropriate, imagine the sphere of protection you created slowly returning to the earth as well. (Note: In many cases, if you are doing protective work, you may choose to keep it up in some form so it can continue to protect the area. The decision about this should be a case-by-case basis.)

5. Thank the spirits in respect.

After closing a space, particularly after doing intensive work, you will likely want to engage in some self-care practices (see chapter 9). It is useful to eat or drink something for further grounding. Choose nutrient-dense foods that are healthy, such as fruit, eggs, lean meats, or vegetables.

# Raising or Lowering Energy

Now that we have a sense of what energy is, the kinds of energy we might work with, and a few tools for working with it, we can talk more generally about what to do with that energy. Energetic work is necessary for nearly all energetic land healing, useful for physical land healing, and often appropriate for palliative care and helping spirits pass. In this section I offer general principles that will be expanded on in specific ways in future chapters.

Let's return a moment to our wassail ritual. The wassail ritual is a nice example of a group of people raising energy and directing that energy into a chosen vessel (the tree) to then radiate that energy out to the broader land. The ritual uses a variety of methods for raising energy, including circling/ dancing around the tree, singing, and drumming/noisemaking. These all are physical and embodied methods of raising energy and work particularly well in groups. One theory about why this works is that while physically expending energy, using quick movements and sound, we raise the energetic vibration of a space and then direct that energy. Individuals can use these approaches too: a good drumbeat or rattle, a dance, a song, a chant, or even a forest frolic all can raise the energy needed to send elsewhere. So sound and physical movement are two options for raising energy.

A second method of raising energy is more metaphysical and mental. One can raise energy and direct it by using quiet breath work, focus, or a steady chime or beat. For this, you want to be in a natural place where you can connect to sources of power outside you (the sun, the moon, mountains, the seven elements, etc.). As you meditate, imagine drawing that energy into you (to be directed back outward) or into an object or place for healing. You might draw upon the seven elements as part of raising this energy.

A third method of raising energy is directly connected to nature's power. With permission and gratitude, tie your working into an existing powerful and natural energy source, such as moving water, wind, or energy of a storm. Thus, you can borrow some of that energy to direct toward a specific purpose in healing by envisioning a connection between the energy source and where you need to direct it.

A fourth method works directly with the energy of spirit: deities, spirit guides, or other beings that you already have existing relationships with. Many choose to work with deities in this way, so you might call on a nature-oriented deity such as Elen, Cernunnos, Radagast, or Frau Hollie. The specifics of this would be negotiated on the basis of the spirit or deity and the relationships you established with them.

Lowering energy involves the opposite of the above—attuning with the current energetic frequency and finding ways of slowing it down or lessening it. For land-healing purposes, energy lowering typically comes in a few situations: when the spirits of the land are angry and that anger is no longer productive and is getting in the way of moving on (so this would be some kind of releasing magic), or when you want to help land go to sleep so that it can avoid trauma and pain—present or future. These approaches are discussed more specifically in chapters 6 and 8.

Different kinds of land-healing work may be suited for different ways of raising and directing energy. Thus, you may find that physical movement is well suited to helping engage in energetic healing for a forest, but quiet distance work is better for a site that needs palliative care. The important thing to recognize at this stage is that these energy practices matter. If this concept is new to you, I would suggest some practice—open up a sacred grove. Raise energy in the space with one of the methods above and then, once at its peak, gently bring it back down or send it into your crane bag and working tools. Remember that much of land healing is based on sets of skills—skills that the more you practice, the more effective you will be in anything you want to set your mind to.

Because we spend so much time in deep listening as land healers, action is necessarily varied, flexible, and intuitive. None of the rituals or practices given in this book have to be done as they are written—consider them templates that you can work from and adapt for your current circumstances. The basic formula is to start with deep listening and preliminary practices first. Once you know the course of action, open up sacred space. Set intentions. Make offerings. Do energy work of some kind. Engage in more deep listening. Offer gratitude and close, then practice self-care and grounding. It can be that simple—and a lot of the specific rituals and workings in this book use some variant on the basic formula.

# Distance Work and Levels of Energetic Connection

Often, engaging in land healing is very local work: you work with the plants, animals, bodies of water, insect life, and many other aspects of life that are where you are. Depending on where you live, even within a mile or 10 miles, there may be a lot for you to do. Some work is better done at a distance, while other work, such as physical land regeneration (chapter 7), must be done in person.

Land healers also feel led to do work at a distance on behalf of a place—perhaps a place you visited or one that is calling to you for healing or a place where you once lived but no longer do. Even though you live far away or cannot reach that place, you want to help. Distance energetic work is necessary for a variety of reasons: lack of access to a site due to it being on someone else's property or in the middle of a extraction zone (e.g., fracking well, mountaintop removal site, factory), mobility and transportation issues, safety, or because the site is too far away for you to reach it physically.

Distance-healing techniques are more-advanced techniques that require confidence in a variety of spirit communication and protection techniques: deep listening, spirit communication, visualization, grounding, and protection. You need to focus for long periods of time and be open to the messages of spirit (see the suggestions for building this focus in chapter 2). You have to be able to protect yourself, since any energetic healing requires a deep energetic connection—and that connection goes both ways. You have to be able to raise and direct energy effectively. If you are still learning these techniques, you should work on developing them further before doing serious distance-healing work, particularly on sites that have extensive damage or require palliative care.

Any distance work is based on a connection that you establish between yourself and the land (be it a piece of land, body of water, specific animal or group of animals, plants or groups of plants, etc.). If it is land you visited before, you can use your own memory or any mementos or tokens you may have gathered. If you haven't ever visited the site but still want to do healing, it's helpful to have something that represents the land, such as a natural object, memento, or photograph. The idea behind connecting at a distance is that you will establish some energetic line between you and the land you are working to heal, and through this line, you can send energy, activate sigils, chant, work magic, and much more.

There are at least three different energetic levels of connection you can make with the land, and understanding the differences is important for distance work.

*Communicative.* The first level is being able to sense and communicate—enough to do deep-listening work, enough to ascertain what state the land is in energetically. This is a lot like standing on a peak and overlooking a mountain below or talking to a friend on the phone—you see what's going on, but you aren't quite close enough to be affected energetically in a significant way. This level of connection allows you to communicate and sense energy but not actually affect it deeply (which is good for those new to these practices). This connection can allow you to do witnessing, communication, apology, and some space-holding techniques (chapter 2).

*Energetic.* The second level is an energetic connection, where you can raise or lower energy, send energy, and receive energy back. It is at this level that you can work magic, where you can do chanting magic, raise and direct energy, and do any number of energetic healing techniques found in chapters 4, 5, 6, and 8.

*Attunement.* The third level—what I call attunement—happens only over prolonged contact with the land, where you are always in deep connection with the land. This happens after years of direct working with the land, interacting with it, and a period of time where you have lived on the land or regularly visited (the Grove of Renewal practices, in chapter 7, can help establish this deep connection over time). With attunement, there is always some energetic connection present, and that connection can be sensed and activated on either side very simply. Work can easily be done at a distance through that existing link that is always present. This attunement usually takes years or decades to achieve and is a slow process.

## ENGAGING IN DISTANCE WORK

To connect with land at a distance, begin finding a quiet place where you will not be interrupted. Begin by engaging in shielding techniques, such as the Sphere of Protection ritual offered earlier in this chapter, or your own that you regularly use. No distance work should take place without protection. Once you are properly protected, make yourself as comfortable as possible (sitting or lying on the ground). If you have any objects or images to connect with, hold them in your hand or place them before you.

*Communicative:* **Finding the thread of connection.** Envision the place or person that needs healing (land/waterway/plant/animal) before you. See it in your mind's eye; focus on the object or image. Speak aloud, asking to connect. Sense the connection between you, like a small golden thread, connecting you to that part of the land you want to connect with. If you have been there before or have met this being before, this thread may already be established. If you haven't met before, you might need to establish the thread by reaching out through the object/image with your mind's eye and establishing the connection through visualization. Breathe, allowing the connection to unfold out and be established. Then, go about deep listening or any other practices you want to do (such as those in chapter 2). This connection should allow for basic communication and deep-listening techniques.

*Energetic*: **Feeling the heartbeat of the land.** The second stage of connection establishes an energetic link that can go both ways so you can do ritual at a distance, including land blessings (this chapter), energetic land healing (chapter 5), and palliative care (chapter 6). All land and beings have their own rhythms, and if you focus, you can align with the heartbeat of the land/being/plant. To do this, once you have connected at a distance and have clear permission, slow your breathing down and quiet yourself as much as you can. Now, feel your own heartbeat. As you listen to yours, widen your range and feel the beat of the land / tree / body of water, etc. If you have an object from the land, hold the object in your hand while you do so. Sometimes this can take time.

Once you have the beat, match it on a drum, rattle, gong, bell branch, or any other instrument. If you don't have any of these, simply clapping, snapping, or slapping your hand on your leg will work perfectly fine. Spend some time aligning to this second beat. This gives you a good connection to the land, even at a distance. From this point, you can do many different kinds of energetic healing and palliative care.

*Attunement:* **Establishing permanent connection.** Deep attunement requires long-term physical connection to the land, or to a particular species or body of water. This is intuitive work with the land. Live on and work on a piece of land long enough, and you will grow attuned to it and it will be easy to connect with at any point or any time, even if you are at a distance. The connection is always present, whether or not you are actively aware of it.

# Chapter 5:

ENERGETIC LAND HEALING

**A group of forty druids gather as the sun** is setting in the old Eastern Hemlock grove, just above the river. Tall, majestic, and serene, these Hemlocks are a keystone species in eastern North America; their presence represents the final step in ecological succession for US East Coast forests. However, these Hemlocks are suffering. They have recently been afflicted with the Hemlock Woolly Adelgid, a tiny aphid-like invasive insect that will slowly suck the sap—their lifeblood—from their branches until they die. For about a decade, the Hemlock Woolly Adelgid has slowly made its way west—and now it has reached this sacred place. We druids form a circle. A ring of fires are lit, and fire tenders stand ready. We open a sacred space, calling to the directions, making offerings to the ancestors of our tradition, ancestors of the land, and to the spirits who may be watching. We join hands and form concentric circles around three Hemlock trees. The fire tenders begin to quietly chant as they hold our space, to create a container for the energy we are raising. Three concentric circles of people link hands, then move and chant around the trees. When the energy is literally crackling in the air, all groups move toward the center and place many hands on the trunks of those ancient Hemlock trees. All the energy we raised goes into those Hemlocks, which, through the same magic that allows wassailing ceremonies to be so successful, spreads to the other Hemlocks in the area and then across the land. We smile, we ground, we cheer—good work was done this evening. Whether this will turn the tide of the battle against the Hemlock Woolly Adelgid is yet to be seen, but we have raised healing energy for the good of the land.

The Eastern Hemlock illustrates a key point for land-healing work, a point that can help you distinguish between energetic healing (this chapter) and palliative care (chapter 6). When approaching the Hemlocks to do the ritual (as part of deep-listening work; see chapter 3), the question we asked was "What do the Hemlocks want? Do they want us to help soothe the burden and pain of the adelgid infestation, or do they want us to raise energy for a fight?" In the case of the Hemlock story, the clear message we received from the land was that the trees wanted to live and fight, and thus, raising a powerful amount of energy by using the techniques in this chapter was the right approach. If they wanted to pass on in peace, then it would be more appropriate to use the palliative-care methods.

To explore this distinction further, let's return to our earlier metaphor of a person who is in need of healing. You have a friend who has recently had a serious surgery. Right now, that friend is weak, bedridden, yet positive about recovery. What can you do for your friend? You might bring them gifts. You would certainly go visit them and let them know that you care. You might also offer various kinds of healing and blessing ceremonies to aid in their recovery. Your friend, at various points, may ask you to get something or do something for them that they can't do on their own. While your friend's own body has to do the healing, your own time, care, and magic can powerfully support the process. We can apply this same kind of philosophy to energetic land healing— and the work of this chapter.

Most of the rituals in this chapter are variations on a similar formula— you set intentions for the ritual, raise energy, and then do something to direct it out. That "something" to direct it out can be either passive or active. Rituals that have a specific focus of releasing the energy at the end of them are more active. Setting standing stones or constructing mandalas that you may leave upon the landscape for long-term work is more passive. Once you have the general pattern of how these rituals work, you can create your own. This chapter offers suggestions for different approaches—solo and group— to energetic land healing. You can choose an approach that is based both on what you want to accomplish and which ones you are most drawn to for your specific situation.

Here we focus on raising energy for healing and growth: this work is best for places where healing can happen, or where the raising energy can do good (as in the case of the hemlock ritual described above). In other words, these are spaces that are ready for the healing energy that we can offer—a forest after a fire, a new piece of land, land that has been cleared and replanted, land that is battling a destructive invasive species, and so on. You can do this kind of healing both on a larger scale or for individual trees, animals, or small plots of land. Thus, this chapter offers six different approaches to energetic land healing, as well as insights on large-scale healing and visioning practices.

# Approach 1:
## Working with the Seven Elements and Visualization

On the most basic level, a very effective energetic working can be done employing the seven-element framework from chapter 4. This is what I consider to be my "go to" land-healing approach and the one that I use most frequently, because it is effective, consistent, and powerful. The ritual that is presented here is a variation of the seven-element blessing and Sphere of Protection ritual and uses both visualization and connecting to the seven elements as its primary sources of energy raising. To do this work, you will need to choose a focal point—a stone, a tree, a plant, or some other natural feature. If you want to do this ritual at a different site and bring the energy elsewhere, you can use a small stone as a focal point, wrap it in cotton or linen cloth after the ritual, and transport it to a site for healing. You can also use this ritual at a distance.

Obviously, you can do a number of variations on this with more tools, words, drumming, dancing, music, and more. This is the basic energetic form. I often perform it as written, or I use a drum or flute improvisation for each of the directions. Use and modify it as you see fit.

## Seven-Element Land-Healing Ritual

**Optional materials:** Blessed oil or water, growth sigil, offering

Take a moment to breathe deeply and center yourself before you begin. If you have an herbal-healing oil or blessed water, dip your fingers in the water or oil and then run them over the focal point. If you have created a healing-sigil set, place a sigil near the focal point.

Stand facing the east. Take a moment to attune with the energies of the air. If you are outside, observe the east and the air, breathing, seeing the wind blow through the trees, feeling the air on your face. Breathe deeply, bringing the element of air to your focal point, a yellow and bright light. Take all the time you need to establish this visualization. Repeat the visual at the remaining three quarters: fire in the south (envisioning a red light), water in the west (envisioning a blue light), and earth in the north (envisioning a green light). If you want to include words at each of the quarters, you can do so as you feel led.

Next, place your hands on the earth around or near your focal point. Connect with the deep heart of the earth and feel the rising of the telluric currents and energy from Mother Earth herself. Connect to this source, feeling it rising into your focal point, a green-gold light.

Stand tall and reach your hands to the sky, above or near your focal point. Connect with the heat of the sun and the turning wheel of the heavens. Feel that vibrant solar energy descending down into your focal point, filling it with the golden light of the solar current.

Take several deep breaths and place your hands over your focal point. Feel the energies in the focal point mixing and growing stronger. Imagine them coming from the six directions and spiraling into a single white light, the light of healing, growth, and peace. Focus on this as strongly as you can.

Once this is firmly established, place your hands on the focal point and radiate this healing energy outward to the land; see it ripple from the focal point to the other places it needs to go.

Bow your head and thank the spirits for their gifts. Leave an offering at your focal point.

# Approach 2:
## Land Healing through Chanting Magic

Chanting magic has been used globally in many cultures to help focus the mind, bring healing, raise energy, offer reverence, and many other practices. These include the (narrating/telling) chants of Bahkti yoga originating in India in the sixth century, the traditional Norse chant (incantation/*galdr*), and ancient Irish Imbas (chanting, inspiration). Many traditions and religions around the world use chanting as a basic spiritual practice. For land-healing purposes, chanting magic is a simple, effective, and enjoyable way of raising energy for active healing as well as energetic blessings of the land.

The chants here use the Celtic tree alphabet, ogham, as their basis, and a basic guide to selecting an ogham for your chant is below. However, if you prefer, you can substitute any other words or divination system for your chant, such as the runes. The important thing here is to use something that you are comfortable using, that you can select or draw from, and that can be the basis for your chant magic.

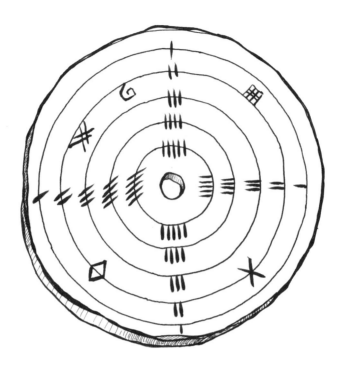

**THE OGHAM**

The ogham (pronounced *OH-um*) is an ancient tree alphabet[19] found in the British Isles, often inscribed into ancient stones in vertical or circular patterns. Each ogham few has a sacred tree attached to it, a symbol, a letter, and a divination meaning. (A few refers to the symbol itself, often painted or engraved on a piece of wood from the tree, which is usually referred to as a "stave.") They are frequently used within various nature-centered spiritual traditions and thus make an excellent option for chant magic for land-healing work. Here is a list of the ogham with basic meanings and pronunciations,[20] as well as suggestions for the kinds of land work you might do with them.

| Original ogham | Keywords | Land healing use | Pronunciation |
|---|---|---|---|
| ASPEN (Eadha) | Hard work, endurance, courage, bending rather than breaking | Apology | EH-yuh |
| GROVE (Koad) | Balance, community, conflict resolution, communication, listening | Apology | KO-ud |

| Original ogham | Keywords | Land healing use | Pronunciation |
| --- | --- | --- | --- |
| PINE (Ifin) | Vision, awareness, making amends, self-work, guilt | Apology | EE-van |
| SPINDLE (Oir) | Obligations, honoring commitments, persistence | Apology | OR |
| APPLE (Quert) | Celebration, love, harvest, contentment | Blessing | KWEIRT |
| ASH (Nuinn) | Interconnection, magic, connection | Blessing | NOO-un |
| FIR (Ailm) | Vision, understanding, perspective | Blessing | AHL-m |
| VINE (Muinn) | Freedom, honesty, prophecy | Blessing | MUHN |
| BIRCH (Beith) | Beginnings, rebirth, purification, regrowth | Growth | BEH |
| GORSE (Onn) | Hope, potential, learning, possibility | Growth | UHN |
| OAK (Duir) | Power, strength, durability, grounding | Growth | DOO-er |
| WILLOW (Saille) | Change, cycles, fluidity, receptivity, flexibility | Growth | SAHL-yuh |
| HAZEL (Coll) | Creativity, inspiration, awen, artistry, craft | Healing | CULL |
| HEATHER (Ur) | Spiritual power, spirit connection, energy | Healing | OOR |
| YEW (Ioho) | Legacy, things that abide, wisdom from experience, eldership | Healing | EE-yoh |
| REED (Ngetal) | Swiftness, speed, transformation, healing | Healing | NYEH-tal |
| ALDER (Fearn) | Bridge between spirit and matter; spirit, transitions, individuality | Passage | FAIR-n |

| Original ogham | Keywords | Land healing use | Pronunciation |
|---|---|---|---|
| BLACKTHORN (Straif) | Upheaval, fate, external forces, unavoidable change | Passage | STRAHF |
| ELDER (Ruis) | Resolution, endings, permanent change, otherworld | Passage | RWEESH |
| HAWTHORN (Huath) | Patience, restriction, danger, protection | Protection | OO-ah |
| HOLLY (Tinne) | Courage, challenge, opposition | Protection | CHIN-yuh |
| ROWAN (Luis) | Protection, judgment, discernment | Protection | LWEESH |
| BEECH (Phagos) | Wisdom, learning, history, ancient knowledge, memory | Sleep | FAH-gus |
| HONEYSUCKLE (Uilleand) | Hidden meanings, secrets, subtle influences, mysteries | Sleep | ULL-enth |
| IVY (Gort) | Entanglements, slow progress, determination | Sleep | GORT |

## DESIGNING A CHANTING RITUAL

While this chapter focuses on land healing (and offers two examples of healing chanting rituals that follow), you can use chanting work for all the different practices in this book: apology, witnessing, remembrance, palliative care, energetic land healing, helping spirits pass, and self-care. Chanting rituals are easy to do, require minimal planning, and yet can be extremely effective.

The general formula is as follows. First, engage in deep-listening work. Next, set your intentions which you have co-created with the land through deep listening techniques. Third, you will draw or select your ogham (see more below). Fourth, you will perform your chant ritual, raising and directing energy as necessary. Finally, you can conclude by expressing gratitude, placing sigils, leaving offerings, and more.

# SELECTING OR DRAWING OGHAM

*Drawing ogham.* Your first option is to allow the spirits to choose their own energies for the chant. If you have an ogham set (or are using runes or another divination system), you can leave the choice of what ogham you will draw up to spirit. At the beginning of your chant ritual or before, you can simply close your eyes and draw several staves (I usually draw one or three, depending on my intentions). Then, you can use that ogham to chant, knowing that whatever energies you will be bringing will be directed by spirit.

*Selecting ogham.* The alternative to drawing ogham is to carefully select your ogham to develop a unique energetic overlay for your ritual. As the previous list demonstrates, the ogham offers a variety of different energies and foci. Here are some sample lists for use for different land-healing situations:

- **Land blessing:** Apple (Quert), Birch (Beith), and Oak (Duir)
- **Physical land healing:** Birch (Beith), Willow (Saille), and Hazel (Coll)
- **Land protection:** Hawthorn (Huath), Holly (Tinne), Rowan (Luis)
- **Apology:** Fir (Ailm), Aspen (Eadha), Spindle (Oir)
- **Sleep:** Honeysuckle (Uilleand), Beech (Phagos), Ivy (Gort)
- **Passage:** Blackthorn (Straif), Elder (Ruis), Alder (Fearn)

You can, of course, create your own combinations for a specific situation. In the case of impending logging on a friend's property line to put in an awful tar sands oil pipeline, I used a combination of three trees carefully chosen to let the land know of my sorrow, to encourage the land to sleep, and to offer protection to the surrounding land: Grove (KO-ud), Beech (FAH-gus), and Hawthorn (OO-ah). I chose Grove and Beech because my friend's land was used for community and teaching, and I wanted that energy present as part of the work to acknowledge the sorrow of the community. I chose Hawthorn because of the presence of actual hawthorn trees in the path of the new pipeline and for their protective qualities. As a second example, the chant ritual that opened up this chapter was a more elaborate version of a chanting ritual that included movement and a larger number of people. In the case of the hemlock ritual, we spent several months in communion with multiple trees as well as researching the different ogham letters to find trees who would work with us and lend us their energy for our very specific healing ritual. We used Apple, Blackthorn, Birch, and Oak. Prior to that ritual, the ritual leaders connected with each of these trees to help us develop the energetic connections to raise energy for the ritual.

## CHANTING OPTIONS

Once you have selected or drawn your ogham, you want to develop your chant. There are a few options here. The first is to simply chant the ogham in a quiet voice, perhaps accompanied by a steady beat of the drum. You can vary the pitch, length, and tone of your chant as you want, keeping it monotone or making it more musical in nature, almost like a song.

The second option is to break down the single word into multiple syllables, similar to the current practices that some of the Norse traditions use for *galdr* chanting. So if you were connecting to Duir, the Oak, it might sound something like this:

> *DOO-ir, DOO-ir, DOO-ir*
>
> *Dooo Ahhh Iiiirr*
>
> *Du Du Du Du*
>
> *Ir Ir Ir Ir*
>
> *DOO-ir*

Regardless of your approach, you want to allow the chant to be fully embodied as you do it, to lose yourself in the chant. As you chant, draw deep breaths and let your full breath be part of the chant. Open your mouth wide. Dance and move if you feel led. Be fearless with your chanting—the more you can put yourself into the chant, the more the healing magic will take root.

# A Simple Healing Chant

This healing chant ritual can be used anytime you want to offer healing energy for the land. This ritual is very simple.

After engaging in deep listening and setting intentions, open up a sacred space. Select three ogham trees for your healing. Three is a very powerful number, tied to the three elements of earth, sea, and sky; the three stages of life; and three aspects of time: past, present, and future. Thus, it is a powerful choice for the healing chant, allowing you to interweave energy of the three trees. Take three deep breaths to root and ground yourself in the moment. Focus your attention on the focal point you would like to heal. Begin to chant your first tree. Spend a few moments chanting, until you feel as though that energy is settled. Move to your second tree, again taking as much time as you need to bring that energy forward. Finish with your third tree. You can add drumming, music, movement, signing, and more as you weave your chants.

At the conclusion, cross your arms and thank the trees: "I thank the sacred trees for their healing energy." Leave an offering, anoint the focal point with a blessing oil or leave a sigil, and close your space.

As the example from the opening of this chapter demonstrated, you can "scale up" an ogham chant ritual to include any number of people.

# Approach 3:
# **Sacred Fires and Smoke Prayer Bundles**

Smoke cleansing and blessing practices have been used throughout human history and in many cultures as a blessing and purifying agent—this ritual uses burning sacred herbs in a large bundle along with other prayers to send healing energy to the broader land. This prayer bundle uses a combination of sacred herbs, visualization, and a sacred fire to work healing upon the broader land.

One of the challenges with land healing, particularly on a larger scale, is that you don't always have physical access to the land you want to heal. Thus, this ritual technique is very useful for spaces, far and wide, that are otherwise inaccessible: around here that would be large swaths of logging, strip mines, polluted waterways, etc. It is also very useful for healing more-distant concerns: the plight of polar bears in the Arctic or deforestation in the Amazon, the oceans, burning fires in Australia or North America, or some other "faraway" issue. Or maybe you want to do land-healing work for the entire globe, just sending healing energy out there to wherever it may be needed. Thus, this technique is one that you can use to send healing and blessing energy to the lands nearby—or quite distant, using air and smoke as a carrier.

Thus, this technique has three parts. Each of these three parts has both a physical component and an energetic component. The parts include

1.  creating a bundle that will turn to smoke and bring that energy, through the currents of the air, to other places;

2.  creating a fire in a sacred manner and opening a sacred space; and

3.  burning and releasing the bundle and directing energy, then closing your space.

If you are an urban druid without access to a large fire or outdoor fire pit, I offer an alternative to the healing prayer bundle at the bottom of this section.

**PART 1:** MAKING YOUR HEALING PRAYER BUNDLE

Your prayer bundle can be made up of anything that will burn and release smoke: dried herbs, sticks, papers rolled with prayers, string, leaves, and more. Everything in your prayer bundles should be all natural, coming directly from nature. This is because you are burning the objects, so obviously you don't want to burn something that pollutes the air. So, for example, if you are using string, it should be cotton, hemp, or jute (string can be plastic), coated with wax (use soy wax or beeswax). Nonnatural materials can release harmful chemicals into the air, thereby rendering any healing work you want to do ineffective.

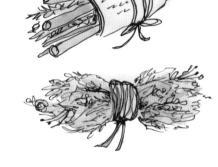

Like most magical workings, I think that the physical form it takes is less important; more important are the intentions you bring. Work with what you have, and don't worry about replicating what I have here—rather, create things from your local environment that speak to you, things that you can ethically obtain and harvest. While any size of bundle will work, a larger-sized bundle (12" or more across) certainly does give a good ritual effect, which is something you might want to consider. Small ones work great too, but large ones burn longer, giving you more time to focus healing energies in a particular direction.

*Set your intentions.* Begin by setting your intentions for the ritual you will be doing. Do you want to send healing energy to a particular place? Do you want to raise energy for the land as a whole? Do you want to offer blessings? Once you've set your intentions, you can begin to construct your healing prayer bundle.

*Creating your prayers.* Start with a brown paper bag or white recycled paper. In a quiet place, take some time to write your intentions and prayers. You can write one or many such pieces of paper. As you write your prayer, feel your intentions going into the paper to be later released. Prayers can be simple or complex—this is up to you and your goals for the ritual.

*Put your bundle together.* Now you will combine your prayers and construct your bundle. You can wrap your prayers on sticks or tuck them into the bundle once you make it. Here are some options for making your bundle:

- **The herbal-healing bundle:** This approach is best for people who do regular wild foraging, who know where to get wild and abundant healing herbs, or who grow their own herbs. For these, you can use most any common healing or culinary herbs. Any material (other than Poison ivy or other poisonous plants) would work fine for such a bundle, but I think it's particularly good with aromatic healing herbs that burn well: Rosemary, Sage, Thyme, Mint, Scented geranium, Wormwood, Mugwort, etc. If you have loose dried herbs, I suggest using a paper bag (which you can write your intentions on and then place the herbs inside) and wrap it tight with cotton string. Depending on the nature of the herbs, you might be able to make your bundle without the bag, especially if you have a lot of long plant stalks. If you are using green/fresh herbs, you will want to just bundle them without the bag; using cotton string, you might just want to tie them together. To this bundle you can add fresh conifer leaves/needles, resins (which burn well and smell wonderful), or pine cones.

- **Shapes, rings, and effigies:** Rather than putting your materials in a bag, you might instead choose to shape some form—a wreath, for example, offers additional symbolism. Certain kinds of herbs and plants are obviously better for this than others. An easy way to do this is to get a wooden ring started with willow or another bendable wood and then from there, you can use cotton string to wrap dried or fresh herbs around the ring, layering until you have something you are happy with. Or you can use cornstalks, dried grasses, and some cotton string to create your bundle. Again, use your intuition here—it doesn't have to look good—it's the intention that matters.

- **The wax-and-herb bundle:** An alternative to the large bundle described above is to use one or more beeswax candles wrapped in herbs. Beeswax will burn very brightly and give off powerful light and thus is particularly good when you want to be bringing that kind of energy into a situation. Take one or two beeswax candles (or a small brick of beeswax) and then layer the outside with herbs. Or, you can heat wax up until it is just a little soft, then roll herbs into the candle. When you throw this into the fire, it will burn brightly and send energy outward quickly.

- **The wooden message bundle:** A final option is to use wood itself to fashion something—a bundle of sticks, wrapped with messages or healing words. You could also use a log or a wooden round with woodburning or natural ink messages, a wooden object bound together with string, a vine wreath with tucked in messages, and so on. My favorite approach is to get sticks, wrap my prayers around them, tie them with string, and then wrap a number of these together. Then I tuck in herbs and a beeswax candle.

The bundles can be made anytime in advance of your fire ritual. You can also make them together before your ritual, as a grove or group of people.

## PART 2: A SACRED FIRE

I suggest choosing a fortuitous day for your ritual. I find that the four neopagan fire festivals—Beltane, Lughnassadh, Samhain, and Imbolc, are excellent choices for the timing for these rituals. Given weather and other issues, any day is also a good day for your ritual—whatever day you can get an outdoor fire going. You can also use a fireplace for this ritual, provided that what you are burning is not resinous (thus, I would stick with herbs or sticks and not use any conifers, wax candles, or resins).

Prep your fire for lighting and open your sacred space. I have found that it is best either to light your sacred fire after you open your ritual or have your fire in a place where the fire doesn't need tending for a while.

Make an offering to your fire to honor the flames. Fire has their own spirit and their own energy, and I think it's useful to acknowledge that the fire spirit, in this case, is your partner and ally in this work. I like to offer the fire a branch of fresh white cedar, which quickly crackles and burns. High-proof alcohol can also be a nice fire offering, as is your herbal-offering blend or a few drops of your herbal-healing oil (chapter 3).

## PART 3: BURNING YOUR BUNDLE AND SENDING ENERGY OUT

Once you are ready, place your bundle before you. Bless your bundle and energize it however you see fit. There are no right or wrong ways to do this—just trust your intuition. With that said, here are a few ideas: I like to do an elemental blessing of my bundle at the fire, blessing it with the seven elements: earth, air, fire, water, above, below, and within, inviting those elements into the bundle to help with the healing work. Envision the light of the solar and telluric currents flowing into the bundle. If you are a Reiki practitioner, you could send some Reiki energy into the bundle, for instance. You can use chanting magic, as described in this chapter. You might also raise energy in the bundle in other ways; drumming a steady beat into the bundle also works great.

You might add your bundle (especially one that contains conifers and wax) to a blazing fire and watch it flare up and release the energy into the world. Or, you might wait until the fire dies, or rake out some coals and place the bundle on the coals, letting it smolder. As it burns, envision that energy going to where you want it to—that the winds take that energy to the places you wish it to travel. This may take some time, and my suggestion is to hold space for the duration of the bundle burning and smoldering.

At this point, if you want to use some divination (e.g., Tarot, ogham, runes) to ascertain how the healing energy will be received, and if you have any additional work to do, this is a perfect time. Once you are done, close out the space and, if at all possible, allow the fire to burn out naturally.

# Approach 4:
# Land-Healing Mandalas

A woman comes to a clearing in the recently burned forest with a basket of stones, sticks, and nuts in her arms that she has gathered from the surrounding landscape. She begins to sing, laugh, and dance as she creates a beautiful series of circles with the materials. As she weaves her healing magic, the design of the circle grows more complex, spiraling inward and outward. She finishes her work and sits with it quietly for a time, before leaving it in place to do its own work.

Land-healing mandalas represent a different approach to blessing, and healing can be done through the creation of a natural mandala. This is an intuitive magical approach that does not use formal ritual per se but instead works with the connection of your own subconscious to the living Earth. C. G. Jung, esoteric psychologist, spoke of the benefits of creating such mandalas as a way of seeing deeply into the psyche and allowing for the cyclical process of self-development.[21] Mandalas have been used in a variety of traditions, as he describes, primarily for inner spirit work—as the mandala is constructed, understanding, enlightenment, or healing may come. Mandalas can also have a similar function in the practice of land healing and blessing. A mandala can be done in combination with other practices (such as the healing and blessing rituals in this book or using particular healing sigils), or they can be done on its own. Mandalas can also be done by anyone, regardless of their ability to raise energy, visualize, or engage in any other advanced ritual techniques.

Before you begin your mandala, approach the land in the same way you would for any other working: practice deep-listening work and make sure such a practice will be welcome (see chapter 2). Then select a flat space for constructing the healing mandala: a flat riverbank or shore, a sandbar, a bare spot in the forest, a space in the lawn in your backyard, etc. These can be large or small, permanent or ephemeral, and can be done in places where water can wash them away (a beach at low tide, the edge of a stream that will eventually flood, the forest where leaves will cover in the fall, etc.). If you live in a snowy region, you can also walk mandalas in the snow, which will melt at some point, bringing the energies into the Earth.

In terms of the design of the mandala, many options are possible, some intentional and some intuitive. To begin, you can use the healing-sigil patterns provided in chapter 3 or do modified versions of those sigils. Jung noted that many mandalas in other cultures unfolded in a circular fourfold pattern, tying to the four elements and other fourfold patterns in the universe. While we see fourfold patterns in nature (e.g., in the flowers of a Dogwood or in the small flowers in the Arugula plant), this is only one possible pattern nature provides. The flowers of Apples and hawthorns show us a fivefold pattern, the shell of a snail shows us a spiral pattern, and the flower of a Trillium shows us a threefold pattern. These and many other patterns can be used for inspiration. You can create these as intentionally or intuitively as you want.

You can create intuitive designs, setting your intention, putting yourself in a meditative place, and letting your subconscious guide you to create the mandala. If you are going to use this approach, I suggest that before you begin, you spend time communing with the land as described in chapter 3. Walking with the land, hearing the voices of the spirits in the wind, in your inner mind, feeling the energies present. Attune with those, and when you feel connected and centered with this place, create. This becomes a kind of intuitive healing sigil that you manifest for the specific land and its needs. This approach allows you to connect with the land and bring forth a design that is unique to the land, to your interaction, and to the place. This can lead to some really amazing designs and experiences. Here are some possibilities for your mandalas and how to create them:

*Nature mandala with sticks, shells, stones, and other things.* Begin gathering the materials for the mandala, using your intuition. A basket here also helps! As you gather, be careful not to disrupt the ecosystem (e.g., use fallen sticks, leaves, small stones; leave big stones where they are). When you have gathered your materials, begin to organize them in some circular or spiral fashion. There is no right or wrong way; just flow with the spirits of the land. With each piece of the mandala, you can set intentions for the healing of the land (e.g., "This leaf represents the new growth of spring," "This stone represents the health of the insect life," and so forth).

*Nature mandala with snow.* If you are in an area with snowfall and an accumulation of snow, another approach is to weave your mandala into the snow itself. To do this, simply close your eyes and visualize the shape you want your mandala to take—or just start walking. You can use a big, open area or you can use a wooded area where you work the trees, stones, and other natural features into your design. Walk your mandala each day the snow is present, if possible, to leave lasting healing on the landscape.

*Nature mandala with sand or soil.* Another option for a nature mandala is in the sand or bare soil. You might use a stick to trace patterns, adding stones or shells. You might use your feet to trace, to walk a larger path of the mandala. Mandalas on the shore, placed at the low-tide line, will be taken by the sea and thus can be used as a blessing for the oceans. Mandalas placed higher on the shore can bless the land around them. Mandalas on the edges of riverbanks can be done in a similar manner, since rivers flood.

*Stone mandala.* A more permanent option is to create a mandala with stones, leaving it somewhere to simply "be." I would suggest this only at sites that have already had major disruption, since you do not want to disrupt the ecosystem itself by moving stones. A piece of land that is in the path of a pipeline, septic line, or something else is a good option for this, as is a grove of renewal (chapter 7) that you will tend regularly.

When you complete your mandala, you have several options in terms of what you will do next. You can use it as an anchor point for other ritual activity in this chapter (Seven-Element Healing, chanting). You can chant "Healing for the land, radiating outward" over it or drum with it to raise energy. Or, you can simply be present with it for a time and then let it be, knowing that work continues on nature's time.

One last point—make sure that in your mandala creating, you don't disrupt the natural world. Stones of any size are often home to insects and other life, and removing them can disrupt the ecosystem. Don't remove large stones or take them from rivers, etc. Pick up and use things that are already ephemeral: small stones that are moved by the river or waves, nuts, sticks, leaves, acorn caps, etc.

# Approach 5:
# Setting and Blessing Standing Stones for Long-Term Land Healing

Ancient peoples set standing stones and built other stone structures all across the world. In the British Isles, Iceland, Africa, and South America, you can often still find ancient standing stones. While their many uses are shrouded in antiquity and subject to some speculation, the seven-element framework offers one clear way of using stones as a land-healing practice. As John Michael Greer describes in *The Druid Magic Handbook*, standing stones can channel the solar current into the telluric current, which offers blessing and healing to the land. As he describes, setting a permanent standing stone is a way of offering long-term healing and blessing. This approach uses a stone of any size (a small one you can manage yourself is fine) to engage in long-term energetic healing for a place.

Begin by looking for a stone that you could manage to carry and set on your own or with a small group of people. Standing stones are ideal if they are able to be placed one-third in the ground and two-thirds out of it, somewhere that gets regular sun. Thus, the best standing stones are ones that are long, but not necessarily very thick or wide. That's a general guideline, however, and your stone might end up being something shaped very differently. Stones that contain some quartz are ideal (since quartz is an excellent transmitter of energy). Where I live, we have mostly shale and sandstone, so I'd choose sandstone because it has a higher quartz content.

If you decide to use this approach, understand that setting a standing stone is a journey. Begin by setting your intentions of the need for such a stone. Take your time looking for your standing stone. Look for the stone when you are hiking, in your yard, walking along streams, just being out in the world, etc. A standing stone will find you when the time is right.

Once you have your stone, find the right place to set the stone—a place where you feel inspired by spirit to do so. This could be anywhere—at an edge of a forest or field, in your backyard, at a local preserve, on a damaged land. You can even set a stone in a pot of soil on your patio (if you use this option, consider then moving your "energized" soil to places in need of healing). Like all other aspects of land healing, make sure that you engage in appropriate deep listening to make sure that (1) setting the standing stone is appropriate and wanted, and (2) that you have the right time and location to do such work.

To set your stone, choose a fortuitous day and time. The most fortuitous day of a year and timing for setting a standing stone is noon at the summer solstice, since you are calling upon the energy of the sun, and setting the stone when the solar energy is at its peak both in time of day and year will be powerful. You can choose any other day or time that is fortuitous, however, but I do suggest you set the stone at noon if at all possible, when the solar energy is at its highest.

The following ritual can be used to set your stone. The ritual is most effective if you visit the stone and continue to offer healing and blessing. After the initial setting of the stone, you might come back every solstice and equinox and do a full season of healing rituals (see the following), or use it as a focal point for other work (such as a grove of renewal or a refugium garden; see chapter 7).

Finally, a variant on this is to find an existing stone that is partially in the ground and partially out of the ground, and do the blessing that follows.

## Ritual for Setting a Standing Stone

*Materials.* Assemble all of your supplies prior to beginning your ritual. This should include tools needed to move and place your stone (such as a shovel or posthole digger), as well as blessing materials to bless the hole. Many of the tools described in chapter 3 would work for this: a blessing sigil, a blend of sacred herbs, sacred waters, a blessing oil, and so forth. The ritual that follows uses an herbal tea made from fresh healing herbs: Rosemary, Sage, Oregano, and Lavender with a few drops of sacred water, as well as a blessing sigil.

*Open up your sacred grove.* Begin by stating your intentions for the healing to take place. While I highly recommend you use your own words, you can also use the words here: "Land before me. What a journey you have had to get to this place. And now, your healing is coming forth. As you regrow, as you heal, know that I am with you. I set this standing stone today to aid you with your healing, that you may grow bountiful and diverse."

*Bless your stone.* Pour some of the tea over the stone and bless the stones in your own words. Or you can say, "Sacred stone, ancestor who has been on this land for millennia, thank you for lending your healing power as a channel for the solar current."

*Prepare to dig the hole.* Say, "Spirits of nature, powers of this land, I offer my energy to prepare this Earth."

*Dig the hole.* As you dig, focus your mind on healing for the land.

*Bless the hole.* After you dig the hole, bless the hole with your own words or say, "Sacred earth, oh cradle for this stone. Hold this stone firm and be a conduit for healing to radiate forth." Pour the remainder of the healing waters in the hole. Place a blessing sigil in the hole as well.

*Set the stone.* Place your stone, making sure you firmly tamp down the soil all around the hole.

*Energetic visualization.* After you finish, say, "From above to below, from the solar to the telluric, may this stone radiate healing energy. Each day as the sun rises until the sun sets, this stone will serve as a conduit to channel nywfre (noo-IV-ruh) throughout this land." Visualize the rays of the sun warming the stone, then envision the stone channeling those rays into the earth, a beautiful golden light emanating from the stone in all directions. Visualize those rays of golden energy helping plants regrow, seeds take root, eggs hatch, and young ones grow. Imagine the land before you as a healthy, strong, and abundant place for all.

*Offer your vow (optional).* Offer your own vow as a custodian of the land. Say, "As I close this ceremony, I offer myself as a force of good and healing in service to this land. Lead me as to what you need me to do. Speak, and I will listen. Spirits of the land, I honor you and heed your call." Bow your head and cross your arms.

*Close the ritual space.*

# Approach 6:
# A Full Season of Rituals: **Infusing with the Blessing of the Sun**

As we've explored in this book so far, land healing is a long-term process that we can support. Just like the regrowth of the forest after a fire or logging, nature takes time to heal. Working in a ritual way on nature's timeline can support healing efforts long term. As a final suggestion, then, any of the rituals or other energetic-healing methods presented in this chapter can be done over a period of time rather than just at a single point in time. You can do the rituals once every full moon, once every season, or even once a year to help speed healing along. Repeating rituals at regular times of power can help enhance the ritual energy and healing with greater effect. Build this into your own wheel of spiritual practices as you see fit.

You can also alter your ritual structure to do different rituals as healing progresses: starting with some rituals aimed at clearing out energetic darkness or dealing with the grief in the land, and moving toward infusing the energy with light and long-term healing. You can figure out what to do by using the deep-listening techniques and develop your own ritual structure.

Here's one sample ritual structure that uses the solstices and equinoxes for healing. This was the ritual structure that I used when I first moved to my Pennsylvania homestead. Six months before I purchased my home, the previous owners decided to log a number of acres of the land, including most of the land I purchased. When I stepped foot on the land, I could sense the grief in the landscape from the logging. My first year on the land focused not only on land healing but also on addressing the grief and rebuilding human-land connections. These are the techniques I used in the first year to work with the land (I moved in October, so I started the rituals at Samhain).

- **Winter solstice**: Deep-listening ritual. For this I simply open up a sacred space and then use divination or inner-listening tools (see chapter 3) to listen to what the spirits of the land have to say, and to leave an offering.

- **Spring equinox**: Seven-Element Land-Blessing ceremony (chapter 4)

- **Summer solstice**: Land-Healing ceremony using ogham chanting (chapter 5)

- **Fall equinox or winter solstice (or both)**: Setting a standing stone, doing tree planting, and land healing with a mandala (chapter 5)

- **Yearly after that**: Seven-Element Land-Blessing ceremony and wassail ceremonies (chapter 4)

## Dealing with Large-Scale Land-Healing Issues:
# Fires, Floods, Pollution, and Climate Change

This last section of the chapter focuses on working to heal and send positive energy to larger-scale issues that we are facing as a planet. While I believe that we can be at our best as land healers when working as locally as possible, I also realize that sometimes we want to offer healing and support for larger issues that are impacting other places. In the years that I've taught and explored these practices, I often get asked about how to help a situation that is unfolding somewhere else in the world, by people who feel compelled to do something. And thus, I offer these suggestions—in the context of energetic healing.

After three centuries of human activity and abuses to our lands, we are now in the age of the Anthropocene, a time when humans drive climate change, and many species and life are at risk. In this age, we are seeing increasing climate instability, which is creating more-extreme weather patterns: wildfires, floods, droughts, tsunamis, hurricanes, heat waves, and more. These weather patterns may cause temporary or long-term damage. In fact, as I type these words, most of western Pennsylvania is bordering on a drought caused by months of little rain combined with sweltering temperatures—and I am witnessing the wilt of the plants and trees and the pain of the parched, cracked Earth. What we know from weather patterns globally is that these kinds of extreme weather patterns and weather-related disasters are only going to increase in their frequency and severity in the coming years.

And the truth is, nearly all humans living in industrialized nations have contributed to large-scale changes to our climate patterns and an increase in the overall global temperature. It doesn't matter if you live near a disaster area or not—we each are responsible for our part in global carbon emissions, the sixth great extinction, and climate change through the everyday choices we make, the products we buy, and how we live our lives.[22] Thus, I believe it is our responsibility to respond to these kinds of situations. We have both an energetic responsibility to the Earth that we hold as sacred as well as a physical responsibility to reduce our carbon emissions as much as possible. In this section, I'll share some long-term healing strategies.

Before I do, I want to remind you that in these kinds of situations, it is very wise to ascertain what kind of healing needs to happen: energetic healing or palliative care? If it is energetic healing, then all the approaches offered above in this chapter can be done at a distance, using the distance connection techniques described in chapter 4.

## WILDFIRES AND DROUGHTS:
## RITUALS AND SIGILS FOR RAIN AND PROTECTION

Wildfires in the western United States, Canada, Australia, Russia, and other places are now an unfortunate and common occurrence and are an area that you might feel called to for energetic healing. We are also seeing increasing numbers of droughts and heat waves, which harm and threaten life. What a fire- or drought-ravaged place needs are gentle rains and cooling temperatures to stop the fires. The following are three techniques here that can be used—individually or combined—to help bring rains and stop the wildfires and such loss of life. I will also note that some may also ask to pray for wisdom for our leaders and protection for those fighting the fires—all of these are potentially good approaches.

*Rain visualization.* For this first technique, begin with some deep breathing. Find yourself in a place of quiet, of grounding, of connection to the land and world around you. Feel that peace within you. Now, visualize the place where the fires are burning or the drought is happening. As you visualize, imagine gentle rains coming to calm the fires, putting them out. Imagine the animals, insects, and all life returning to these ravaged places. Send peace, calm, and healing to those lands.

*Object focus work.* You can combine the above visualization with a simple physical representation. Gather something you can use to represent the land that is being ravaged by fire or drought—a stone, a leaf, a stick, a slice of wood, or even a piece of paper with the shape of the continent drawn on it. Now, take some pure water (rainwater, snowmelt, spring, or your healing water from chapter 2), and as you visualize, flick some drops of water onto the object. You can do this daily to help send that energy forth.

*A rain and protective sigil (see next page for image).* Drawing from the folk traditions of the Pennsylvania Dutch (German), which are part of my own heritage, we can use hex signs as another way to raise and direct energy. Throughout Pennsylvania, farmers paint various hex signs on their barns so that they can protect their crops, call the rain, protect livestock, and bring abundance and fertility to the land. These hex signs are colorful, always circular, and have embedded layers of meaning. Thus, we have many different kinds of signs in the tradition, including symbols for protection and for rain. A rain sign uses raindrops swirling around each other, while the pentacle and pentagram feature prominently as a protective symbol in this tradition. You can use this sigil as a focus for meditation, distance work, and some of the other rituals in this book.

I share this rain work with a caveat: be very careful in your wording and intention. Weather magic is notoriously challenging and fickle—inadvertent weather magic can cause floods, hail, and more, shifting the balance from one extreme to another. From Pennsylvania Dutch country, there is a story of a man who created a barn rain hex sign and prominently displayed it in his yard, upturned to the skies. For the next three weeks, rains came down so hard that it caused flooding and four million dollars in damage. Finally, his neighbors forced him to remove his hex sign, and the rains abated. The point is that we are seeking balance with any kind of weather visualization, object work, or sigil work—we aren't seeking to move from one extreme to another.

## FLOODS, HURRICANES, TSUNAMIS, AND OTHER SEVERE STORMS

On the other side of climate change, we have the challenges posed by severe storms, including flooding, hurricanes, tsunamis, and other storm damage. You might do any of the following if you want to provide energetic healing:

*If a storm is on its way*: Storms can have an energy and life of their own. Connecting with the elemental spirits of the storm (usually air and water; sylphs and undines) and asking for gentleness is one approach. These kinds of prayers can be sent both at a distance or if you are in the path of the storm. Sometimes, an offering and a prayer go a long way to calming the angry energies of a storm.

*If a storm has already caused damage*: The aftereffects of storms can be severe both for human and nonhuman life, especially in ecologically sensitive places or coastal areas. Doing some kind of distance-healing work is quite effective in this case—I like to use the herbal-smoke-bundle approach described earlier in this chapter to send healing smoke or do visualization, as described in the last section.

## PRAYERS FOR THE LEADERS AND LAND WARRIORS

One of the few things that can turn the tide in this current situation is for the leaders of the world and of individual nations to radically alter course and help us come to an ecological balance with carbon emissions, deforestation, waste, and the myriad of other factors that are contributing to our current predicament. Toward that end, I say prayers for the world's leaders that they would have the wisdom to turn us toward a different path. I say prayers that those who take up the mantle of leadership will have wisdom to consider future generations. I also say prayers for those who are putting themselves on the front lines of local, countrywide, or global battles to save our future. These prayers can be simple[23] and heartfelt. Here is a sample of a prayer for the world's leaders:

> *I pray for the leaders of the world.*
>
> *I pray for their wisdom.*
>
> *And I pray for their compassion*
>
> *That their decisions be just, fair, and honorable,*
>
> *That they choose to protect life, health, and land*
>
> *So that we can envision a brighter tomorrow.*
>
> *Blessings.*

And here is one for the land warriors, water protectors, and those who are on the front lines fighting for the planet:

> *A blessing to the land warriors, the water protectors, the defenders of life.*
>
> *I pray for their bodies to stand strong and unharmed.*
>
> *I pray that their voices will be heard as their cause is just.*
>
> *I honor the work that they do on behalf of all life.*
>
> *I pray for justice, peace, and life to prevail.*

These are simple prayers but send a blessing into the world that focuses on bringing peace and justice to the challenges we face. To ask for compassion and strength for those to fight to prevail.

# A Vision of a Healed and Abundant World

The more people that we have envisioning and working for a future that embraces life and choices that will honor and protect life on this planet long term, the more chance that we will bring this future into being. Within the occult traditions, the concept of the group egregore is a useful one to consider here. Egregores[24] are thought forms created—sometimes consciously but often unconsciously—by people in groups, whose energies, perspectives, and even unconscious desires can shape the ways that the group energy manifests. I'm sure you've experienced this in some ways—some groups have a good energy to them, and some do not—that's part of the egregore and how people are feeding it. When a group is putting forth a particular energy and going in a particular direction, you can sense it. People who practice magic have long understood that like anything else, we can influence this thought form directly.

Right now, I think there are a lot of mixed emotions over the future of the planet. Many people who care deeply are suffering from compassion fatigue, burnout, and feeling as if things keep getting worse rather than better. I struggle with these feelings myself (and it's one reason that I engage in land healing as my primary spiritual practice and why this book was written). Yet, the more that we focus on feeling hopeless or demoralized, or the more despair about the future, the more we put that into the larger egregore that is driving this situation. What if, instead, we visualized our world and its peoples making planet-honoring and compassionate decisions, policies that save our earth and its many lives, and envisioning that brighter future? That we envision and work to enact that healed, vibrant, and healthy planet? Here are two potential approaches to doing this work.

## NEW-MOON VISIONING FOR LIFE

At each new moon, I like to spend some time at my land-healing altar doing visioning work and the future that I'd like to see. I start by doing a grove opening and then sitting comfortably in front of a candle. I close my eyes and spend time visualizing a better world: clean rivers flowing with fish; forests with old growth trees; agriculture that is restorative, organic, and holistic; people connecting and honoring nature; livestock living good lives on pasture; our world on a path to peace. I hold these images firm in my mind and then send out peace and hope to the core of our planet. I then close the space.

## A VISION BOARD FOR A HEALED PLANET

Another take on this is to create a vision board for a healed world. Vision boards are intuitive pieces of art, usually in collage form, that are created by a meditative art practice.[25] They are meant to help visualize and set intentions for the future. They are generally made of collaged materials that are cut out and intuitively placed on a piece of poster board.

To create a vision board, start with magazines, photos, newspapers, and any other materials that you can cut words and images from. You will also need glue, scissors, and a large piece of card stock or poster board. Open up a sacred space and put on some relaxing music. Speak your intentions for the vision board (bringing peace and healing to the world, visioning healed landscapes that are abundant and restored, praying for clean and healthy oceans) and try to keep this intention in your mind as you create your board. Spread out the magazines, newspapers, and other materials in front of you. Working in a meditative and quiet way, select things that stand out to you—words, phrases, and images. At some point you will feel "done" and can move on to constructing your board. Lay out the photos and images that spoke to you and start assembling them on your board with glue. If you don't end up using everything, that's okay! Just let your intuition work and don't worry about if it "looks good" or has high artistic value—that's not the point of the vision board. When you are finished, sit with your vision board and use the practice from the New Moon Visioning for Life to strongly visualize the change you want to see in the world. Finally, close out your sacred space and place your vision board somewhere prominent where you can see it and interact with it often.

While I've framed this practice in terms of visioning a healed world more broadly, you can also use a vision board to focus on more-local land-healing issues: such as regenerating a piece of land you purchased, having a space for a community garden to open up, and so on. A vision board can be set for any intention!

# Chapter 6:

# ENERGETIC PALLIATIVE CARE

**Some years ago,** I picked a trail out in our local forest park that I hadn't hiked on for quite a while, and I set off. My hike turned in a very unfortunate direction as I came across over a half-dozen very recently installed gas-fracking wells. The land still bore the marks—acres of cut-down trees with leaves still wilting, upended soil, and a silence where there used to be birds. After coming upon the sixth well on what would otherwise be this beautiful landscape, I broke down. I lay under a giant Tulip poplar tree near the well, and I cried into the earth. I felt lost, as if the landscape of my ancestors had been turned into some kind of dystopian site of energy extraction, and I couldn't escape it. I went home with a heavy heart. But this experience helped reaffirm the importance of land-healing work—and the constant need for this in today's world. After deep meditation, I went back to those woods to engage in deep listening and apology work, holding space as described in chapter 3. Then I built a healing altar (also in this chapter) and offered protection and growth sigils (chapter 3). I could sense the land settle, the spirits calm. After the ritual, the spirits invited me to lie back down in the spot where I had cried before. I did so. And they gave back in the form of this beautiful healing light, healing of my weary soul. This was reciprocal healing, helping us both.

I'm sure, dear reader, that you have your own stories and experiences just like this one—where land you loved was destroyed or is going to be destroyed, and you were surrounded by the death of the inhabitants of the land. This kind of situation makes you feel powerless and helpless. In fact, when people reach out to me about land healing, it's almost always these kinds of situations that spark their desire to do something—anything—knowing that they likely can't stop the engines of profit and so-called progress.[26] Because of the death, suffering, and pain that are present, the most knee-jerk reaction is to look away, disengage, or despair due to your own powerlessness. Palliative-care practices in this chapter offer you an alternative powerful skill set, allowing us to do some of the deepest spirit work. Consider palliative care to be the first stage in the healing process—you are setting the stage for what is to come. You are easing the pain and suffering and laying the foundation for the eventual healing that will come, even if it is decades away.

# Deepening Our Understanding of Palliative Care

As I write this chapter, the forest that I grew up in, where my parents still live, is having a huge part cut out of it to make way for a septic line, a 40'–60' cut that will go for miles and miles through forests and wild places. It's coming directly through the refugium garden that my parents and I have worked for years to tend and cultivate (see chapter 7), where the Ramps, Wild Ginseng, Bloodroot, hardwood nut trees, and so many others grow. The situation is extremely heartbreaking to me and my family—we have done everything we can to fight, but even the lawyer we hired says it can't be stopped. There has been serious talk among the family of us chaining ourselves to the big cherry tree that grows in the middle of the land, but we know that will only lead to jail time for us, and the project will continue as before.

In yet another example, thousands of miles of streams in my region suffer from acid mine drainage (AMD). Our streams are so polluted from old mine runoff (mines that were put in place before regulations), and we have thousands of miles of lifeless and polluted orange-stained rivers. Most of our streams in the coal-mining regions of Pennsylvania have looked like this not only during my life, but during the lives of my parents, grandparents, and even great-grandparents. Once a mine starts producing AMD, it is almost impossible to stop it, but there are mitigation efforts (often quite expensive) that can be done. While work is being done to address these water issues at a community and statewide level, we still have thousands of miles of dead streams today.

The three situations I've laid out above—a recently installed fracking well, the soon-to-be-destroyed forest, and the long-term pollution of streams—represent the triad of circumstances for which palliative care is often the most effective. The fracking well represents a place that was recently damaged and is angry and full of pain. The soon-to-be-cleared land that will house the septic line represents life and habitat that will be destroyed. The acid mine drainage pollution represents a multitude of long-standing damaged waterways where healing is not yet possible. In addition to these kinds of sites, we are surrounded by places that continue to pollute (strip mines, factories, toxic waste storage sites, mountaintop removal, gravel pits, sites where continual pollution happens), as well as sites where the natural world is prevented from returning to a place of health through chemical or mechanical intervention (lawns, pipelines, golf courses, etc.).

Notice that all these examples are putting the land in a long-term state of damage. The major difference between when to choose palliative care versus energetic or physical healing (chapters 5 and 7) has to do with the future of the land. Is this circumstance a temporary one from which the land can regrow and heal? If it's temporary, the energetic-healing approaches in chapter 5 are most appropriate. Or, is this damage ongoing or irreversible (at least in the immediate future)? If the answer is yes, palliative care is more appropriate.

I am really stressing these differences throughout this book because choosing the wrong kind of energetic work not only may be ineffective but can be damaging to the spirits of the land. A sleep working, part of palliative care, would not be appropriate for the AMD stream for a forest that has been logged and can now regrow. A sleep working would certainly be appropriate for the forest on my parents' property, where it will not be allowed to regrow because the company will keep the septic line clear of plants/trees (most certainly using chemical means). These two situations are different and thus would require different kinds of interventions.

Another aspect of palliative care is to recognize that the specific circumstances surrounding the damage, the severity of the damage, and the length of time that something has been damaged also have energetic effects. Thus, energetic differences exist among a site that will be destroyed (the forest that will be cut), one that has recently been heavily damaged (the fracking well), and one that has been damaged over a long period of time (the AMD-polluted stream). A site that is not yet destroyed has a vitality to it and is often abundant with life—the work then becomes how to transition that site and prepare it for what is inevitably going to come. A site that was recently destroyed is often a place of deep pain and anger—think about a person who was recently violated and their reactionary responses as they try to make sense of what just happened. This requires a different approach. A site that has been polluted or damaged over a long period of time has yet a third energetic signature—this kind of site loses the energies of life (Nywfre) over time and has a kind of energetic darkness that fills the void where that Nywfre would be. This chapter offers rituals and techniques to provide palliative care for all three such kinds of circumstances.

You may not know the history of a site or how long it is damaged, but you can teach yourself to sense such energetic differences. One of these approaches is through the deep-listening strategies of chapter 3—spending time sensing the energy of a site and communicating with that site will help you understand the nature of the damage. There's also just your general "energy sense" that you will invariably cultivate as someone who is engaging in regular land healing. When you do a ritual such as the Sphere of Protection ritual in a place that is healed, you will feel the energies of life flow into you—you can literally summon Nywfre to come into you. When you walk into a healthy ecosystem (such as a forest, desert, plain, beach, etc.), you can likewise sense that Nywfre—this is why places like these are vitalizing and refreshing. When you come across a site that is in active pain, you are going to feel something very different—many people feel this in the pit of their stomach or in their heart, a kind of tightness, weight, or wrongness. The dead places are the worst. You will feel this deadness deep within you, like darkness or a heavy weight pulling you down—that's a sign that the land has been deeply suffering. So now let us consider these different approaches—and for all palliative-care practices, remember that you are making a difference. You are doing what can and needs to be done, and not only is that work valuable and appreciated, it is enough.

# Protection and Self-Care

Anytime you are working as a healer of the land, you are coming into a relationship with the energy (and often physical presence) of the land. For sites that have damage and suffering, including many of the sites described previously, it is important to practice good protective techniques, such as the Sphere of Protection. If you take on the energy or pain of the land while it is in this state, particularly over a long period of time, it can lead you to emotional burnout, mental instability, or even physical harm. Thus, making sure you protect and take care of yourself for any techniques here is of paramount concern.

In chapter 4, the Sphere of Protection was given as one such shielding technique, and it is an excellent one to employ for the work here. Prior to doing any work with damaged lands, you want to perform the Sphere of Protection ritual to offer a basic "energetic" buffer—you do not want to take any of this energy into yourself. During any work, pay attention to how you are feeling, and work to not take on the energy or emotions of the land into yourself by keeping that sphere of protection strong. Another approach is to use an herbal smoke stick (chapter 3) to surround yourself with smoke before doing this work. You may also find protective stone jewelry (particularly black tourmaline) to be useful to you during this work. Also realize that there are limits to what you can do and times you need to take a break from this very difficult work. It's okay to take that time or to say "no" if you are not up to it in the moment.

After the work, check in with yourself and practice any number of basic grounding and self-care techniques (many of which can be found in chapter 9). Two particularly useful ones for doing the work of palliative care is a cleansing bath or healing bath (e.g., soaking or showering and using herbs, salt, or vinegar for cleansing) and spending time communing with healthy places in nature (such as a favorite tree, hiking trail, or stream). A final thing that might help is using stones or herbs as additional protectors. Cultivating a relationship with a protective plant, such as Hawthorn, can help strengthen and protect you for this difficult work. Palliative care is the most challenging work that we can do as land healers, and thus this work should be done with an understanding that you will also need grounding, shielding, and self-care.

# Working with Sites That Will Be Destroyed

I think one of the most tragic situations at present is working with land or trees that are currently healthy but that will soon be damaged, logged, bulldozed, poisoned, or otherwise destroyed by human hands. The septic line on my family's land that I described above is a good example of this kind of site—as I was writing this, the forest went from a place that was healthy and vibrant to one that was bulldozed and destroyed. Recognize that this kind of situation is extremely disempowering. You want, more than anything, to stop something from occurring, but powers beyond you have destined this land, tree, or habitat for destruction. This kind of thing happens on individual levels as well as community levels. For example, here in the US, many communities are fighting against oil pipelines and often losing those battles, having pipelines come through ecologically sensitive areas and through their backyards. If the decision has been made and there is no stopping it on the physical world, this is when we turn our attention to what can be done metaphysically.

My recommendation for this kind of situation is to do three things: move plants or save seeds to preserve the genetic legacy of what will be lost, do the hibernation ritual on the space (either physically present or at a distance) to assist the land with this fate, and be prepared to hold space while it happens (for holding space, see the next section). We'll now consider these in turn.

## PRESERVING THE GENETIC LEGACY OF THE LAND

Preserving the genetic legacy of the land or a tree, or doing whatever you can to save small parts of the being or place's genetic legacy, is really important. All life deeply cares about passing on a genetic legacy—helping spread and preserve that genetic legacy is a very healing practice. You aren't going to be able to move a whole forest, or even every plant or species growing there. But what you can do is save a few: dig up a few young seedling trees and move them. Save seeds and plant/scatter them elsewhere—or bring them back in to replant later if the site will be allowed to return to health after the destruction. Even if you are able to move only one kind of plant, the act of doing this is a powerful one and sends a message to the land that it is valued and that you care.

## PUTTING THE LAND TO SLEEP:
## THE HIBERNATION RITUAL AND SLEEP SIGIL

The septic line that came through my parents' property was extremely destructive—bulldozers came through literally knocking over trees, and massive amounts of heavy machinery moved through the area. About four months before the bulldozers arrived, but after we knew we couldn't stop it, my sister and I (both of us grew up on that land) met and performed a hibernation ritual. This ritual recognizes that trees, forests, and other wild spaces can feel the pain of death just like anyone else, and the ritual does work to help soothe that passing as much as possible. Thus, the ritual has several goals: the primary one is to induce an energetic hibernation, helping to soothe the inevitable pain of what will come. You might think about this as being comparable to a sick friend who is struggling with a lot of pain at the end of their life—the goal is to make them comfortable and take away as much of the pain as possible. A second goal for the hibernation ritual is showing respect: communicating what will happen and why it is happening, offer an acknowledgment and sorrow for what is happening, and make a physical offering in solidarity. Finally, you set a sigil to be activated when those who will destroy the land show up to do their deed: the deep slumber activates and the land will not feel as much pain.

You can perform the following ceremony either at a distance or physically on the land. You can also perform it around a single tree or anything else that will be destroyed. If you have to do it at a distance, you should do your best to get an object that is from the land/tree (a stone, stick, etc.) or else get something that strongly connects you to the land. The absolute best is to be present at the land, but that's not always possible. If you are at the land or tree, you can do the ritual below. If you are doing distance work, you should refer to my earlier comments on distance work at the end of chapter 4 and use an object that represents the land in the center of your space.

The timing of this ritual should also be considered. I suggest doing this ritual as far in advance as you can. Remember that nature works on a slower time frame, and so the more time that passes, the more the land will be able to sink into a deep hibernation. A few months or weeks is a good time frame; that gives the land or tree time to attune to the lowered energy level and get deeply into a long and deep sleep. After your work has been done, you can visit the land, walk on the land, and so forth, but I suggest not doing any energy work or communication work—the last thing you want to do is raise energy or awaken the land after you've put the land to rest. For example, while this ritual was done four months before the bulldozers arrived, the evening before they began bulldozing the property, I visited the land to say goodbye. The ritual was in effect; the land was at peace. I reinforced the sleep sigil, helped replant a number of small trees and plants from the path of the bulldozers, and knew there was nothing else I could do.

Finally, the ritual that follows includes setting a sigil on the land that will both reinforce the energy present from the ritual, and activate when the actual destruction begins. The sigil should be placed right in the center of the path where the machinery will come through, if at all possible. When they bring their heavy machines in, they will invariably run over the sleep sigil, activating it and pushing that final deep sleep energy into the land.

After you finish the ritual, I suggest engaging in self-care practices (chapter 9). Perhaps go hiking somewhere and spend time in a place that is not under threat, that is whole, that is vibrant. Take some time for you. It is hard to do the work I've outlined above, because it means facing the reality of what is happening to the land and not looking away. It is particularly hard if this is land that you love or have spent a lot of time on. Thus, self-care must be a critical part of this work.

Despite the challenges, there is a silver lining to this work. Land may go into hibernation with the help of ritual or simply through repeated abuse. When the land is ready for long-term healing, you can help bring the land out of slumber and into health with a blessing or land-healing ceremony (as described in chapter 4 or 5). Let us hope that more opportunities are present for blessing and healing than the need to do this work here.

# The Hibernation Ritual

Needed materials:

- representations of the elements or other materials for opening sacred space
- an offering to give to the land (see chapter 3)
- some way of hearing the voice of the land (techniques in chapter 2: a pendulum or another divination tool)
- materials to construct or draw your sleep sigil (gathered locally)
- *If at a distance:* a representative of the land; paper and pen for drawing the sigil
- a drum, rattle, or another instrument that can connect you with the heartbeat of the land (you can bang two sticks together; it doesn't have to be elaborate)

*Open up a sacred space.* Begin the ritual by opening up a sacred space (see chapter 4). Attune with yourself and the land by taking a few deep breaths and settling your mind for the work to come.

*Make an offering.* As you make your offering, acknowledge the land/tree in your own words. For example, for a tree that will be cut, "Friend, I see you growing strong. I climbed your branches when I was a little girl. I walk with you now as a grown woman. I make this offering to honor you, honor the time we have spent together, and honor our friendship through the years."

*Explain what will happen, and offer condolences.* Next, explain to the tree/land what will be happening, again, in your own words. Share how you feel about this. For example: "Friend, we have fought to stop the loggers from coming here to clear this land and dig a septic line. We have failed. When the leaves begin to come back on the trees, they will come and clear this land down to bare earth. I am heartbroken for what will happen. I want you to hear this from me, a friend. I am so sorry that this will happen. I am here for you."

*Ask if there is anything you can do.* Before moving on to the hibernation part of the ritual, ask the land/tree if there is anything you can do. You might get asked to move seeds, stone, or soil or do some other task. Do whatever task is asked of you in the moment or, if it cannot be done at this time, agree to do it in the future.

*Offer sleep and distance from pain.* Offer the spirits of the land distance and slumber, again, in your own words. Here's an example for a forest to be logged: "Friend, because I know they will come, this will cause you great pain. The trees here will be cut. The forest creatures will be driven away. The soil will be torn up. I offer you distance from this suffering; I offer to help the spirits of this place go into a deep sleep, to awaken again when the pain is over and when you can regrow. Please let me know if you would like me to help you sleep through this suffering."

*Wait to hear a response.* It may take some time to hear a response; be patient. It is possible that when you offer this, the land will not want you to help perform the rest of this ritual, or the land may want you to come back at a later point. Again, feel out the will of the land and honor the will of the land and her spirits. Use any spirit communication or divination tools to aid you with this approach. If the spirits decline, thank them, spend some more time on the land, and then close out the space. If they agree, complete the rest of the ritual.

*Construct the sleep sigil.* If the land allows you to continue, begin by drawing or constructing the sleep sigil on the ground as large as you can (but done in such a way that it will not be obvious). You can draw it in the dirt, create the symbol with stones or sticks, or, if it is snowy and frozen, walk it in the snow. Place the sigil somewhere that will be directly in the path of what is to come, which will help "activate" it when necessary. If you are working with a single tree, you can trace the sigil on the tree in healing oil (see chapter 2). If you are at a distance, you can draw it on a piece of paper or stone and then take the sigil to the location and leave it there. As you draw/construct the sigil, you can chant three ogham letters tied with this work as described in chapter 5: Pine (Ifin), Honeysuckle (Uilleand), and Elder (Ruis). Chant for as long as you feel it necessary, and spend time building up energy.

*Spend time connecting to the heartbeat of the land/tree.* Sit near or within the sigil you created and now connect to the heartbeat of the land. Clear your mind, take a few deep breaths, and then feel the energy of the land. Feel the wind in the leaves; feel the soil beneath you. Be fully present here in this place, breathing deeply and attuning to the space. Eventually, you will feel or hear a heartbeat or other rhythm; that is the steady rhythm of this land. Let that rhythm sink into your body, and feel yourself align with that rhythm.

*Put the land/tree into hibernation.* Picking up your drum or rattle, match that heartbeat of the land. For a time, simply play with the heartbeat of the land as you hear it, connecting yourself and that drum to the energy as deeply as possible. As you drum, imagine that you are holding that heartbeat with your drum. Now, intentionally, begin to slow down that beat. Take your time doing this, understanding that it can take awhile for the land to respond. Keep the beat going slower and lower until it is very quiet. At this point, you might sit or even lie on the ground, in rest, beating the drum so very faintly. Feel the heartbeat of the land now, lower and slower, as it slides into deep slumber. Eventually, stop your drumming entirely and simply sit with the land, feeling the lower vibration. The heartbeat will not be gone, but it might be much more quiet and slower than before—that's exactly what you are working toward.

*Close your space.* Quietly thank the elements (a simple nod to the quarters will do) and close your sacred space. Leave the land for a time, letting it fall deeply into hibernation.

## EMPOWERING YOUR SLEEP SIGIL

The drumbeat part of this ritual can be used to empower your sleep sigil. For this, open a sacred grove, using the methods in chapter 4. Place your sleep sigils at the center of your sacred-grove space. Using a drum, start with a fast beat. As you beat the drum, circle your sigils, drumming the energy into them. Then, just as you would if you were performing the sleep ceremony, slowly drop the volume and tempo of your drum until the drum is quiet and the beats are very soft. Feel the energy of sleep going into your sigils, seeing a gold-green light entering them. After some quiet time, stop the drumbeat and sit in silence. With the ritual concluded, close your sacred grove.

## DISTANCE VARIANT FOR THE HIBERNATION RITUAL

Perhaps you want to do this work for land, but you do not have access due to it being someone else's property, mobility or transportation issues, or simply being far away. The main modification you will need to do is to spiritually connect with the land at the start of the ritual and use that connection for each of the parts of the ritual. Here's the modified ritual structure: open up a sacred space, establish a distance connection to the land (see chapter 4), make an offering, explain what will happen and offer condolences, offer sleep and distance from the pain, construct a sleep sigil, connect with the heartbeat of the land, put the land/tree to sleep, and close your space. If at all possible, place the sleep sigil on the land that will be destroyed. If this is not possible, create a small altar for the work and place the sigil on the altar. Leave the altar undisturbed until after the event has occurred.

# Working with Sites That Are Suffering or Damaged

When something is actively suffering, with no end in sight—a tree, friend, place, animal, plant, forest, waterway, field, lawn—this is the work of palliative care. This is especially true with places that have ongoing issues with damage or pollution: fracking wells, polluted streams, mountaintop removal, active mines, factory farms, active dumps, Superfund sites, and so on. This may also be true of places that are repeatedly sprayed with chemicals, fighting declining populations, or for species that are endangered, losing habitats, fighting an invasive species, and much more. Unfortunately, we have an overabundance of places on our beautiful planet that fall into this category—and more places are being damaged each day.

Let's return to our metaphor of a sick friend in order to think more about this work. You wish you could do something to help this person, but it's not in your power to heal them of the illness at present. Instead, you sit quietly with them, laugh, talk, let them know they are not alone, and maybe do some energetic work for them. I'll now offer two strategies for this kind of work.

## HOLDING SPACE

Holding space is a powerful form of palliative care for the land. It's the difference between suffering in silence, afraid and alone, and having someone there. Your very presence as a land healer can be calming and soothing and can resonate: "I am here for you, I see your suffering, and you are loved." We cannot abandon our Earth mother during these dark times—if we want to walk the path of land healers, we must quietly and firmly stand with her even in her darkest times, holding space for her in the most damaged of places. Holding space is about investing your time and energy. It's being available and simply there, for however long is needed. It's being strong even when you see suffering you'd rather not see. Doing the work of land healing in this day and age can be tremendously difficult and isolating because the damage never seems to end—but holding space gives us the peace of knowing we are doing something, and that something is important.

Most of the Eastern Hemlock trees in my town and region are currently fighting the Hemlock Woolly Adelgid, which I shared details about in chapter 5. This is a small, aphid-like beetle that has been making its way east and destroying our Hemlock populations. Millions of little adelgids suck the sap out of the trees until they die. I discovered that some of the trees in our town were infected recently. This experience is deeply painful to me, since Eastern Hemlock is one of my closest tree friends. There's a part of me that is tempted to look away, to take a different path on my walk to work, because the pain of this is so great. But instead, I choose to walk by them each day. To hold space for these trees, I visit them often. I put my hand on their trunks and send them a bit of healing energy. I bring blessed stones with sigils painted on them in walnut ink, and bury them at the roots. I offer healing waters and anoint their tree trunks with my healing oil. I acknowledge what is happening and ask how I can help. I have collected their small cones with seeds to put into my freezer to save to plant later. I know that in this act, I'm not just holding space for these specific Hemlocks; this work can reach many other Hemlocks who are going through this transition—the tens of thousands of them here, in this county, the millions and millions in this state, and more beyond.

My story of holding space for the Hemlocks in my town illustrates a number of useful "space-holding" techniques. Unlike some of the other material in this book that can be formalized and ritualized, I think that holding space should be an intuitive thing where you do what feels right in the moment and what the spirits ask of you. Here is a list of possible techniques for space holding:

*Be present.* Your presence and attentiveness, just acknowledging what is happening, are excellent ways to begin to hold space for something that is suffering. Be present, visit often, and acknowledge what is occurring. Sit quietly and be still, being present for the land.

*Make offerings.* Making a simple offering is an excellent way to hold space, particularly for land or waterways that are suffering. An offering demonstrates reciprocation and honor between you and the land.

*Play music, sing, or drum.* Bring an instrument or your own voice and spend some time playing music, drumming, or singing for the land. Allowing the land to hear your song and your voice as it carries through the air is a powerful healing aid. You can also do this kind of palliative care even among other people—it can be a very subtle but effective way to work in public areas.

*Place a sigil.* Consider using some of the land-healing sigils as part of this work—sleep most likely being appropriate, but possibly others. You can create the sigils in advance and bury them on the land or create them from materials found at the site.

*Practice deep listening.* Listen to what the spirits of the land in this place have to say. Hear their words, acknowledge them, and act on anything that they may ask for. Some of the requests may seem odd or strange, but do your best.

*Do a smoke cleansing.* Using a smoke-cleansing stick (see my 2021 book *Sacred Actions: Living the Wheel of the Year Through Earth-Centered Sustainable Practices* for more on how to create smoking cleansing sticks) or any other kind of incense, walk the land and allow the smoke to clear some of the pain. When I do this work, I will usually use a whole stick for the space, burning it until it is finished (this is why I like to make my own smoke-cleansing sticks—I can go through a lot of them even at a single site, and buying them gets expensive!).

*Anoint with oil or healing water.* Offer a bit of healing water or anoint the tree/land with oil. While you do this, hold space, feel their pain, and work to soothe them as best you can.

## PALLIATIVE-CARE ALTARS

Another powerful way of helping the land with active suffering is to create an altar to energetically help dull the pain. Altars represent ongoing work where you can continue to focus energies—or allow energies to permeate—long term. Altars can serve several purposes, as we'll discuss here. In terms of building altars, I suggest you use what materials are local and available and do not have an environmental cost: stones, sticks, leaves, shells, your own herbs or herbal blends, etc. Any of the items we use as part of palliative care should come from the earth without harm and return to her without harm.

### ON-SITE PALLIATIVE-CARE ALTAR
The on-location palliative-care altar is simply a space that you set up that you can come to regularly (possibly to do holding-space techniques) and to offer a presence for the land while you are not there. Perhaps you create a simple stone cairn and pour blessed waters over it every season.
Perhaps you plant a flower and surround it with stones. The actual altar, and what goes into it, can be intuitive—the act of creating it and tending it is what matters, less so how it looks. It can be as simple as a stack of stones on an old stump or a little ceramic heart hanging on a tree.

These altars are like a light in the darkness. For land that is suffering, what your shrine does is give the land a focal point and lets the spirits of that land know that someone is thinking about them, wishing them well, and saying that we are here in support, even when we are not physically present. I have made many such shrines over the years—small places, hidden places, places that I quietly go and visit. You will get a sense, from the land itself, about how often you need to come and what you can do while you are there—altar work can include any of the holding-space ideas previously mentioned. Find a regular pattern to work this altar (each new moon, each solstice and equinox, etc.).

### DISTANCE PALLIATIVE-CARE ALTAR

A distance altar is particularly useful if you want to work with a site over a period of time and that site is not easily accessible. This technique uses an altar that is at a different location (ideally, a location that is in vibrant health or indoors). Again, the nature of the altar doesn't matter. What you want to do is build it and include something from the site or a representation of the site (e.g., a photograph) and place it on the altar. Now, do regular "holding space" work, mentioned previously, or develop a set of chants for this altar (see chapter 5). Regular work at this altar is critical.

# Advanced Work:
## Pain Management, Energy Moving, and Herbal Allies

A final set of techniques are the equivalent of using high-powered painkillers for the land: these are techniques that use energetic work to help dull or lessen the pain. These techniques can be used not only at sites that require palliative care, but also at sites where destruction will happen. As I shared at the beginning of this chapter and in my introduction, you do *not* want to send large amounts of energy into a site that needs palliative care—this is kind of like making a sick friend who is sleeping wake up and be too active, which causes additional suffering. But what you can do is the opposite— moving the pain away from the site and grounding it in a very specific way to release it. I offer three techniques, the first of which is accessible to beginners, and the last of which should be practiced only by advanced land healers. The reason that they should be practiced only by advanced land healers and those used to grounding, shielding, and moving energy is that you are going to come into direct contact with that pain and suffering, and what you do not want to do is take it into yourself, even inadvertently.

# GROUNDING OUT THE PAIN BY USING HEALING HERBAL ALLIES TO HELP THE PAIN

Within any local ecosystem or community, there are certain herbal allies that may be willing to lend their powers to help lessen or deaden pain and can be energetically used to assist the land through visualization. Usually, these herbal allies have a long history of human use for pain management, although the stronger painkilling allies also may not be legal, depending on where you live. This technique involves establishing a relationship with one such herbal ally so that you can use this ally's power to help assist the land.

There are many such herbal allies found all over the world. These allies include but are not limited to Black Birch (*Betula lenta*), Cannabis (*Cannabis sativa, Cannabis indica*), Ghost Pipe (*Monotropa uniflora*), Kava Kava (*Piper methysticum*), Lavender (*Lavandula* spp.), Rosemary (*Salvia rosmarinus*), Willow (*Salix nigra*), and Turmeric (*Curcuma longa*). If nothing on this list works for you, you can study plants and herbs local to your area and learn what plants are often used for pain relief in your region, and you can start there. I strongly recommend that you use a plant that can and does grow in your ecosystem if at all possible (e.g., in western Pennsylvania, I'm drawn to Black Birch and Ghost Pipe as two such allies because they are native here, and I'm likely not going to work with Turmeric or Kava Kava since they belong to other ecosystems in far-off places). Make sure that, for these techniques at least, you focus on a plant that has pain-numbing properties, not just general healing properties—since the last thing you want to do is energize a space that needs palliative care.

The first thing you need to do to use this technique is establish a relationship with one of these such allies.[27] This will be a plant spirit ally that you work with for a specific purpose of land healing, and that relationship should be strong before you call on this plant's aid. Begin by meditating with a bit of plant matter or a live plant. Focus on the plant and ask the plant spirit (using deep-listening techniques described in this book) for assistance with land healing. Make offerings and do other things to bring this plant into your life in this new way. In a second and third meditation session, again sit with the plant and make an offering. This time, focus on visualizing the plant in its most vibrant and powerful form—the large Poppy in full bloom, the beautiful Black Willow tree by the lake, or the blooming Lavender hedge 3 feet tall. Work with this image firmly in your mind. Feel the energy of this plant and its potent pain-relief properties. In a final meditation, if you are able, imbibe the plant—drink a tea, eat a small part of the plant, or otherwise find a way to take this plant within you. Focus on the energetic connection being established from this act. Once you've done all three of these things, you can start to work with this plant as a plant-healing ally in damaged places.

Once you've done the groundwork, the technique itself is actually quite simple and can be done at the site itself or at any distance. You can do this in combination with space-holding techniques and altar work.

Begin by taking a few deep breaths to clear your mind and focus on the work in that moment. Ask permission of the land to work to numb the pain. Assuming you have permission, first feel the pain-numbing energy of your plant ally. Now, visualize that plant ally growing up in this space, covering it, and numbing the pain. Hold this visualization as long as you can. If you have a small bit of the plant you can leave (infused in oil, as a dried plant, or in a tea), you can do so, but the energy and visualization of this technique are really where the power lies. You can also, of course, plant the plants themselves in an area if you are able to.

## DEEP PALLIATIVE CARE THROUGH GROUNDING OBJECTS:
### For Fracking Wells, Oil Fields, Strip Mines, Deforestation, and Other Seriously Damaged Places

For deeply damaged places, where ongoing human extraction takes a serious toll on the landscape, additional techniques may be needed. I developed the following rituals and techniques after many years of working with fracking wells. Fracking wells are terrible places that cause pollution to rivers, aquifers, and the landscape, as well as ongoing disruption as the wells are maintained and, eventually, abandoned, often without proper closure due to poor regulations. Fracking-well sites are excellent examples of places that can use deep palliative-care techniques. Often, one of these sites is in so much active pain that sleep rituals aren't effective—so grounding out some of the pain prior to a sleep ritual is necessary. The basic ritual involves gathering two stones from near a site and linking them through ritual. Then, one stone is placed back at the site of pain, while the other is placed where the stone can help ground out the energy coming from the palliative site—kind of like a pain relief. In my case, I took two stones from a central fracking well in a cluster of wells and linked them. With permission of the spirits of the land, I left one stone on an isolated island in a local state park that was accessible by kayak (and that I visit often enough to check on regularly), and returned the other to the fracking-well site. The island stone helps ground out some of the worst of the suffering from the fracking well, using healing techniques as only nature can and water to soothe the pain. I check on the island stone regularly to make sure the work is proceeding without ill effects to the island or surrounding lake. Bodies of water are particularly good for this work.

This technique is the most advanced one that I'm offering in this chapter, and should be done with the utmost care. Do this work only if you feel directly led to do it, if you are experienced in feeling the flow and direction of energy, and if you have good protection techniques. If you do this incorrectly, you can inadvertently transfer some of the pain and suffering to yourself or to a new site. This technique is best used for sites that are actively in pain and who ask for relief. I would also try this technique only after doing other palliative-care techniques—I consider this a "last resort" technique. Often, once you've used this ritual to stave off the worst of the pain, you can then move back into other palliative-care techniques shared earlier in this chapter. I also recommend reading through this entirely and finding your "grounding site" in advance before undertaking the work.

Go to the site you are working to heal and find two stones. If you can't visit the site directly, find stones that would represent that site. Take these stones to a place where you can do deep ritual work without being disturbed. You will first scope out both potential sites—the damaged site and a location that can be used to help with grounding for the damaged site. Once you've selected both of these sites (see details that follow), you will perform an initial ritual to link the two stones. Then, one object or altar is left at the site where the damage is taking place. The second object or altar is placed somewhere that can help channel the pain away from the first site and ground it, releasing it harmlessly back into the earth. The link between the two stones is activated and the palliative care can begin.

*Linking the stones.* Open up a sacred space and place the two stones in the center of your working area. If you have a land-healing altar or shrine, this would be an ideal location to do this work. Begin by focusing on the stones themselves. Provide a blessing to each of the stones—pour over some sacred healing water—and do whatever else you feel led to do (smoke cleansing, seven-element blessing, etc.). Next, visualize the connection between these two stones: feel their similar history, their similar composition, their similar energy. Mark each of these with a sigil or ogham (I usually use the protection sigil for this work). As you mark them, say, "These two stones are linked for the purposes of palliative care. May these stones work for the good of the land and may all energy transferred through these stones be returned to the earth and rendered harmless. When I intone the rune of the Elder (Ruis), the link between these will become active." Close your ritual space and wrap the two stones in cotton or linen cloth until you use them again.

*Anchor stone.* Now, return to your site that is in need of palliative care with one stone, your anchor stone. When I place a stone in this way, I build a small altar or mandala (see chapter 5) that helps connect it with the site and channel the energy. Spend time visualizing the energy of the site connecting to the stone. Do not touch the stone while you do this or for the remainder of the ceremony. When you have this visual firmly in your mind, place your hands over the stone and chant "Ruis" to activate the connection. Make an offering and do deep listening before leaving the site.

*Grounding-stone site.* To place the second stone, your grounding stone, you will need to find a place to leave the grounding stone to help transfer away some of the pain of the damaged site. This should be a protected and healed location that is willing to help ground out this pain. Often, healed landscapes or waterways are willing to do this work. I have found that the best sites for this kind of work are islands or other sites that have some water feature—for example, you can put the stone in a stream, on a lakeshore, or on a small island on a lake, where the water itself can help dissipate any residual pain. I suspect you can find other such "buffer" sites in other kinds of ecosystems as well; these are just the ones that work in my own ecosystem. The principle here is that nature knows how to heal, and she has her own methods of grounding and healing. Nature can take so much pain and transform it harmlessly back to energy and send it deep into the earth.

Once you have found a potential site, use deep-listening techniques, offerings, and other inner work to determine if the spirits of the land are willing to help with the grounding work and have the capacity (as described in chapter 3). Before placing your second stone, you will want to spend time in silent communion, making sure that any place is willing to support this work and has the capacity to ground the pain without harm.

After determining that the site will be willing to ground out the pain from the other site, you can bring your grounding stone. Build an altar for the stone, if possible, and spend time visualizing the stone's energy traveling harmlessly into the earth. When you have this visual firmly in your mind, place your hands over the stone and chant "Ruis" to activate the grounding stone. Sit in the spot for a while once the connection is made. Again, do not touch this stone. Sense the flow of energy through the damaged site's stone to the stone in front of you. Feel the flow of energy returning harmlessly to the earth, where it is grounded out and rendered harmless. If all is feeling good, thank the spirits, leave an offering, and let the stones to do their work.

This ritual is an ongoing one that can be in place for a short or long period of time. I strongly recommend returning regularly to the grounding site to check on the status of the stone. I also recommend going back to the site with the pain—it is possible that, in time, enough of the pain will have drained off that you can close this ritual (by severing the link and returning the grounding stone) and then put the site to sleep, which is a better long-term option. If you sense something is amiss (at any point), you can place your hands over the stone and chant "Ruis" to sever the connection between the stones. Then, return the grounding stone to the damaged site.

## "DEAD" ENERGY AT SEVERELY DAMAGED SITES

Another kind of situation you may encounter is a site that has been so energetically damaged that the site feels dead. You don't sense spirit activity at these kinds of sites, and usually there is no Nywfre at all. When I visit these sites, I usually get a heavy feeling in the pit of my stomach. You'll get this feeling near nuclear power plants, active strip mines (especially ones that have been established for some time), toxic factories, severely polluted rivers, or other sites where toxic waste has been spilled (extremely polluted sites, known as Superfunds in the US). These are sites that have been severely damaged, and at present and in the foreseeable future, no active healing can take place. These sites often have an energetic deadness present at sites that have been damaged for some time period (decades, centuries), and the local land spirits have given up and fled.

When you find a site like this, you might be tempted to intervene. But I would suggest, in nearly all cases, leaving the site alone. Think about it this way—the deadness is better than pain, in that there is no active suffering. The land has figured out how to numb itself, and the spirits have retreated. I might say a small prayer or acknowledgment, but otherwise I leave the site be. I am certainly not going to do anything to "wake" that site back up or call those spirits back until it is time and active healing work can begin. When it is time for real healing to take place, though, the "deadened" land then needs you to come in and give the site a burst of light and life by channeling the solar current downward (see chapter 5). Again, the sick-person metaphor helps here—you have a very sick friend who has fallen into a deep sleep. Let them stay asleep as long as possible; waking them will simply cause more hurt.

Other sites that fit the previous description may have a different energetic signature, a kind of dark intensity to them, and the energy may feel really "wrong" and "awful" just being near them. For example, when I was visiting a friend in West Virginia not too long ago, I was driving and was struck with this horribly awful feeling as I rounded the bend. Turned out, just around the next bend was a huge gravel/sand pit, cutting into the mountainside—and that was the source of the suffering. Because this site is energetically awake and suffering, many of the palliative-care strategies described in this chapter would be appropriate.

## Palliative Care for the Waterways

When I was still in college, I would go to an overlook for the Monongahela River, in California, Pennsylvania, in the western part of the state, which bordered the edge of campus. The "Mon," as it was locally called, was extremely polluted—its waters often had a bad odor, and the water was usually a very pale green/gray and opaque. No fish or other life was present in the Mon due to so much pollution—there were many factories located along the Mon, and for several centuries now it was more of an "industrial river" than a scenic one. I would sit with the river, despite the smell and the heavy feeling in the pit of my stomach, because as a land healer, I felt it was necessary for me to hold space. As I've described in this chapter, like the Mon, we have so many streams, rivers, and

lakes, and even now our oceans, that are polluted and poisoned due to human activity. We have waterways under threat from chemical fertilizers, creating dead zones and toxic algae blooms, and waterways under threat from long-term mine drainage. We have pollution from factories, oil pipeline spills, and plastic filling our oceans. Our waterways need some love. Water is life. Without water, we all will perish. Working with our waters, especially those bodies of water that are suffering, can be good work for land healers.

Many of the techniques shared earlier in this chapter are appropriate for waterways, in addition to the ritual on the next page. The ritual below is best for rivers such as the Mon, rivers that have long-term damage and are, at present, not able to be healed. In chapter 2, I suggested one powerful tool for engaging in land-healing work by creating your own sacred waters—these approaches use the sacred waters for palliative care.

In terms of sacred timing, for water healing and palliative care, consider doing this kind of work when the energies of water are at their peak in your region. For where I live in western Pennsylvania, I prefer to do healing work on waterways in the spring (between Imbolc and the summer solstice), since this is the most powerful time of flow on my landscape. The snows melt, the rains come, the Sugar Maples run, and ephemeral springs usher forth. If you live in an area that has a dry and a rainy season, the start of the rainy season would be most appropriate. Here are a few techniques that are specific to waterways.

As I was finishing revisions on this book, we had the driest summer in recent history. By August, with months of no rain, the landscape was wilting, trees were suffering, and many smaller plants and life were dying. This was the direct result of human-caused climate change, because the jet stream that drives much of our weather is no longer stable or predictable. In fact, these days, the summers continue to be hotter and drier, and I anticipate many of us will need this kind of ritual in the coming years.

A drought becomes an issue of palliative care as long as the conditions of the drought hold out—the longer the drought continues, the more important it is to do some energetic palliative care. If a drought lasts more than a season, doing some hibernation work may be appropriate. For shorter droughts, the approach offered here is of use. This approach is a variant of the Grove of Renewal approach offered in chapter 7. This work also assumes you are living in an area that is directly affected by the drought.

# Offering the Waters of Life

The first way is a simple offering. To prepare my water offering, I get a pot and take rainwater or spring water and put three drops of my sacred waters (see chapter 2) into the pot. I bring this to a boil and, as I am preparing the water, send healing and soothing energy into the waters.[28] Let the water cool, and take your waters of life to your polluted body of water or waterway, offering a simple chant for soothing and peace:

> *Waters of life*
>
> *Waters of healing*
>
> *Soothe this waterway*
>
> *Waters of life*
>
> *Waters of healing*
>
> *Be a balm to this waterway's suffering*
>
> *May peace be present this day and always*

# Prayer in a Bottle

A variation on the "message in a bottle," this technique uses a small glass bottle that is tightly lidded to send prayers and healing energy into the waterway. Begin by finding a small glass bottle that can be corked or lidded. Opening up a sacred grove, you will want to craft your prayer bottle for the waterway and its specific needs (active healing, palliative care, hibernation, etc.). To the bottle, I recommend adding a prayer (written on paper and rolled up) along with herbs, a bit of your offering blend, sacred healing oil, or anything else you feel led to add. Make sure anything you add would be harmless to the waterway. You can seal the lid with beeswax from a candle. Close your sacred space and take your prayer bottle with you. When you get to the river, release your bottle with a simple prayer or chant. As the bottle is taken by the waters, the prayer flows through the waterway.

## A FLOWER OFFERING

Another kind of soothing offering for a damaged waterway can be done an impromptu way. With permission and offering, gather either living flowers or the dead and dried seed heads of flowers in the winter months. Go to the edge of the waterway and offer your flowers. You can structure your offering any way you like, including

- throwing each flower in individually and speaking of hope for the future,
- throwing in the bundle of flowers with a simple palliative care chant using three ogham—Spindle (Or), Oak (Duir), Alder (Fearn),
- visualizing the flowers by using the seven-element framework as a blessing or strengthening for the spirits of the river and then making the offering, or
- combining the flowers with singing, drumming, or music.

# The Ritual

Choose a small, natural area or a single plant that you can regularly water. This might be a single plant on your running path that you can offer the contents of your water bottle to, or a small section of forest that you can stretch your hose to. The size is less important than the intent. Every few days, at least once a week, water this area as thoroughly as you can. Offer a short prayer as you water (use your own or this one):

> *Dried and parched land, I feel your pain.*
>
> *Dried and parched land, I see how you wilt and wither.*
>
> *Let this offering of water soothe your suffering.*
>
> *Let this offering of water soothe your spirit.*
>
> *The rains will return in their time, but that time is not yet come.*
>
> *Be at rest until this time is done.*

See this water like a balm to the surrounding landscape, reminding the land that at some point, the waters will return.

# Chapter 7:

# PHYSICAL LAND HEALING

**In this chapter,** we turn our attention to physically healing nature through replanting, regrowing, scattering seeds, and tending the wilds. While some of the work of this chapter assumes that you have access to land, others do not, with the hope that each of us can heal in whatever ways we have opportunity to do so.

Nearly all the healing practices that I describe in this book are about you building relationships with nature and the spirits of nature for promoting healing, alleviating suffering, and engaging in the work of repair. But what is the nature of that relationship with the physical Earth? I remember one influential druid speaking at a major event and saying, "The best thing you can do in nature is pick up the garbage and get out." From a certain standpoint, this perspective makes a lot of sense. It is the same perspective held by many conservationists trying to preserve ecologically sensitive lands. In a world where most humans lack basic understanding, knowledge, and care about the natural world, it is a reasonable perspective. This is a perspective ultimately rooted in the desire to care for nature, to preserve nature, and to do good. Unfortunately, this perspective assumes that people's actions are always bad, and therefore it is better if we keep nature at a distance and not engage. We hear that "the Earth should be protected" while not really teaching us how to engage in that protection but instead sending the message that the best thing we can do is remove ourselves from it.

The importance of traditional nature-caretaking roles for humans is well documented, as explored in *Tending the Wild*[29] by M. Kat Anderson and also through *Sand Talk: How Indigenous Thinking Can Save the World* by Tyson Yunkaporta. One of the concepts that Anderson describes is the view of Indigenous peoples of California on "wilderness." While in the English language the concept of "wilderness" is positive, in that it has been untouched by humans, the concept of "wilderness" for the Indigenous peoples of California is very negative. As Anderson describes, it meant that land was unloved, untended, and not under anyone's care. For Western people, humans touching nature is assumed to be bad/destructive, so wild places that are untouched are therefore good. But for the Indigenous Californians, touching nature and interaction are good, and nature that was left to go "wild" was a sad thing. Indigenous peoples all over the world and all people's ancestors, if you go back far enough, understood that if we are going to survive, and thrive, we do so in partnership with nature.

Thus, the perspective I'm advocating for in this chapter is not one of picking up the garbage and getting out but instead building ecological knowledge, actively tending nature, and regenerating ecosystems through careful, thoughtful, and knowledge-based actions. It is a perspective rooted in connection, wisdom, and a deep-rooted responsibility. What we need—as a society and as individuals—are tools for being *proactive* and directly engaging in *long-term regeneration*: healing the land, healing the planet, healing ourselves, and rebuilding the sacred relationship between humans and nature. We need tools to help us regain our active status as caretakers of our own lands, to learn about them, and to learn how to heal. This chapter makes the case, then, that the tools we might consider are those for "active regeneration" of damaged ecosystems. Some places that need healing are quite obvious: the pipeline recently installed, the logged forest, or the construction site now abandoned. But some places that are also in need of our healing may be much less obvious because we are surrounded by them each day: the typical lawn, for example, or local forests that are damaged or in decline due to repeated long-term logging. I think it's helpful to talk about how to recognize the different places that could use healing, and consider interventions that you can engage in. Thus, this chapter offers insights into how to do the work of physical land healing and some different suggestions for people in different life circumstances.

## Physical Land-Healing Primer:
# How Do I Know What to Do?

In chapter 1, I offered a discussion of what ecosystems were and how ecological succession is nature's way of healing over time. In this chapter, we look at some specific functions of ecosystems and talk about the knowledge necessary to help rebuild ecosystems and cultivate them. This chapter primarily focuses on soil, seeds, and plants for physical land-healing work. This is because plants and soil (along with water and sunlight) are the cornerstone of most life. A key reason for such loss of animal and insect biodiversity is loss of habitat—thus, restoring habitat can be a primary concern. Further, learning about plants is often fairly straightforward—there is an abundance of courses, books, and other learning opportunities for most bioregions on Earth. Focusing on plants isn't the only way to engage in land healing, but I think it is one of the most effective and

accessible for many people to do. If you create the right conditions with soil and plant life, animal, bird, reptile, amphibian, and insect life is sure to follow!

Tending the lands as active and contributing members of an ecosystem requires that we build our knowledge. This is not knowledge that likely was taught to us in the present-day education systems, but it was certainly part of the body of knowledge our ancestors held. Thus, learning to tend the wilds is also about connecting with our ancient ancestors and the ancestors of the land—how they lived, how they tended the wilds, and what they did. This knowledge has many benefits beyond land healing, including helping us develop a deeper appreciation and connection with nature, making us feel "part of" nature rather than removed from it, and learning a host of useful uses for plants (food, medicine, crafts, fiber, etc.). Not to mention helping us "rewild" and ground in practices that tie us directly to the living Earth.

In the first part of this chapter, I'll cover a variety of different kinds of information that can help you focus on answering this question: How do I know what to do? Obviously, I can't tell you about the specific plants in your ecosystem, what roles they play, which are under threat, or what you should plant. I could tell you those things about my own ecosystem, but that would be of limited use to those readers who are not in my small bioregion in the Pittsburgh Plateau and Laurel Highlands in western Pennsylvania. Instead, I'm going to share with you some ways of learning about the plants in your ecosystem and how to begin to build ecological knowledge. After that, we will look at how ecosystems function generally, and some planning decisions you can make when figuring out what to do.

## BASIC PRINCIPLES FOR LEARNING

Before you do anything, it is critical to take the time to learn about your local ecosystem: What does a healthy ecosystem look like in your bioregion? What does a pinnacle ecosystem look like? What plants are native to this area? Where do I start? You don't have to start by healing every damaged patch of soil—pick one or two places to target your energies, pick one or two species of plants to work with, and start there. These and many other questions can be answered by engaging in the following.

*Careful observation.* There is no substitute for direct experience. Start to learn how to identify plants, insects, and animal tracks, and go out into your local ecosystem often and in all seasons. Take note of the variety of the plants. Where do they grow? How robust is the ecosystem that they grow in? The question of "How do I know what to plant?" must be asked and answered as locally as possible—what your lands need depends on what they are lacking, and you figuring out what that might be. It can be very helpful to visit healthy ecosystems and take note of what is growing compared to those that have been disrupted. As I explained in chapter 1, not all "healthy looking" ecosystems are actually healthy, so finding older ecosystem that have not been disrupted for 50 or 100 years is one of the best methods, if possible.

*Building ecological knowledge.* The more ecological knowledge you have, the more effective you will be at any of the land-healing strategies offered in the second half of this chapter. Ecological knowledge can be found everywhere: books are a great place to start, especially books that talk about plants in relationship to one another and that consider whole ecosystems. John Eastman's collection of books[30] is particularly useful for this for the eastern US regions— his book covers not only what plants look like, but what ecological roles and functions they play and also what key species depend on those plants. Learning from classes and teachers is another fabulous way to build your knowledge. In the US, many parks and nonprofit organizations offer free classes about aspects of nature. Online resources, particularly materials from state extension offices and other organizations, are other good ways to learn. Visit your local library and see what resources there are to get you started.

*Organizations and lists.* You can learn a lot from looking at organizations that specialize in creating lists of endangered plants, insects, and animals. For example, the United Plant Savers has a list of currently endangered plants, or near to becoming endangered, that is specific to ecosystems along the eastern US. When you study this list, you can see that the plants fall into a couple of different bioregions and a couple of different groupings. Similar organizations, such as the International Union for Conservation of Nature (IUCN.org), offer these kinds of lists at the local or global level. I have found my state's Department of Conservation of Natural Resources website to be a very useful place to learn about what animals, plants, fish, and insects are endangered where I live. This allows me to focus my efforts in particular directions.

*Ecological and natural histories.* I would also draw your attention to ecological and natural histories of the area—what exactly grew in your region, in the various biodiverse microclimates, before the present day? Are there areas that have been either protected (e.g., old-growth forests) or replanted that you can go visit and learn from? A few years ago, I found an old, hardbound report from the Pennsylvania Department of Agriculture's forestry division published in 1890. They had a list of the makeup of Pennsylvania's forests, with percentages of trees that allowed me to know exactly what trees were here once, and what trees had thrived here prior to the clear-cutting that spanned most of my state. I compared this to what I find in the forests now, and I have a good sense of what kinds of nuts and tree seeds I want to bring back (hardwoods such as Oak, Hickory, Walnut, Butternut, and Chestnut top my list—especially blight-resistant American Chestnut, which used to compose almost 30 percent of our forests).

*State extension office and stewardship programs.* In your region, especially if you live in the US, there are often lots of resources available to you for free or at low cost. If you live in the United States, you can contact your state extension office for opportunities not only to learn but to volunteer. Volunteering in a local park system, for example, can put you in direct contact with knowledgeable people and allow you to learn more about conservation and tending the land.

## OVERCOMING FEAR

I also want to speak here about fear. The "pick up the garbage and get out" mentality unfortunately creates this idea in our minds that all we can do is harm nature if we interact. When I share these strategies through writings and workshops, a lot of people are eager to do something but hold themselves back because of fear. I suggest using your mind and your heart. In terms of using your mind, as long as you research carefully, stick with native or naturalized species, and target areas that really need your help (see below), it's hard to do something wrong or cause more damage. It's also important to use your heart. Trust your intuition here, listen to the voices of the land, and know that your heart is in the right place. Recognize that your ancestors' blood flows through you—and you are drawing upon their interactions and wisdom as you do this work.

# Fostering Ecosystems

Regardless of where you live, it is helpful to understand some basic information about ecosystems, ecological roles, and the different layers of plant life that make up a typical ecosystem. We now consider these in turn.

## THE SOIL WEB OF LIFE

Before we get into higher forms of life, it's useful to know a bit about soil and the soil web of life. Soil is the building block upon which nearly all terrestrial life on Earth is based, and is a complex living system. A single teaspoon of rich soil from a forest or garden can hold up to one billion bacteria, several yards of fungal filaments, several thousand protozoa, and scores of nematodes. Healthy soil contains bacteria and engages in complex chemical conversions to move nutrients into plants, store carbon, and more. Generating only 3 inches of topsoil takes almost a thousand years using natural processes. The soil web of life also often includes mycorrhizal fungi and fungi hyphae, networks of what are essentially mushroom roots that help plants move and uptake nutrients and moisture and promote plant health. Given this powerful web of life, soil is one of the most sacred things; it is what everything else is based on.

Unfortunately, our soils are currently under severe threat. According to the UN's Food and Agricultural Organization, about one-third of the world's soil is already considerably degraded, and most of the world's topsoil could be gone in as little as sixty years.[31] Conventional industrialized agriculture uses chemicals in place of natural processes and contributes to soil pollution, agriculture runoff, overgrazing, and soil depletion. Soil and soil health are now major concerns for long-term sustainability and human food systems, and thus this is an excellent area to consider regenerative work. Later in this chapter we will discuss soil-building and soil-honoring techniques— and since soil is the foundation of life, this is good work to do.

## ECOLOGICAL ROLES

Just as each microorganism in soil has its own ecological role, so too do many plants. As you learn more about ecology, you'll start to understand that a healthy ecosystem has a variety of self-sustaining systems, with each element within the ecosystem filling one or more roles. Our goal, as land healers, should be to help cultivate these self-sustaining plant systems and reintroduce plants that were once part of these healthy ecosystems. Here are some of the common roles that plants may play.

*Nectary plants.* These are plants that provide nectar to bees, butterflies, flies, bugs, and hummingbirds. Nectary plants are often the primary food source for a host of invertebrates that provide pollination and forage for larger animals and birds up the food chain. Pollinators are critical to the production of nuts, fruits, and many other crops, as well as seed production.

*Nitrogen-fixing plants.* Some plants are able to feed the soil by bringing nutrients from the air into the plants. Legumes, lupines, and clovers, for example, are nitrogen-fixing plants; they take nitrogen from the air and store it in their leaves and roots. These are particularly critical for areas that have had depleted soil or soil removed.

*Habitat plants.* Plants may offer habitat to animals, birds, or insect life. Some of these plants are very specialized, as in the case of the monarch butterfly larva, which needs common Milkweed (*Asclepias syriaca*) to thrive.

*Animal forage plants.* Some plants are useful for animals to forage; certain animals depend on plants (or their nuts, seeds, or flowers) as primary food

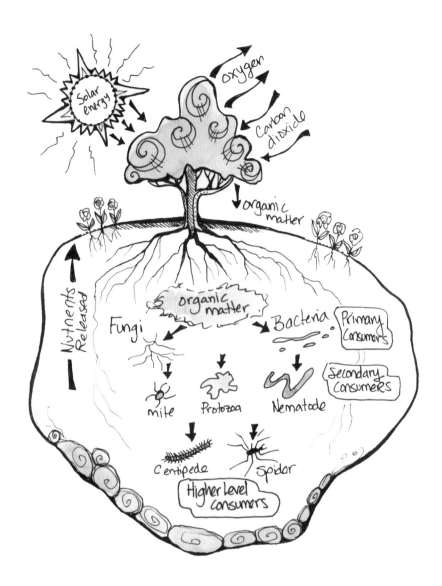

sources. Nuts, berries, plant matter, and more all can fall into this category. Some relationships are very specific (e.g., a bird species that lives primarily off one food source), while others are more general.

*Dynamic accumulator plants.* Some plants with deep roots (such as trees or Comfrey) are able to bring nutrients from deep in the soil and store them in bioavailable form. This is very useful for rebuilding soil.

*Biomass / mulch plants.* Soil building takes time, and each successive layer of plant matter on the surface of the soil helps build soil. As the dead plant matter breaks down, it holds in moisture, adds carbon, and adds nutrients to build a new layer of soil. Some plants can also be used as a "living mulch" during the season (Comfrey again is one of the popular ones for gardening, while layers of leaves function in the same way in a forest setting).

*Soil-compaction-remediation plants.* When we are looking to regenerate something such as an old farm field, a lawn, or a recently installed oil pipeline, soil compaction is a serious issue. The soil becomes so hard that it is difficult for many plants to take root and thrive. Certain plants have deep taproots and can help break up compact soils to pave the way for other plants. One set of annual plants that are very good at doing this are Daikon Radish and Purple-top Turnips. After one season, they rot away and allow new plants to grow with soil. For example, in remediating the land around an oil pipeline that was recently installed, where heavy machinery compacted the soil, the first year might include covers, radish, and turnip. Subsequent years would follow with native plant seeds.

*Medicinal, craft, and useful plants.* Of course, humans also can find many of their basic needs fulfilled by plants. We have medicinal plants and herbs, fiber plants that can be used to create clothing, dye and ink plants, and plants that can offer us methods of building shelters, fire, fine crafts, and more. While these uses aren't directly tied to healing, they are indirectly tied to healing: the more "value" something has, the more likely someone will work to protect it.

As we can see, one plant does not make up an ecosystem. Rather, it is groups of plants, functioning in multiple ways along with insects, birds, animals, mushrooms, and a host of other things, that contribute to a healthy and resilient ecosystem. Resilient ecosystems are able to better fend off disease, produce more food, and produce more habitat than those that are impoverished. I'll also note that I'm talking only about plants here—there's also fungal activity and the soil web of life, animal foraging, insects, weather, microclimates, and much more, all working together.

## POLYCULTURES AND ECOLOGICAL DIVERSITY
Another feature of a healthy ecosystem is the existence of polycultures. Polycultures refers to multiple kinds of plants, an abundant diversity of plants, growing together. Healthy ecosystems have polycultures—large groupings of plants, animals, and insects that depend on each other for survival. Those plants have different ecological roles. Thus, as we are planting, thinking about how to move from monocultures (such as the lawn or conventional agriculture) to polycultures is a useful way of thinking.

Also, it's hard to tell what a healthy piece of land looks like from the outset. For example, here, if you walk into a forest, unless it is a sanctuary or old-growth forest, chances are that it is not nearly as biologically diverse as undisturbed land. For example, I grew up on the edge of a large forest. Roughly 90 percent of it has been repeatedly logged about every twenty-five to thirty years, at least since the time of my grandfather. There is a small section in this forest that is owned by someone else, and this area has not been logged. It is the same as the rest of the forest in terms of light, climate, and rainfall, except for the logging. Abundant Ramps, along with Blue Cohosh, White and Red Trillium, Mayapples, and Trout

Lilies, are all over this small piece of land. Everything I've listed, with the exception of Trout Lilies, shows up on one of the United Plant Savers "at risk" or "to watch" lists—endangered medicinal and key species of plants, now disappearing from our lands. An invisible line is present in that forest; as soon as you step into the areas that have been logged within the last thirty years, the forest floor is no longer carpeted with these spring plants. Instead, it's mostly bare on the forest floor, or, in areas where there is no tree cover, it is full of brambles and Birches. Only knowing the history of this land, and what area has been disturbed and what hasn't been, allows me to understand the dividing line between ecological sanctuary and ecological wasteland. There are lots of spaces just like this forest— spaces that used to have important plants and biodiversity but, due to various human activities, no longer do. Only knowing what once grew there can help us bring it back. The practice of wild tending and seed scattering is putting the tools—the plants—back in nature's hands for healing work.

## ECOLOGICAL SUCCESSION

As discussed in chapter 1, nature is always engaging in ecological succession to move toward the pinnacle ecosystem, with lots of steps along the way. One of the key decisions you have to make is what kind of ecosystem you want to help establish or support.

Permaculture design typically recognizes seven kinds of plants in terms of the height of the plant (called a plant horizon), which determines how far along you are in terms of ecological succession. For example, in a mature oak-hickory forest, common in my bioregion, seven layers are present. These differing layers are best viewed on the edge of the forest ecosystem. These include the tree canopy (overstory: Tulip Poplar, White Pine, Oak), the understory trees (shade-tolerant and shorter trees such as Hawthorn, Pawpaw, and Hemlock), shrubs (Blueberry, Spicebush, Blackberry), herbaceous plants (Stoneroot, Ferns, Blue Cohosh), ground cover (Ramps, Wintergreen, Partridge Berry), vining plants (Ground nut, Wild Grape), and the root zone (which itself has different levels). Fields, edge zones, and the like may not have all seven layers. Logged forests or those that lack ecological diversity likewise might not have all seven layers. One of the things you might want to think about is how far along ecological succession is in the area you might want to work with, and what your goals are for ecological succession.

Here's why this matters: not everywhere that you work to heal may be appropriate for a pinnacle ecosystem. If you want to convert a small patch of lawn into a wildflower garden for bees and butterflies, planting giant oaks is probably not in line with your goals.

## A NOTE ON "INVASIVE PLANTS"

"Invasive plants" is a sticky subject, being intertwined deeply with power, money, and politics. My perspective as a land healer is simple: nature is good.

But there are some plants that have been introduced by humans, often on purpose, that offset ecological balance at present. These plants are not "bad" or "evil" in any way in themselves, but as displaced plants, they may find themselves able to occupy ecological niches that cause problems for other plant, animal, or insect species, particularly in a radically shifting world where humans are driving change in every ecosystem, often in drastic and destructive ways. Nonnative plants also may be opportunistic species, able to regrow in damaged ecosystems much faster than native varieties. Human activity often creates ecological opportunity for opportunistic species. While these opportunistic species may bring nature temporarily out of balance, given time (on a broader time scale than a human life), nature will find ways of balancing out that which is currently out of balance. This is literally what nature does—evolve and adapt. If new plant, animal, or insect species come into an ecosystem, nature herself will rectify that imbalance over time through evolution on the larger scale. This perspective is starting to be present in the scientific literature,[32] where ecologists realize that the radical reshaping of the earth during the age of the Anthropocene has led to the development of "novel ecosystems" (Dalby 2013) that are driven by evolutionary necessity. The truth is—humanity has radically altered all parts of our Earth. We cannot return to a pristine past, but nature will find a way forward, and some of these "opportunistic plants" are how nature is adapting.

As a land healer, and someone committed to nurturing, care, and healing, I strongly reject the mainstream ways of thinking about "invasives" and the ways of framing them as evil or bad. I see the invasive-plant problem as a problem with human practices, not a problem of the plants themselves. When you strip the land bare and create an ecological opening, in my ecosystem the "invasives," including Burdock, Dandelion, Yellow Dock, and other first-aid species, will populate what's left. That's not a problem with burdock; it's a problem of human destruction of ecosystems, which seems to be entirely absent from the conversations surrounding invasives. Nearly all the so-called invasives in my ecosystem thrive in areas of disruption. You don't see invasive plants in old-growth forests; you see them in fields where the forest was logged and on the edges where chemical spraying is happening. Invasive plants show up at areas of disruption in most cases (there are exceptions to this, of course). Thus, the problem isn't plants; it's human behavior that is upsetting ecological balance.

Most advocates of removing invasives suggest chemical controls, since they are efficient and effective at killing plants. It appears that narratives about "invasive plants" are largely driven by chemical companies who want to sell weed killer. Dumping pesticides and herbicides on the land—for any purpose—to me is the antithesis of what I do as a land healer. I don't mind pulling plants by hand that are taking over, or foraging for them and using them as medicine and food to help reduce their populations, but I will never use chemicals as a way to "heal." You might disagree with me, and that's certainly your right. But I cannot see any circumstance where dumping tons of poison into the environment is an act of healing.

## Putting It All Together:
# What Should I Do?

Now that we have some background information about soil, plants, and ecology, we can put it all together to return to the initial question: What should I do? As complex as these systems may be, they also break into a few distinct considerations we can use when selecting what actions and plants we can consider for direct land healing.

1.   Do you need to remediate the soil?

2.   What is the height of the plant and growth habits? (e.g., do you want trees or are you focusing on a field?)

3.   What are the plants' needs for soil, light, water, and temperature?

4.   What does the plant offer in terms of functions (food, nectar, etc.)?

5.   What is the plant's endangered status more broadly or its specific population locally? How can you select plants that can support rebuilding endangered ecosystems?

6.   Are certain plants going to assist other endangered or at-risk species in your ecosystem? How can you facilitate habitat for them?

7.   What is the distinct context you are planting? You should consider both long-term growth and other people's potential actions.

## Approach 1:
# Wild-Tending Practices

Wild tending is a practice where we tend the local lands around us (not necessarily lands we own) to foster ecological succession, encourage biological diversity, and create sanctuaries of life. By tending the lands around you, you do not have to be focused only on growing a specific space. Rather, all lands are in need of your help and might benefit from more-subversive healing practices. I believe that wild tending is something that all of us can do, in large and small spaces, as the need arises. And wild tending was certainly a core practice for our hunter-gatherer ancestors in all parts of the world where they lived. There are at least three core wild-tending practices: scattering and planting seeds, cleaning up, and interacting spiritually and physically with the space. Not all spaces may require you to engage in all three of these practices—you'll have to gauge your local-area needs and the needs of the space you want to tend.

The first practice is seed scattering. The most important thing to understand about physical land healing is this: *Nature already knows how to heal herself.* All we have to do is to help *set up the right conditions for healing and offer her tools to do so.* When we can directly intervene on behalf of nature, we can foster much-faster ecological succession and literally help build healthy ecosystems from the ground up. The problem we face today is simple: nature doesn't always have the resources she needs to heal, because of human actions. We have a tremendous loss of biodiversity (both plant and animal life) caused by severe damage to our lands, from clear-cutting or logging forests, to the creation of monocrop industrialized agriculture and lawns, to industrialized forests created by the logging industry, to spraying and toxins. A monocrop, or monoculture, is where, due to human intervention, a single crop such as corn or grass dominates. Compare this to a forest, which is a polyculture, which hosts millions of different kinds of life in ecological balance. On top of this, human activities and infrastructure prevent the natural spread of seeds and roots. Further, the decline in bird populations and wildlife that would spread the seeds means that fewer seeds are spread.

If you already go out into wild places, consider making yourself a wild-tending kit as part of your healer's crane bag. Have some seeds or nuts with you that are appropriate for the areas where you'll be planting (also use seed balls; see chapter 2), and carry them with you. Seeds are resilient—even if they are planted at the wrong season, they can often survive in the wild and come back up the following spring. The very first and best thing you can do is to start scattering seeds that are appropriate, popping nuts in the ground, and going from there. Or, if you see small seedling trees coming up that won't make it where they are sprouting, dig them up and take them somewhere they will thrive. This work is simple and can be built into your existing forays into this great, beautiful planet. If you aren't sure where to start, look at my lists in chapter 2 for different kinds of seed balls or just focus on one species that you have access to (or grow to gather seeds from to spread).

Another approach to seed scattering is working with small and endangered populations. This involves learning to identify rare plants, gathering their seeds, and scattering them slightly beyond their range. For example, in a recent foray into a local state park, I noticed a small patch of Blue Cohosh in seed. Blue Cohosh is a rare forest medicinal plant that is currently under threat due to its medicinal uses and is being overharvested in our region for profit (hence why to be careful with the "wild-harvested" label on many herbs). I gathered the seeds and tossed them in farther than the patch of plants, to help scatter them and expand the patch. I also took some and scattered them a little farther on my walk in areas where Blue Cohosh might grow well. This practice required that I know how to identify Blue Cohosh and its status as an at-risk plant, and also observing what the growing conditions were so I could scatter seeds in other areas where the plant would do well.

The second is picking up the garbage. It is truly incredible how much trash humanity generates. Estimates now suggest that there is more trash in the ocean than fish. Anywhere I go, I always make it a point to bring a biodegradable garbage bag with me, and when I start walking I start picking up the trash. For some spaces, particularly beaches, this might be the best kind of wild tending you can do—simply removing refuse for more life to be present. It is simple and effective and honors the land and her spirits.

Interacting physically and spiritually with the space is the third core wild-tending practice. For this, we spend time there. We let the spirits of the land know that we care and we are there to help. Sit quietly and listen to the land and her spirits. Interact. Observe. See how the space changes over time. Simply invest your time in this piece of land and let the land know that you are here to do good. The more that you interact, the more you will understand that specific space and the needs that space may have for future wild tending.

## PLACES TO WILD-TEND

*Places nobody cares about as places to wild-tend.* In *Geography of Nowhere*, James Howard Kunsler[33] talks at length about the places and spaces that "nobody cares about" in relationship to urban planning and architecture. I believe we can apply this same principle to our lands. The strip of bare earth behind a strip mall, the insipid monocrops along our highways, utility land areas, the recent construction site stripped bare of its soil, a trash-filled water drainage pipe area, a logged forest, a riverbank behind a shopping mall, abandoned fields, the logged forest quickly regrowing—you get the idea. Lots of spaces like these are present all through our landscapes. But these spaces are part of our world; they once grew abundantly and they can again. These places, places that have been exploited and stripped, are prime areas for us to begin our wild-tending work. Why? They are places that nobody cares about, that nobody is tending—and those are the places that need wild tenders the most. For example, near where I live are these spaces called "boney dumps" (known in other parts of the world as soil tips). They are from old mines where the slate and other rock that was dug up that wasn't coal was amassed into giant mountain-sized piles. This "boney" is hard for plants to establish, and because of its mostly dark colors, it gets really hot in the summer. I've been working slowly on soil building at the edges of boney dumps to try to help some of them recover more quickly, using seed-scattering techniques. Consider adopting a small piece of land, a place nobody cares about, such as a strip along a side of a highway or an abandoned lot, and work with it.

*Mountaintop removal, fracking, strip mining, and other such activities.* Logging, fracking, and other extraction activities are another potential site for wild tending, especially once these sites are abandoned. These sites often extract what is under the surface for five to ten years, and then the company "replants" the land (usually in a monocrop) and leaves. These are useful places to hone your wild-tending skills. Even a visit to them one or two times a year to plant nuts and scatter seeds could help shave off fifty or a hundred years of ecological succession. Where I live, there are lots of these kinds of places. Where you live, you may have other kinds of industry—so look around.

*Recent construction.* Often, you see new sewage lines put in or other kinds of construction activities. Construction activities are horribly ecologically disruptive, and wild-tending practices can help these areas heal.

*Abandoned lots and spaces.* In urban and suburban areas, we often find abandoned lots, abandoned houses with yards, and so on. I like to do a little wild tending in these spaces, tossing in seed balls rich with native flower seeds and blessings.

*Spaces near retail areas.* For some reason, at least here in the US, retail areas have a lot of abandoned spaces—the ditch by the side of the road that is full of garbage and was graded when a store went in, and so on. You might find such a space near your workplace or where you shop. Tossing some seeds in these places and picking up the garbage can go a long way to replanting and healing.

# Approach 2:
# Engaging in Conservation and Replanting Work

Consider joining one or more volunteer organizations that regularly do conservation work. Even if you do not have land yourself, you can partner with others to help lend your energy to this work. Planting trees along a riverbank to help establish a riparian zone, engaging in hand pulling of nonnative plants and replanting natives, doing river or trail cleanups, and building new rain gardens all are ways to help engage in physical land healing. While I do this work, I often bring growth sigils or blessing sigils with me (see chapter 2) and subtly deposit those along with my physical contribution.

Usually, volunteer conservation work is not too difficult to find. Most parks, forests, or other preserved lands have attached volunteer citizen groups—and if they don't, you can consider starting one. Conservation organizations working regionally or locally often have volunteer days where you can get involved. Conservation organizations may focus on particular areas, watersheds, parks, or more. Communities may also come together to plant rain gardens, meadows, butterfly gardens, and more in urban areas.

## THREE SOIL-REGENERATIVE STRATEGIES

Before we move on to the last two approaches, both of which are kinds of sacred gardens, I want to share a few key strategies for regenerative agriculture by focusing on soil and soil building. Soil and soil fertility are absolutely critical for successful land regeneration—consider soil a primary building block for all life to flourish. Many of the soils that you find in typical landscapes are highly degraded: mowers and other heavy machinery compact the soil, making it hard for plants to take root. Most soil is also stripped of nutrients (for a variety of reasons, including modern construction practices, which strip fertile topsoil and sell the soil before putting in new housing). Finally, most soil does not have a healthy soil web of life (with nematodes, fungal hyphae, bacteria, protozoa, and much more), and thus it is harder for plants to take up nutrients or flourish.

One of the ways to recognize good soil fertility is through observing the soil on a forest floor. The forest is not compacted (no heavy machinery, and animals travel light). The soil has an amazing web that is not disturbed by tilling, and the soil is rich in humus (dark, organic matter). At the end of each season, leaves fall from the trees and add another layer of mulch, which retains moisture and slowly adds humus. It can take up to a thousand years to build 1" of topsoil in the forest, but we can mimic this process and have healthy soil in a few years' time.

### ADDRESS SOIL COMPACTION

If you want to start growing in an area that has traditionally been mowed or well trafficked, you will need to address soil compaction. The easiest way to do this is to simply break up the soil by using a garden fork and gently lifting and continuing to break up the soil. Go down as far as you can (at least 6"–8") and just use your fork tines and weight to gently add holes and gaps in the soil. Do this in the entire area where you plan on planting. If you are physically unable to do this or are happy to take a longer approach, you can use plants that break up compact soil. Rake the topsoil, add a few inches of compost, and plant a thick layer of Turnips and Daikon Radish. Let them grow for a full season and either harvest them or let them rot down at the end of the year—and now your bed will be ready to plant.

## ADDRESS SOIL FERTILITY

Soil fertility methods vary widely but most involve bringing outside materials (organic compost, worm casings, nutrients) in to address soil deficiency. To know what challenges and strengths your soil has, you can start with a soil test. Soil test kits can be purchased for home use. Additionally, in the US, most state extension offices will have low-cost soil kits that offer much more information than a home test kit. The remedy to most issues is adding compost; however, if you have a severe deficiency in some nutrient, you might also add amendments.

If you can produce your own compost, either through composting or worm composting, this creates a great resource for any soil fertility work. See my book *Sacred Actions* for a lot more information about composting techniques!

*Sheet mulching.* To build soil fertility and mimic the forest floor, I recommend sheet mulching (also known as lasagna gardening). In my bioregion, fall is a great time to do this technique due to the abundance of fall leaves readily available (you can almost always get as many as you need if you simply drive around a suburban area and pick up the bags of leaves). Sheet mulching can use any organic matter (compost, used straw bedding from animals, weeds from your garden, manure from a local farm, fall leaves, pine needles, weeds, coffee grounds from the local coffee shop, etc.). You will want a good amount so that you can build in many layers, and your piles will originally be several feet high—but will quickly break down into 6" of beautiful soil.

Start by aerating your soil with a garden fork as described above. You do not have to "weed" your bed—just layer right on top of the grass or weeds. Saturate the aerated ground with water. If you have any weedy materials that have seeds that could sprout in the following season, place them next and wet the layer down. You can layer these up to 12". Layer newspaper or cardboard (a thick layer, making sure to overlap at least 4" any edges) on top of your grass or weed layer—this prevents any seeds or grass from coming through. Now, layer leaves, finished or unfinished compost, straw bedding, or whatever else you have. Try to keep your leaf layers less than 6" thick and intersperse these layers with finished compost, food waste, or fresh manure. Wet down each layer as you work. Finish the layers with a 4"–6" layer of compost and a final layer of leaves or straw. When you are finished, you will have a bed several feet high—let the bed break down over the winter and plant the bed in the spring.

## ADDRESS MOISTURE CONTENT

Moisture content is another critical component of your garden, and you will want to find ways of adding and retaining moisture. One of the things you can do is find ways of directing water to your garden or retaining water (or both). By directing water through rain gardens, swales, and rain barrels, you can capitalize on natural water flows rather than turning on the tap. Once you have soil to plant in, you will want to make sure you mulch your plants well. Mulching your plants mimics the forest floor and holds in moisture much more effectively— avoid bare soil at all costs. Mulch can be in the form of ground hardwood mulch (you can often get this for free if there is local tree work happening in your area), straw, or even dried-out grass clippings. Keep the mulch directly away from any roots and put in at least a 2"–3" layer. As your plants grow taller, you can add more mulch.[34] Armed with these simple soil-building techniques, you can now turn your attention to creating several kinds of land-healing gardens that work within and without.

# Approach 3:
## Creating Refugia

Refugia is a concept discussed by E. C. Pielou in *After the Ice Age: The Return of Life to Glaciated North America*.[35] In a nutshell, refugia (also called "fuges") were small pockets of life that were protected for various reasons from the worst of the effects of the last ice age. These isolated pockets survived as a sheltered spot, a microclimate, a high point on a cliff face, and so on. When the glaciers receded and left a bare landscape devoid of topsoil, seeds, or life, it was these refugia that allowed life to spread outward again, repopulating areas in North America that had been covered by glaciers. Of course, refugia are not limited to North America; they are a worldwide phenomenon, and even our human ancestors, at various points in our history, have used them to survive challenging environmental conditions.

In the Anthropocene, the loss of biodiversity and presence of essentially inhospitable landscape can pretty much sum up the 40,000,000 acres of lawns currently in cultivation in the US, or the 914,527,657 acres of conventional farmland, and the amount of concrete and houses taking up land (statistics for which I cannot find). Combine this with other resource-based extraction activities, and we can see how we have a situation where a biological life, generally, has a lot less space to grow and thrive unhindered. This is part of why we have the sixth mass extinction happening globally—because of the loss of habitat due to human demand.

Given this, I believe that the concept of refugia is extraordinarily powerful and is something that can make a serious difference. Most of us have no control over what is happening in the land and world around us, but we can work to help cultivate small spaces of intense biodiversity, spaces that preserve important

plant species, then we can put more of the building blocks back into nature's hands for the long-term healing of our lands. From a land-healing perspective, creating or preserving refugia is one of the most powerful physical practices that you can do. If you combine creating refugia with wild tending, you are able to create a seed bank that you can then use to scatter far and wide, helping replant key species that are struggling.

## CREATING REFUGIA: GOALS

We can cultivate refugia in human-dominated spaces (e.g., lawns), or we can create them in wild spaces (e.g., forests, wild fields) that we know will be safe from extraction activities or human interference for some time. In the permaculture and organic-gardening communities, people have long been creating spaces that are intensely planted, that may be perennial or annual in nature, but they might be creating them with different goals. Most often in permaculture practice, the goals are intensely focused on the site—the goal of bringing a degraded piece of land back into healthy production, with a range of yields, some of which are beneficial to humans and some of which are beneficial to other life. In other words, permaculture designers often use a kind of sanctuary model. For organic farmers, they may have many of the same goals, but different (more annual) means; both may be interested in some economic benefits as well (such as selling at a farmers' market). Working to actively create refugia can add and complement these existing goals in the sense that we are creating a protected place (physically and magically) that is richly biodiverse, with the idea that this biodiversity can be spread beyond the refugia.

I would like to suggest that each of us, as we are able, create biologically diverse refugia—small spaces, rich in diversity and life—that can help our lands "weather the storm," and a place where we can grow seeds, nuts, and roots to scatter far and wide. Or if we are already cultivating biologically diverse gardens, homesteads, sacred gardens, and the like, we add the goal of becoming refugia to our plans—and plant accordingly. This is not only physical land healing, but deeply sacred work.

## SET GOALS

In order to create refugia, it's useful to have some goals to help guide your work. Here are the goals that I set when beginning to create my own refugium at our 5-acre homestead in western Pennsylvania. Your goals might be different depending on your situation, but I thought I'd share mine as an example. The refugium garden will contain plants that

1. are native or naturalized to this region;
2. currently are rare or nonexistent in the surrounding ecosystem (but were traditionally located here);
3. are slow growing or hard to establish;
4. offer some key benefit to the ecosystem (nectary, nitrogen fixer, dynamic accumulator, wildlife food, etc.);
5. offer some key benefit to humans (medicine, dye, fiber, food, beauty, spiritual significance);
6. are able to grow without human influence or cultivation long term (perennial focus or self-seeding annuals);
7. can be spread by nut, root, rhizome, or seed (to think about how to repopulate these species outward); and
8. are well positioned in terms of how my climate will be changing in the upcoming century (e.g., adapted to a warming climate).

The refugium garden will be

1.  a teaching and demonstration site for others;

2.  a sacred place for humans to commune, reconnect, and grow; and

3.  a site of ecological diversity and healing for all life.

## REFUGIA GARDEN PLANTS

You will want to think carefully about what kind of ecosystem you are designing your refugium garden for—is it full sun? Dry? Part shade? Moist? A woodland? Use the material in the first part of this chapter (see "Physical Land Healing and Fostering Ecosystems") to design your own refugia. Remember that while you are focusing on plant life as a way to invite insect and animal life in, you might also choose to release certain kinds of insect life (such as butterflies) into your space.

I have several refugia at my homestead to propagate plants outward. The first is a full-sun garden refugium that also functions as a meditation space. The meditation garden refugium focuses on a number of wildflower nectary species that have been declining in abundance in our bioregion. These I work to cultivate and make into seed balls (see chapter 2): several species of Milkweed, several Aster species, St. John's Wort, Echinacea, and more. The second is a forest refugium. I collect nuts from our Hickories and Oaks for planting in damaged areas. I've also worked to bring the forest floor into a refugium for declining woodland species by planting and tending Ginseng, Goldenseal, Black Cohosh, Blue Cohosh, Ramps, Trillium, and more. Sometimes these plants take a long time to establish and produce seeds, but the effort is worth it. In examining the endangered plant lists for our county (produced by our state's conservation department), we have also added a rare Violet (*Violeta alleghensis*) that is severely threatened in our county and will continue to add more plants over time. This work is ongoing, but we are starting to produce seeds and extra roots that we can then work to propagate elsewhere and share these resources with others looking to do the same.

# Approach 4:
# **The Grove of Renewal**

Part of the challenge we have in the ecological reality of the twenty-first century is time. Everything is fast: fast food, fast lives, fast jobs, fast relationships. The speed doesn't just influence us: it also means that nature is being consumed/ destroyed/damaged much faster than she can heal. Part of the challenge, too, is that the earth takes time for damage to show: melting ice caps and glaciers aren't responding to today; they are responding to previous years or even decades, and we won't see the full effects of today's carbon emissions for some time. But nature's own powerful lesson resonates deeply here: with healing, time moves differently. This is true of land healing as much as it is true of our own heart healing. If we think about time as a primary force for change, we can work with time both physically and magically to engage in powerful healing practices.

A "grove of renewal" uses the approaches explored in chapter 4 (microcosm to macrocosm) to create a healed, vibrant small space where life is cared for and flourishing in the physical world, and then radiates that energy outward energetically to the surrounding land. Often when we think of ritual, we think of a single event, a single sacred moment in time. We do a ritual, it is good, and the energy radiates outward. This is also true of a lot of land-healing rituals and work in this book: we do a ritual to heal the land and move on to the next problem because there is so much need. The grove of renewal takes a different approach. It cultivates an intentional space for healing as an "extended" ritual over time, using both physical land healing as well as land blessing (chapter 4) and energetic healing (chapter 5). By focusing efforts on a small space, that healing energy can radiate outward to the broader landscape for the benefit of all (using the micro/macro magical techniques described in chapter 4's discussion of the wassail ceremony). Envision a garden, combined with a ritual space, that radiates healing and life out into the surrounding landscape.

When you begin planning and planting your "grove of renewal," you will likely focus on regenerating and healing that space—for several years, your effort may be on simply getting it established and supporting it through rituals. As time passes, more healing happens both physically and energetically. At some point, your grove of renewal is a healed and healthy space, so much so that you can now direct that healing energy outward in a much-broader way. It's important to note that this is slow magic, very slow magic. It unfolds over a period of years and thus requires patience, peace, and connection. You are building a relationship with a piece of land as a healer, observing and interacting, and doing regular work. You are on nature's time.

## STEP 1: CHOOSING YOUR "GROVE OF RENEWAL" SPACE

For your grove of renewal, you'll want to choose a small physical space to help heal. Perhaps it's a segment of lawn you want to convert to a native plant garden and butterfly sanctuary. Perhaps it's a strip of land behind an alley nobody cares about that you can plant. Perhaps it's a new piece of land you just moved to, and you can now tend. Wherever the space is, how great or small, you can make this place a center of land healing. You can certainly—and are encouraged— to also make this space a refugium (see earlier in this chapter).

On the physical level, this should be a space where physical land healing can happen. That is, it should be a space that is protected in some way and that you can keep safe for a time. It should also be a space that you have direct and regular access to. It might be on your own land, on a friend's or family's land, or just in a local space that you can visit often (such as a space that nobody else cares about; see above). On the metaphysical level, you also need the "go-ahead" from spirit— that you are working in accordance with the spirits of the land and their wisdom. Selection of the right space is critical, since you will be working this space extensively over a long period of time. Take as much time as you need for this step—remember, this is slow healing, slow time. Make offerings, visit a number of times, and allow yourself to resonate with the space. You might even choose to observe and interact for a year and a day before actually planting. When you are certain it is the right place and the right time, move on to step 2.

## STEP 2: CREATE YOUR PLAN

Because your grove of renewal will function as a shrine for physical and energetic land healing, you want to consider what kinds of things would work best with that intention and any other specific intentions you may have.

*On the physical level*: Create a plan for the plant life, soil support, and animal, insect, bird, reptile, or amphibian life that you want to invite to the space. If you are working from scratch, you might be able to carefully design it. If there is already life there, you will want to work with that life and tend that life, perhaps adding additional plants or other features. Use the strategies described in this chapter to make decisions about what and how to plant.

In order to do this work on the physical level, you will need to carefully observe and interact with the space over a period of time. Think about the wind, light, soil, water, and potential pollutants, and how you might intervene. Consider what you want the final result to be in ten or twenty years: a forest environment, a wetland, a meadow with wildflowers, and so on. Consider what plants may grow there that are rare and endangered. Consider what insect life and wildlife that may need a space to live. Look at what may already be growing there—what will you do with what is there? Will you remove what is there (with honor) and plant natives? Will you work with what is growing? Think also about the lands immediately surrounding your potential grove of renewal. Are there needs that aren't being met (e.g., no wetlands) that you could meet?

Another serious consideration for thinking about a grove of renewal long term is to think about how climate change will impact future growing seasons. In my own grove of renewal, I used *hügelkultur* techniques, where you bury logs in the ground below the beds, and as the logs break down, they hold moisture and facilitate an excellent soil web. I combined them with deep mulching, making sure we never had any exposed soil. We did so specifically because both of these approaches can help hold more water and thus help the plants through hotter and drier summers.

*On the spiritual level.* Since the grove of renewal also functions as a ritual space, you may also want to physically represent the spiritual aspect. Thus, sacred objects can be included in the plan but should be naturally based and locally sourced. You might create a stone altar or stone cairn, use statuary, decorate the space with found natural objects (shells, bones, stones, etc.), hang flags, and so forth. I recommend finding things to use that are natural and do not take any additional burden from the earth, things that you can create from the land itself.

*Putting it all together.* Once you have the pieces in place, create a plan: What do you need to do first? Second? Third? Realize also that the best-laid plans can be changed, so be ready to adapt as necessary. Let this unfold on nature's time and enjoy the healing that it brings—to the immediate space, to the surrounding landscape, and to you as a land healer.

## STEP 3: CREATE THE SPACE, FOCUSING ON INNER AND OUTER WORK

Creating the space itself should be a ritual activity, working on both the inner and outer planes. I suggest timing your beginning of the work to one of the eight festivals in the typical wheel of the year: Samhain, Winter Solstice, Imbolc, Spring Equinox, Beltane, Summer Solstice, Lughnassadh, and Fall Equinox (see more about a "Year of Rituals" in chapter 5, and the blessing ceremonies in chapter 4). When you are ready to begin, take your first step and start the work. You are working both on the physical level and the level of spirit.

*Spiritual work: A permanent sacred space.* Begin by creating a permanent sacred space where your grove of renewal will be. For this, I recommend beginning by opening your permanent sacred space by doing the Seven-Element Land-Blessing ritual offered in chapter 4, yearly on the day you have established your grove and at least once every three months for the first year. Place seven stones in your grove that represent the seven elements, and when you call in the seven directions, envision that energy channeling into the stones. Do not close the sacred space but, rather, envision the energy "settling" into place. Do this at least four times (ideally at the solstices and equinoxes). Continue to do regular spiritual work and ritual in your grove and to regularly channel energy into it as a permanent sacred space.

*Physical work.* Physical regeneration of land usually involves building soil fertility, planting trees or other plants, and doing any other cleanup that is needed. This work takes muscle, time, and regular tending. See this work not as a moment in time, but as a process that unfolds (much like growing a vegetable garden—it takes a plan, seed starting, planting out, tending/weeding, and harvesting, all before you begin the cycle again!).

## STEP 4: VISIT YOUR GROVE REGULARLY AND WATCH IT FLOURISH

After your initial work and once you have things in place (which may take you some time), it is time to let nature do its own healing. Visit your space often as it grows and heals; pay attention to the ways that the energies of that space may change. Pay attention to these changes both in an inner and outer way:

- What is growing there that you haven't seen before? Can you identify it?
- If you planted anything, how are the plants growing?
- Observe life: insects, birds, animals, etc. Do you see anything new?
- How does the space change in different seasons?
- Energetically, do you sense any shifts? If so, what are they?
- How do you feel when you are in the space?
- What messages from spirit might you be experiencing?

This step requires us to be very intuitive. You come and visit as you feel led to do so. Another thing sometimes happens: nature tells you to leave the space alone for a while. The space needs its own energy and time, and you may be asked to let time pass without physical intervention before you are asked to return, do more ritual work, and so on. Honor any requests made to you on the part of spirit.

## STEP 5: WHEN THE GROVE OF RENEWAL IS VIBRANT, RADIATE THAT HEALING ENERGY OUTWARD

At some point, your grove of renewal will have a very positive energy, a sense of peace and quietude that only healed spaces can have. Getting the grove to this point may take some seasons. You'll know when the time is right; this space will be bursting with energy and you will feel it start to flow outward. At this point, you can do a seven-element blessing ritual (see chapter 4). When you get to the end of the ritual, rather than containing the energy within the land you are blessing, envision that energy rising from the grove and radiating outward.

# Approach 5:
# **Reestablishing Guardianship**

Humans are part of nature, we come from nature, and, ultimately, we depend on nature for all of our needs. Twenty-first-century humans living in "developed" nations rarely see this relationship, however, leading to many of the challenges that we face and address as land healers. The sacred contract between humans and the land, and the symbiotic relationship between them, is damaged when the land is stripped bare or otherwise harmed. Perhaps you are feeling that you are ready to deeply commit to being a tender and guardian of a particular piece of land: a mountain, a forest, a river. You want to be on this land regularly, listen, and do what is needed. You want to learn about this land: the flora and fauna, the way the land changes in the seasons, and the challenges the land may face. You want to dedicate and commit, in the ways of your ancient ancestors, to this land. If so, making a commitment to being a land guardian may be a calling for you.

First, feel this out very carefully, making sure that this is something that the land wants and that you can commit to long term. Make sure you are stable enough, and rooted enough, for that kind of commitment—you don't plan on moving in the next five years, and you feel that you have ample time to spend on the land and with the land. Each of these relationships is unique, and so I can't offer specific rituals or activities to do, but I can share a few details about what these often entail.

Taking up a path of land guardianship often includes making some kind of oath to the land, committing to being a tender and guardian of the land. Make it clear what you are swearing to, and make sure that whatever you swear to, you intend to uphold.

As part of this work, you will also spend regular time on the land as often as possible. This can be anything: from going to the land and visiting and being open and listening, to picking up trash and paying attention to the needs of the land, to protecting the land from those who would seek to do harm. Regular work on the land should include gaining knowledge about the land: learning its history, learning the dominant species and how they interact, studying botany, learning the names and uses of the trees—enough to know if something is amiss. Spend time on the land—overnight, in quietude, moving around—in all those ways. Build sacred spaces. Bring people there to help heal and grow. Think of this land like your focal point for much of what you do!

The role of guardian of the land is not one to take on lightly, but if you feel compelled to do so, it is a wonderful way of reestablishing those connections and helping the land heal. It is really a lifetime commitment, and I mention it here only because it is so effective for land healing and to understand that it is a possible path for very deep work.

# Chapter 8:

# WORKING WITH PLANT AND ANIMAL SPIRITS WHO PASS

**When I was living** in a rented house in an urban area, my landlords decided to cut down most of the trees on our small lot. I didn't understand why, and pleaded for the trees to remain, but the owners insisted it was to be done. The day the trees were to be taken down had arrived, and I stayed home to bear witness. Killing a tree is no quick process in urban and suburban neighborhoods. It lasts many awful hours, hours with the chainsaws grinding and branches falling. The only solace for me—and the trees—was that by then I had developed extensive spiritual tools to ease the trees' suffering and help them pass to the next life.

Perhaps you are wondering why this chapter, on death, exists in a book on land healing. Returning to our definitions in chapter 1 for land healing, remember that not all healing is about repair; that is, bringing the land back to a healthy place. Some healing is about release, about letting go. As long as I've been on the path of a land healer, I have recognized that I cannot do only the work of physical and energetic renewal; sometimes, the most healing I can do is to help someone pass in peace. All those interested in nature spirituality often have these kinds of experiences—the tree or animal being killed—and because of their intensity and unfortunate frequency, they want to know what to do. This kind of work, working with the death and suffering of the land, is part of the path of a land healer. This kind of work is not easy, but in today's world, it is useful.

This chapter is divided into three parts, depending on how far you've honed your spiritual skills and the kind of work you want to do. The first level is about holding space and honoring, to return to some of our basic principles we explored in chapters 3 and 6. This is work that anyone can do, and requires no more than your time and willingness. The second level is doing this same kind of work on a much-larger scale, honoring extinct species and practicing remembrance through ritual. The third level is more deep and energetic, very advanced work, where you are playing the role of the psychopomp and helping spirits pass. Go as far as you feel led. I will also note that the material in this chapter is not for everyone. If this work doesn't appeal to you, you can certainly pass this by or return to it much later in your journey or not at all.

# Holding Space and Remembering Life That Has Passed

One of the topics that come up a lot in my conversations with other people walking a path of nature spirituality is what to do about death: a tree being cut, an animal who has been killed by a car, and so on. Most death we witness is unnecessary death—the tree coming down in the neighbor's yard because they "don't like it," or the raccoons who are poisoned because they are an inconvenience to landowners. This is particularly hard because in the modern world, in nearly all places, nature has no rights. If a human owns the land, with few exceptions, the human can do anything they like to the other life on the land. Many humans are cold when it comes to nonhuman life, not even seeing this life as life at all.

The first set of practices to address the death of living beings consists of adaptations from the "Apology" and "Witnessing" practices in chapter 3 and the "Holding Space" practices of chapter 6. One of the best things you can do for a being—of any kind—who is suffering or passing on is to hold space for them. Whether or not you have a spiritual calling for deeper work in this area, I believe that all of us can at least hold space for what is happening, see it for what it is, and energetically support those whose lives are being taken before our eyes. You might do this by treating the tree or forest no differently than a friend who is passing on. The same powerlessness exists in that situation as well. You can't do much except be there, listen, and witness. Over time, you might develop your own specific methods for this work if you encounter it often enough. They are methods that are often developed on the basis of your own abilities and gifts. I will also note that it's not so much what you do that's important, but that you do something if you feel led to it—but here some possibilities.

## MUSIC AND SPACE HOLDING

In the process of death, it is useful to hold space for those who are passing. Even if you can't get physically close, sitting at any distance and holding space is useful. One technique that works is as follows. I prefer to play music for those that are in the process of dying or are recently dead (e.g., you can play music while the tree is coming down). I have found that old folk songs are quite effective at easing suffering and allowing a more peaceful passing. The music is really effective for another reason—it can be used almost anywhere, especially when more-overt magical work cannot take place. My favorite folk song for this work is a song called "Poor Wayfaring Stranger," which is an American folk song from the Appalachian Mountains. I use an instrumental version of this song. I learned it on my flute, and I will play it in a somber tone when I see an animal dying or a tree being cut. If I don't have a flute with me, I can hum (or even silently sing the song) in my mind. It is soothing and helps them pass. You can use any song or beat that speaks to you. A simple drumbeat also works here very well—holding and slowing down the heartbeat till it is silent (similar to the Hibernation ritual strategy described in chapter 6). If you find yourself doing this work often, you can have instruments dedicated to this purpose.

As a second space-holding technique, I take the time to simply sit, witness, and watch what is happening unfold. This is important—bearing witness. Letting the being know that they are not alone as they pass. If you are holding space for an animal who is passing or a tree being cut, this can take considerable time. But it is time well spent.

## A Blessing upon Passing

You can also offer a blessing to help the spirit pass. This is a small prayer you can use in combination with a bell or singing bowl:

Friend who has passed through the veil,

Friend whose flame has dwindled to ash.

Go in peace and love, knowing I am here.

Go in peace, knowing that you are honored.

Go in peace, knowing that your passing is witnessed.

Go in peace, knowing that a new life awaits you.

With the three heartbeats, I offer blessing to you.

<Sound a bell or drum three times>
<Pause for a moment of silence>

## PASSAGE SIGIL EMPOWERMENT

You can empower your passage sigils with the "Blessing upon Passing" prayer. For this, open up a sacred grove (see chapter 4). Place your passage sigils at the center of your space. Now, say the prayer for passage three times. As you say the prayer, focus on the sigils themselves and watch the words and sounds enter the sigils. Then, ring the bell or singing bowl nine times. As it rings, imagine the sigils being filled with a gold-green light and the sigil lines themselves glowing. At the end of this ceremony, thank the spirits and close out your grove. Your passage sigils are now empowered.

## HONORING THE CYCLE OF LIFE

Another way to honor the passing of a life is to make sure that the cycle of life can be participated in to the fullest extent possible. If a tree falls or an animal dies in a natural place, such as a forest, nature will immediately begin recycling those remains and bringing forth new life from within them. As I explained with my Eastern Hemlock story in chapter 4, these trees or animals do not need help, because they are participating in the cycle of life within that natural place. If an animal or tree dies in an urban or suburban environment, rarely do they get to participate in this cycle, and the body may end up being carted away or even in the trash. Throwing a body away is incredibly disrespectful. Honoring the cycle of life will vary on the basis of what kind of life you are working with.

For all life, I like to do what I can to return at least something of that being to nature. You can do this same thing with a cut tree—get a piece of it, even a few leaves or branches, and bring it to the forest, where the cycle of life can work. For animals on the side of the road, often, carrion eaters will take care of most of them, leaving bones. I will pick up a bone and take it with me into the woods, offering a burial there where the land will reclaim the bone. If you are holding space for an animal dying, you can return the body to nature. Obviously, here you will want to practice good hygiene and safety.[36]

As I first shared in chapter 6, for trees and plants, if at all possible, see if you can gather some of the seeds/nuts and plant them. For larger trees, sometimes, baby trees come up under the mother tree—save at least one if you can, and plant it in a safe place. This is the best way for life to continue on and honor the legacy of that life.

If I am able to return a piece of the one who died to the wild, I will often build a nature mandala (see chapter 5) made of leaves, sticks, stones, nut caps, and so forth, and place the being there within the center. After building the mandala, you can say a prayer for returning a small bit of one who has died to a natural place:

> Cradle of earth, please accept the remains of one who has fallen.
>
> Soil web of life, please cycle this one back into your womb.
>
> Spirit that has passed, may you find peace beyond the veil.

## THE SIGIL OF PASSAGE

If you decided to make a land-healing sigil set, then the sigil of passage is a useful tool that you can use in combination with any of the work listed here. For example, you can trace the sigil in healing oil, in charcoal or chalk, or in sand or soil where it is needed. You can leave a sigil tucked in a branch or into the soil, or near an animal that has fallen. The sigil carries energy with it that can be used for passage.

## HEALING WORK FOR THOSE THAT REMAIN

Finally, as necessary, you can do positive energy work for the others who have passed in the coming weeks and months—many are still there; they may have witnessed the loss, and they need support. This is especially true of flock animals who lose members of their flock, mated pairs who have had a mate die, or small groups of trees that form a community. Most of the techniques that are described in chapter 4 or 5 are appropriate for this kind of work, especially the Seven-Element Land Blessing.

# Honoring Those Who Have Gone Extinct

Animals die, plants die, insects die. Their spirits live on. In the Anthropocene, even mountains die; they are removed for mining activities all along the Appalachians and in many other places. Rivers die and have been dying for centuries as we fill them with refuse or divert so much water away from them that they dry up. In the Anthropocene, many things die. What happens to that mountain's spirit when the mountain is gone? What is happening now to the millions of nonhuman lives that are dying because of human activity?

As I described in chapter 1, scientists have described the "Anthropocene extinction" due to the widespread habitat loss and environmental degradation due to human activity. Some numbers we know: at the time I wrote this book, almost 50 percent of all animal life has died in the last fifty years, and 75 percent of all life is currently threatened with extinction. Unfortunately, humanity's actions continue to cause the death of so many species and so many individual lives, and given models and projections, the die-off of nonhuman life is expected to get much worse in the next decades. The mass amounts of death and extinction of nonhuman lives are not "natural"; they are directly the result of human activity. This makes humans, collectively and individually, responsible. Not only are we responsible for the actions that cause such death, but also, as land healers and spirit workers, we might consider what happens to those spirits when they die and how we can help.

The two rituals here offer humans a way to "do something" about the tragic losses that are happening on a broader scale. I see these rituals as having two purposes. The first is obviously to help the spirits who are dying, because of human activity, pass on in love and acknowledgment. But the second is to acknowledge our collective responsibility, which I believe may lessen our own karmic debt for these tragedies and help us build a better future where we are not collectively responsible for such death.

# A Ritual for Honoring Species That Have Gone Extinct

This isn't an energetic ritual like many others in this book. This ritual was written for anyone, regardless of their background. (It is not required for this ritual that you practice nature spirituality, magic, or neopaganism or have familiarity with these traditions to perform this ritual.) It's something you could do with friends or family or a spiritual group to recognize and honor extinct species. This ritual was designed for a leader and any number of participants. However, if you are performing this ritual solo, you can simply do both parts.

**All:** Participants gather in a circle, preferably in a natural place or indoors in candlelight.

**Leader:** "We pause in this moment to honor those species who have gone extinct and our unfortunate role in that extinction." [Pause] "Participants, do you wish to acknowledge any species?"

**Participants:** Take turns sharing about one or more extinct species. (Alternatively, the leader can hand out slips of paper that have information about human-caused extinct species for each participant. A list of species is included after this ritual.)

**Leader:** "Does anyone here wish to share their feelings at this moment?"

**Participants:** Allow participants the chance to share as they choose.

**Leader:** "Let us now honor these species and all endangered species with a moment of silence."

[**Optional:** Leader sounds a singing bowl, chime, or bell at the start of the moment of silence.]

**Leader:** "Please say with me, 'Species who have crossed the veil, we honor you.'"

**Participants:** Repeats.

**Leader:** "Species who have suffered, we honor you."

**Participants:** Repeats.

**Leader:** "Species who are forever gone, we honor you. We acknowledge the role of the human in your deaths. And we, on behalf of humanity, are sorry."

[Pause]

**Leader:** "What is one thing you can do, starting today, to help prevent the loss of more species?"

**Participants:** Take turns offering their suggestions for life changes.

**Leader:** "Thank you to all of you who have participated. It is through our own actions and raising the awareness of others that we can help save the species that still live in this world."

[Sound a bell, singing bowl, or chime to end the ritual.]

## EXTINCT SPECIES—LIST FOR PARTICIPANTS
The following list can be shared for use in the ritual.

- **The unknown species.** Many extinctions are in places that are undocumented or unknown. This accounts for insects, invertebrates, and many amphibians and reptiles.

- **The West African Black Rhino.** This beautiful rhino went extinct in 2006, after being poached by hunters for its horn, which was in demand in Yemen and China for its aphrodisiac powers.

- **The Passenger Pigeon.** The Passenger Pigeons were in the millions when Europeans began pillaging and colonizing the Americas. The Pigeon was hunted and consumed to the point of extinction in 1914.

- **The Pyrenean Ibex.** The Pyrenean Ibex, a deer-like creature with beautiful curved horns, was hunted to extinction by year 2000.

- **The Golden Toad.** The Golden Toad, a bright-orange toad living in the Costa Rican rainforest, was destroyed by global warming, pollution, and disease. The last toad was seen in 1989, and it was declared extinct in 1994.

- **The Zanzibar Leopard.** This leopard lived in Tanzania. This animal was hunted and exterminated, both by individuals and the Tanzanian government due to the widespread belief that the Zanzibar Leopard was kept by witches as pets.

- **Po'ouli.** This bird was a native of Maui, Hawaii, living on the southwestern slope of the Haleakala Volcano. The species went extinct in 2004 due to habitat loss and a decline in its food source, native tree snails.

- **Maderian Large White Butterfly.** This butterfly, with yellow-and-black markings, went extinct in the first decade of the twenty-first century due to loss of habitat caused by human construction and pollution from agricultural fertilizers (used for growing olives, figs, pineapples, bananas, and sunflowers).

- **Carolina Parakeet.** Native to the eastern United States, with unusual orange, yellow, and blue markings, the Carolina Parakeet went extinct in 1918. Deforestation and poaching were the main causes; millions of these birds were killed so that their feathers could adorn ladies' hats.

- **Tecopa Pupfish.** Once native to the hot springs of the Mojave Desert, this fish was destroyed by the destruction of their natural habitat by human construction.

- **Pinta Island Tortoise.** This Tortoise was native to the Galápagos Islands and went extinct in 2015. Humans introduced goats who destroyed their native habitats, humans introduced rats who preyed on their young, and humans killed tortoises for their meat.

# A Fire Ritual to Honor Extinct Species

This ritual can be done individually or in a group setting. Before the ritual, gather up materials to build an effigy (very similar to the prayer bundles described in chapter 5). Your effigy will represent one or more extinct species in the world. You can also tuck prayers written on paper and rolled up into your effigy. Construct your effigy only out of natural materials, things that can burn without harming the earth. Before the ritual, build yourself a fire that you can light.

**Open up a sacred space.**

**Build your effigy.** After opening the space, take the time to carefully build your effigy and tuck your prayers inside. As you build, feel the energy of the extinct species enter the effigy. Hold the effigy into the air and speak the name of the species and any other words you feel led to say.

**Burn your effigy.** Place your effigy on the top of your fire. Light the fire. Watch it burn. Drum while it burns. Do anything else that you feel led to do.

**Attend to the energy.** Feel the energy of the species growing calm as it burns. Feel the energy of the sorrow and death being released. As the fire dies down, sit with that fire as long as necessary, till it is nothing but coals and ash. Bid the species farewell and blessings.

**Close the space.**

After this ritual, ground and center yourself and practice good self-care. This is a powerful ritual and can bring the energies of death to you and through you—thus, you should engage in life-focused activities for a few days after this ritual (e.g., gardening, sitting with plants, bringing in light, and healing and blessing). Use the self-care practices in chapter 9 as a guide.

# Helping Spirits Pass and Psychopomp Work

Death is part of life. Death is another journey, and some of us are called or choose to help spirits along that journey in a very active way, by helping them pass beyond the veil. This work has many names, one of the most common being called "psychopomp" work. Psychopomp derives from the from Greek words *pompos*, which means "guide or "connector," and *psyche*, which can be translated as "mind, soul, life, or breath." Other names I have heard for this work include death midwifery, soul midwifery, death walking, and death shamanism, to name a few. Regardless of the term, this work has been a regular part of the healing, magical, and spiritual arts in nearly all cultures across time. Many cultures recognize that humans with certain sets of skills do this work (such as a shaman or another religious leader) along with nonhumans (deities, animal spirits, angels, and other such beings).

This sacred practice of helping spirits pass is largely forgotten in mainstream consumerist life. However, it is still quietly practiced in many Earth-centered, pagan, and New Age spiritual traditions. Most every person whom I have met who does psychopomp work does it for human souls. Human souls may often (but not always) need help crossing over. Humans are complicated, and when we die, our deaths may be complicated too. Humans may get stuck between the worlds, they may die unexpectedly and need to process their death, they may have unfinished business that prevents them from leaving, or they may need assistance to find their path. Psychopomps are the shining beacons in that confusion, helping a wayward soul find his or her path to the next part of their journey. This isn't about human souls. You can learn about that kind of psychopomp work from many other sources. This is about nonhuman souls and the work we can do, given this time, this age, and the current conditions.

The cycle of life and death of animals, plants, insects, amphibians, reptiles, birds, fish, and so on has been going on for as long as life in some form has existed on this planet. Spirits of the land know how to handle their own deaths, and human psychopomps would not typically interact in that way in regular circumstances. Returning to the idea of a death in a forest: if an animal or plant dies, within a span of time (a few days to several decades), those nutrients are completely cycled back into the ecosystem with the help of fungi, worms, bugs, and more. Nothing is wasted, and life continues on. I have always gotten the sense that this same process takes place on the level of spirit as well—the cycles of nature take care of the cycles of life and death.

However, we live in a time when the whole world is threatened. In the last few decades in particular, and with increasing frequency, a much-larger number of nonhuman souls began departing, with some of them being the very last of their kind due to extinction. Some nonhuman souls who pass are exhibiting many of the same characteristics that human souls who pass often exhibit:

anger, confusion, being lost, being stuck, not wanting to go. If a typical cycle of life and death is a gentle forest stream, right now the stream is massively flooded well beyond its banks, causing erosion and destruction. This spillage needs some attention, particularly from humans, who are at the root cause of it. I think another way of framing what is happening is that spirits of these various species are experiencing mass die-off due to human causes, a phenomenon that their own natural cycles of life and death are not adapted to. Anything can adapt over a long enough period of time; that is the nature of evolution. But it is hard to adapt—for any species or spirit—to such frequent and intense change, the kinds of changes driven by relentless human activity in the Anthropocene. And that is where the trouble seems to lie.

The work I describe that follows is extremely advanced. It requires you to have excellent energetic protection, practiced ways of spiritually cleansing yourself, a solid mental state (do not try this if you are mentally unbalanced, depressed, etc.), and excellent self-care strategies (see chapter 9). It also requires you to have developed your spirit communication and spirit journeying skills. Finally, it requires inner contacts (guides, deities, spirits, plant spirits, animal spirits, etc.) who will partner with you for this work; it is very necessary to have individuals on both sides. Some people find themselves drawn to this work intuitively, and for others, they may seek out training, books, teachers, and other such resources. I think that, like anything else, it is a skill you can learn to do, and do well, if you dedicate yourself to it. I also want to stress that this work is not for everyone: there are many other kinds of work we can do in the Anthropocene. I think each of us should do something, but that something should be tied to our gifts and our own journey—this work is clearly not for everyone.

## Stories of Death and Passing

To understand nature psychopomp work and how we can help animals, plants, insects, and others pass, I'm going to share a few examples to help illustrate some of what I understand to be the basic principles.

I remember the year the Christmas trees came. After leaving a sleep sigil in a store where a few cut trees remained (which I first described in chapter 2), their spirits came. Thousands of them, just after the holiday rush was over. They waited for me, patiently, planting themselves in spirit all over my property. I went out and walked among them. They wanted to understand why they had been cut and left to die. These trees, I realized, had never found themselves adorned with gifts in the center of the family home and hearth. Or if they had, once their use was over, they were unceremoniously thrown on the curb without so much as a thanks. Their whole lives—and deaths—were wrapped up in a cycle they did not understand, and they had to understand that cycle in order to pass. I thought it was a fair question. And so I showed them; I talked to them about humans and human life today. I invited representatives from among them to join me for a few days in the world, to see how humans think and what they do, and I shared a human perspective. The representatives asked questions, and eventually they were satisfied. They understood, after seeing me interact with humans and with my translation and explanations, that humans didn't realize that trees had spirits. That humans didn't realize that trees were anything other than objects to be used and discarded. I apologized on behalf of all humans who did not understand. When I felt the time was right, about two weeks after they arrived, I opened up a sacred grove outside. I built a fire and, with the aid of my own spirit guides, helped open a gateway for them to pass. They went through it, one at a time. It took hours to hold the space for them, but when I was finished, I closed the gateway and closed the grove. At the closing, I received a clear message that this work was done, and now, others could pass without my assistance. Afterward, I also did extensive cleansing and self-care, since the energies of the dead are not to be worked with lightly.

In a second experience, I've always been connected deeply with trees and have long done this kind of work for forests who were logged. One forest, however, in particular stands out. It was a section of forest that I had spent time in with my parents as a child on occasion. Some year ago, the township decided that their industrial park was going right in the middle of that beautiful forest. They cleared giant swaths of it and put in power lines, and there it sat. Empty. I drove through it soon after it happened, and I felt such incredible sorrow, loss, anger, and frustration emanating from the stumps of those trees. The spirits of the trees, of that land, of the animals who died, of insects whose lives were over, crowded up around me and demanded to understand why this had been done. Again, I asked them to choose a representative, which ended up being a spirit of a Red Maple. First, I sat in the forest, observing, singing to them, simply honoring them and letting them know that I was there, that they were not alone (work of witnessing and apology; see chapter 3). I walked along that recently cut land, and I found a piece of wood that had been cut, part of a stump. I took it with me, along with some other materials, and made them into a piece of art honoring that forest. The artwork and use of the wood in a spiritual way seemed to appease the spirits. But they still had questions. Their representative went with me, learned what he needed to learn, and then we returned together to that place. I did a ceremony for them (similar to the one I described in the last paragraph) and helped them move on. After that, when I passed other logged sites near there, I got the sense that the spirits were once again taking care of their own work in those kinds of cases. I was welcome to help, but it wasn't necessary for me to do the deep work I did with this forest.

In a third story, on one otherwise ordinary day when I was working from home, I suddenly sensed a very angry presence. Opening up my spiritual eyes, I saw an entire pride of lions. As their eyes bored into me, I felt almost like prey. I could feel their anger, their rage, at their deaths. They demanded answers. I set my work aside and told them I would speak with them, but only if they backed off and calmed down. They left, but a few hours later they were back. I asked them about who they were, where they had come from. They had been poached; they were the last of their tribe in any land as far as they were aware. I listened, acknowledged their hurt, and apologized for their suffering and deaths. As is the way of things, I invited a representative to come with me for a few days, to better understand the way that humans lived. To see. To understand. I did a ceremony similar to those I had done before: opening up a sacred grove, making an offering, inviting any final conversation, working with my guides to open up a gateway, inviting the spirits to pass through the gateway, and then carefully closing the gateway and space. Again, afterward, I did spiritual self-care, cleansing. After a number of these experiences, I realized I needed a permanent space on my land where I could properly honor these spirits. So I did that, creating a shrine that I used to "honor the fallen," and, as any other spirits interacted with me in this way, I would put a representation of them on the shrine.

A final story, that was first shared earlier in this book, is when I visited my favorite place in the world, an old-growth Eastern Hemlock grove in the Laurel Highlands region of western Pennsylvania. I hadn't been there for some months and was absolutely shocked to walk in and see that ten or fifteen of the giant old ones had fallen, leaving giant craters where their roots had been and opening up light in the forest. I immediately sat with the ancient fallen trees and asked the spirits of the forest what I could do and if they needed help. They shared the lesson that is the undercurrent of much of this book and chapter—they were fine. They had died naturally, during a severe storm. They will continue to return to nature as part of that natural process. There was nothing I needed to do, but they thanked me for asking.

## Psychopomping the Anthropocene

These examples are fairly consistent with my larger practices surrounding what I now understand to be some of the psychopomp work of the Anthropocene, at least from my own perspective and experience. So what is the nature of this work? When do you need to do it? How do you do it? We'll now explore it from two perspectives: first, what I call "prerequisites" (i.e., the things you need to bring to the table to do the work), and second, core practices (the things you do surrounding the work itself).

### PREREQUISITES
The first prerequisite is being open to working in this way. You have to be willing to see, be willing to acknowledge, and be willing to spend the necessary

time and energy to do this work—which can be considerable and sometimes quite inconvenient. If you aren't open to it, spirits are not going to come to you, or you aren't going to do them justice.

Second, as I mentioned above, it requires some advanced skills: spirit communication, spirit sight, and solid practices surrounding protection and self-care. It might be that you aren't ready to do this until you've been walking the path for a number of years. I don't recommend that any new person take this on.

Third, you must have guides, spirits, or deities working with you. You need to have those you can trust in the spirit world for this kind of work, both for your own safety but also because this work seems to require it as a balance. You are helping a spirit move from corporeal life to noncorporeal life, and that requires both someone who is corporeal and someone who is noncorporeal to do it properly. You also need a deity or spirit who can balance the energies of life and death—a goddess such as Isis, Frau Hollie, or Elen of the Ways can assist with this, as can certain powerful land spirits who go through a period of seasonal cycles (such as ancient Oak trees). Essentially, if you are going to help envision and open a gateway for a spirit to pass, it has to be opened both from the side of the physical and the metaphysical.

Fourth, you have to find balance and practice good self-care and spiritual cleansing. This is true for everything we do as land healers, and certainly everything in this chapter. It is *especially true* for this kind of deep work. The energies of the dead are not good for the living long term (and if you've ever tended a dying person long term, you'll understand what I mean here). I don't do this work every day or even every week; I do it as necessary, and as individuals or groups of spirits come. You can also refuse this work if you aren't in the right state of mind or aren't feeling able to do it. Don't let the dead stay near you for long periods of time. They must pass, and you must find your way into self-care and balance and embrace the energies of life after they do. Keeping the energies of the dead with you for too long a time can lead to a depletion of your own vital life energy or put you into a serious illness.

Fifth, this work is never about you. You will always have the gratitude of the spirits who pass; however, understand that this is quiet work. It is work that you do on your own, that you don't typically talk about, and that other humans—even those in nature-based spiritual traditions—will not know about. That's okay; the work isn't for humans. If you are someone who needs regular validation from human others, this is probably not work for you.

Finally, a lot of people whom I've spoken with who have gotten into this work one way or another had had some close experience with death, some way that helps them better understand it. These experiences may have involved having a very special person (human or otherwise) die, tending to a dying relative, having a brush with death themselves, or witnessing some other death (such as the logging of a forest they cared about). I think that experience opens up something within you that then can be used to help others.

## CORE PRACTICES OF PSYCHOPOMPING

Given the above, we now turn to some of the core aspects of psychopomping in the Anthropocene.

**To start, you must be open.** If you are doing this work regularly, somehow the spirits sense it and somehow they know. It's like you have an "open for business" sign up on the astral plane. Even if it's just a self-acknowledgment that you are willing to do this work, they will come once you are open to it.

**Be ready to do the work of apology and acknowledgment frequently.** Humans all over this planet are doing awful things and are causing the genocide of many, many lives and species. Why would these spirits of the recently departed trust a human? Because you are acknowledging what is happening, you are compassionate, you can offer them perspective, and, most of all, you can offer them a true and heartfelt apology on behalf of your own species. Acknowledgment and an apology are all that many spirits need to move on.

**Be ready to explain things from a human perspective.** This seems to be very helpful for many spirits and species who are dying in the age of the Anthropocene. They want to know why things are happening, and their minds cannot understand human behavior without your help. My basic strategy is to let them tag along with me for a few days as I'm out and about in the world, explaining to them what they see, answering their questions. This usually helps them understand the complete lack of understanding and regard for other life that most humans have. After no more than three days, I help them ritually move on.

**Be prepared to ritually help spirits move on, if needed.** I always offer, and not all of them accept or need me to help. My basic technique is to open up a sacred space and find a natural gateway such as a fork within two trees. Working with a deity or spirit being on the other side, we open up a gateway, and the spirits can move through it. I say some prayers, drum, and play flute songs while they pass. If I am helping a larger group of spirits (a whole forest) or a species that has gone extinct, I usually light a ritual fire and sit by the fire, since this can sometimes take hours, and the fire can help you stay energized to hold the space and hold the gate. Then we close the gateway. I close the space and then practice self-care to ground and bring the energies of life back in. I don't offer a specific ritual for this, because the ritual changes a bit each time it is done. I would suggest learning specifics for the work for you directly from a spirit, a guide, or a deity that you work with.

**Be prepared to experience spirits who are violent, angry, or upset.** You would be violently angry too if humans killed your family or the last of your kind. It is okay to be firm with these spirits, so say that they must calm themselves before you will work with them, and set firm boundaries.

**Finally, be aware that you may require extreme self-care.** This work can be rewarding but also very draining. You have to take care of yourself and need to make sure to spiritually cleanse carefully after working with the dead. I like to do an herbal vinegar bath drawn from the hoodoo tradition. In preparation, I infuse an apple cider vinegar with herbs, specifically Sage, Mugwort, Rosemary, Bay, Lemon Balm, or Hawthorn (or a combination of these; you can use any herbs you like, but consider herbs that clear and protect). After a few weeks, you can strain your herbal vinegar and put it near your bathtub. I take a few tablespoons of infused herbal vinegar and add it to my bath and scrub myself all over. After I scrub myself, I let the water drain out, and I envision any energy that is not mine or that is unwanted draining away. I let myself drip dry (don't wipe the magic off you!) before putting clothes back on. In addition to the bath, make sure you take time to do what fulfills you most, and let nature heal you! Garden, hike, and spend time with your animals and those filled with vitality and life.

# *Chapter 9:*

# SELF-CARE AND LAND HEALING

**Some parts of land-healing work are regenerative** for both the body and spirit: being able to do the work of physical regeneration, energetic land healing, and land blessing can be work that refreshes and nourishes you. But other kinds of work in this book, particularly palliative care and helping spirits pass, is really difficult work that will require you to invest in self-care practices. When we are engaged in land-healing work, we are often choosing to attend to these kinds of issues more frequently than others, choosing to see rather than ignore, choosing action over inaction. This choice may place us in a position of suffering potentially more psychological duress than those who choose to look away and not engage. When we can keep ourselves in a healed, balanced, and stable place, we are better able to help heal others in the world and continue to do this critically important spiritual work. Not attending to our own self-care as central to our spiritual practice as land healers can lead to burnout.

Attending to self-care is particularly important because psychologists have recently identified the grief and despair that can happen with regard to climate change, called "climate grief." In a 2017 report,[37] the American Psychological Association (APA) noted that climate grief was increasingly affecting the mental health of individuals and communities. Specifically, they note the difference between acute consequences (after a disaster or event) and chronic consequences (large-scale climate change and ecological issues that simply do not go away). The effects both of acute and chronic impacts include everything from posttraumatic stress disorder, compounded stress, anxiety, and depression, to the loss of autonomy and control, the loss of personally important places, and feelings of helplessness, fear, and fatalism. In other words, psychologists recognize that climate change and related events in the twenty-first century can have a profound psychological impact on the well-being of individuals.

Because of these things, when you are doing land healing, you are often exposing yourself to more of what is happening with regards to climate change and extinction than the average person and thus, have a greater need for attending to your self care and grief. Thus, we now consider self-care from a

multitude of spiritual perspectives that offer support specific to land-healing work. In this chapter, I offer many different options for self-care practices and also some background in understanding how to better care for yourself.

## Care for Self:
# The Inner Light and Healing the Land

Each of us has light within us, the light of our souls.[38] This light can be conceived of in many different frameworks. For example, in the druid tradition, this is the light of Nywfre, the vital life force, that which sparks life and supports the energy of life. Joseph Campbell's *Hero with a Thousand Faces* offers another framework where the light must be sought; the hero goes off on their journey, finding their own light, and brings it back to the wider world. This light that radiates so powerfully from us is the light of the spirit and the soul. It is the light through which we can see in the darkness, and in the dark times, and through which we can offer healing to the lands around us.

A modern metaphor for this light is by envisioning an actual lightbulb (a classic roundish lightbulb with filaments). That light, radiating outward from our bulbs, is responsible for so much of what is good and right in the world: our creative gifts, our care and compassion, the blessings we bring, the healing we are able to enact, our passions and our joy, the good we do in the world.

However, as we go through our daily lives, a lot of "stuff" gets sloshed on us. For land-healing work, it might be seeing our beloved forest logged or burning in wildfires, reading climate change reports, being unhappy about the negative action or apathy of other humans in the world, and so on. The daily crud—what we pick up going through our lives—keeps getting splattered on our lightbulb, like splashes of mud or black paint, slowly dimming our light. Emotions and experiences of fear, guilt, depression, anxiety, exhaustion, and sadness add even more grime to our bulbs—until for some of us, it is literally like we dipped our bulb in a bucket of mud, and all light is obscured. Without that light, we cannot offer healing to the world. Without that light, we cannot offer our gifts to anyone.

One of the key principles of self-care is to figure out ways to wipe our lightbulbs clean, so that we can once again manifest our light into the world—that healing energy that we want to bring to the earth. This lightbulb metaphor functions on many levels—the level of the spirit, the level of the mind, the level of the emotions, and the level of the body.

# Developing a Spiritual Self-Care Plan

Part of the challenge we face with regard to self-care is that in many fast-paced cultures, stress is looked upon as a badge of honor rather a cause for concern. Self-care isn't seen as something that is necessary or fruitful. When we combine this with the deep work necessary to engage in land healing, if we aren't careful we can easily burn ourselves out. Spiritual practices can help us cultivate a strong self-care practice and hence be more effective as land healers (as well as just "getting through life"). Let's begin this work by considering two different kinds of spiritual activities that help us understand where we are with regard to self-care and stress responses.

## A SELF-CARE MEDITATION AND ASSESSMENT

In order to begin or deepen a self-care journey, you might want to start by giving yourself a self-care assessment on the mind, body, and spirit level. In a quiet place or in meditation, check in with your body, mind, and spirit. You might use questions such as these:

- What is my emotional state right now? Why am I feeling this way?
- Is my inner lightbulb clear and radiant or is it covered in muck? What is causing it to be that way?
- How often do I feel this way?
- What emotions come up for me over and over again? Are they helpful or detrimental?
- How does my body feel at this moment? Does anything hurt? How often does it hurt?
- Do I feel like my body is healthy?
- Do I feel whole and complete as a person? If not, why not?
- Do I feel like there is "something missing"?
- Am I living my truth?

- Do I feel sharp of mind?
- How do I feel after engaging in land healing? Does it depend on what kind of healing I do?

After reflecting on these questions, you can develop a spiritual self-care plan that can help you keep your light shining forth and the healing happening. The next sections offer you many different suggestions for spiritual self-care work.

## SELF–CARE VISION BOARD

When I started my journey deeply into self-care, I created a vision board to help me understand what it is I was hoping to achieve. This vision board was done in a group setting, with women all creating vision boards for various kinds of healing. We created our vision boards right around the new year and supported each other throughout that year in our visions and goals. The basic practice is simple and is an excellent way to help you move into a plan. Before doing your vision board, you may want to read through the rest of the suggestions presented in this chapter so that you have a sense of possibilities to include in your vision board. You can use the basic strategies given for "A Vision of a Healed and Abundant World" vision-boarding exercise in chapter 5 as a start.

First, begin by opening up a sacred space. Calm your mind and engage in some deep breathing. Then, begin with a short meditation where you go into a garden—the garden of your life. You meet with a guide, hear that guide's messages, and consider what seeds you want to plant in your life and how to prepare the soil. After doing this meditation, you are ready to create the vision board. Come out of our meditation but keep the quietude and peace with you as you do your work. Play soft music with no words for this process.

Spread out the magazines and begin to cut out and tear out images and words that speak to you. Don't try to force anything—just go with what resonates. At this point, don't worry about how the board is going to look. This part of the process can last up to thirty to forty-five minutes.

The third part of the process is the work of putting the board itself together. You begin arranging the board, seeing how things fit together, seeing what messages emerge. Spend time laying out and arranging your images and words, and seeing how they interact with each other. When you have something you like, glue down your images and words. Place your board in a prominent spot in your home, somewhere where you will see it often and allow its magic to work on you on multiple levels.

When your board is done, I would suggest spending some time in meditation with your board. In the process of writing this book, I did three such vision boards. They spoke to me powerfully and meaningfully about not only this book but also my own self-care journey. And later, so many of the things in these boards manifested into reality during the years in which I did them.

## YOUR SELF-CARE PLAN: YOUR BRIGHT LIGHT

Now that you've developed some idea of where you are at present, and potential visioning for your self-care, take time to develop a plan. What will help you brighten your lightbulb, to wipe it clean and allow you and your gifts to radiate into the world? Consider both your overall goals (what you want to achieve) and milestones for how you will get there (smaller steps that help you support your larger goals). Create a plan for yourself—what are you going to do each day, each week, to start or continue your self-care journey? What are the challenges you face in terms of cultivating self-care? (consider making time, navigating family or work demands, honoring yourself, and so on). What will you do to overcome these challenges? Here are a few additional suggestions that may assist you with your self-care plan:

- If you live by your calendar, then I suggest scheduling personal time like any other time; it's like making an appointment with yourself that you can't break. Working with loved ones to ensure that you have quiet time for self-care is also critically important.

- I suggest making the plan colorful or fun, somewhere you can see it and engage with it regularly. Make it something you want to look at, engage with, and see every day. I have found that small self-care reminders and positive messages, placed around my house and office, can really aid me and are a mental reminder to regularly practice these techniques. All over my house, I created little colorful signs that say such things as "You are loved," "Remember to breathe," and "Take care of yourself today!" These little reminders can ask me to slow down for a minute and find my grounding and centering in this busy world.

Be flexible with your plan and try different things until you find the thing that works best for you.

## Care for Our Bodies:
# Managing and Understanding Stress

Managing our stress and stress responses is critical to developing any system of self-care, especially for those attempting to walk the tightrope between spiritual practice and Earth-honoring living, while still living within the broader economic and social systems that are causing massive degradation to the planet. Stress is seen as the body's and mind's response to alarm reactions and perceived threats. In *An Herbal Guide to Stress Relief*, herbalist David Hoffman argues that stress is "experiencing ourselves un-whole," and he argues that stress unbalances are caused, in a large part, by separation from the living earth. He suggests that to truly be destressed, we must work to change our physical and psychological stress patterns, those that are the source of stress and disease (and "dis-ease"). I find his view compelling in its simple truth, also because it implies that some stress can be mitigated by nature-based spiritual practices.

Understanding the body's autonomic nervous system, what stress responses it has, and how it operates is key for engaging in self-care—since so much of our disease, exhaustion, and illness comes from our body's automatic reactions to everyday stressors. Although stress responses are a manifestation of our body's autonomic central nervous system, literally all of the body's systems are interconnected and all are affected by stress. Over time, stress builds up, in the very cells of our bodies, and is also carried in our hearts, minds, and spirits.

To understand how stress can accumulate in our bodies, herbalist Jim McDonald offers this metaphor for stress: the water jar.[39] Imagine that your body and mind is a mason jar half full of water. That water is your stress level. Each major stressor in your life is like a big rock in that jar, raising the level of the water. Lots of other more minor stressors keep going into the jar, raising the water level higher and higher. Soon, your water level is at the very top edge of the jar, and even a tiny pebble or stone (a minor stressor) can spill the water out of the jar. Spilled water might manifest as a nervous breakdown, exhaustion, emotional explosion, numbness, withdrawal, or another emotional or physical event. Many of us have experienced a situation where a very minor issue seems to cause a major reaction in a very stressed person. This is a sign that that person is well beyond their stress limits, and their water jar is full.

Physiologically, our autonomic nervous system has two working modes: the parasympathetic ("rest and digest") and the sympathetic ("fight or flight"). The parasympathetic nervous system slows down many of the body's functions (such as heart rate, blood pressure, and breathing) and increases our sexual functions and digestion. This state is not only where we are able to rest and relax, but also where much of our deep healing happens; the body works to absorb more nutrients, build its reserves, and heal physical damage. Spiritual practices, time in nature, and many of the other practices covered later in this chapter help us find and stay in a parasympathetic nervous system state.

Earlier in our evolution and cultural history, the sympathetic nervous system was used to get us out of immediate danger—we literally fought or fled. This automatic response to stress increases the heart rate and force of contraction, raises our blood pressure, diverts blood to skeletal muscles for quick action, stimulates the brain, speeds up our breathing, dilates our pupils, releases adrenalin via the adrenal medulla, constricts surface blood vessels, and releases the body's stores of fat and glucose, all of this in preparation for our body to move into immediate action. In the sympathetic nervous system state, anything that's not immediately needed for survival, including our digestive system, our immune system, our inflammatory responses (how the body heals from damage), and our sexual organs, are essentially shut down.[40]

The problem for those of us living in the current age is that stress is not as simple as choosing fight or flight, then coming back to a restful state. Most stress in our lives is not stress we can just run away from—rather, it is constant in everyday living, and, as the American Psychological Association report on psychological challenges with climate change describes, it is unavoidable when living in an age of environmental challenge. Additionally, at least here in the United States, we have a culture that shows privilege to self-sacrifice and perpetual overwork; this leads to us feeling that we have to keep going and never stop. Stimulants (e.g., sugar, coffee, caffeine, energy drinks) are used heavily, helping us push further (note that caffeine mimics adrenaline in the body, making it highly addictive). We are barraged with constant advertising, social media, and feeling as though we always have to be on. These are all things that put us in a prolonged sympathetic nervous system state.

Prolonged stress responses make the adrenals release the hormone cortisol into the blood, which mobilizes stored glucose and fat, suppresses the inflammatory response, and further taxes the liver. If the body continues to face stress over a prolonged period of time, the body responds with "general adaptation syndrome," moving into a chronically stressed state, with the adrenal glands releasing all the cortisol they can for as long as they can. This leads to severe digestive problems, muscular tension, poor joint health, high blood pressure, various reproductive-system issues, and compromised mental health. Eventually, if this goes on long enough, the body is exhausted and suffers "adrenal burnout" or "adrenal exhaustion." Our bodies cannot go on forever in a sympathetic nervous system state, and at the adrenal burnout stage, we have a severely decreased ability to deal with further stress and mental and physical exhaustion, and a much-higher susceptibility to illness and disease. When we fail to have good coping mechanisms to reduce the stress and get us out of the sympathetic nervous system state, it can directly lead to depression, withdrawal, and exhaustion. Apathy might be another way to describe this state—literally, the lack of feeling or care.

Persistent feelings of being overwhelmed, overworked, and isolated are key signs of a sympathetic nervous system state. Another sign is exhaustion during relaxation—if you are feeling utterly exhausted when you are relaxing or sleeping, you know that your body has been running in sympathetic mode for quite some time and has few reserves. Because so many people have chronic stress and general adaptation syndrome, when they finally do get back to a parasympathetic state, they immediately fall ill and feel exhausted—this is the body feeling the true state of affairs in your body. A person's inner light is dim at this point, flickering, and on the verge of going out—how, then, can it shine outward? How can we then offer healing to the earth or anyone else? Given healing and time, adrenal fatigue can pass, but rebuilding is slow—and we'll talk about some strategies to deal with this in this chapter.

## Cultivating Self-Care Practices for the Body

We live in our bodies each day, and our bodies, too, can benefit from a variety of self-care practices. In this section, we consider the use of healing herbs, movement and physical activity, and movement meditation practices as tools for self-care.

### PLANT ALLIES FOR PHYSICAL HEALING

Working with plant allies is one way to wipe away the mud on our lightbulbs emotionally and help us physically heal from long-term burnout and fatigue. Since much of our nervous stress comes from a disconnection from the living earth, taking plants within and working with them as healing agents allows us reconnection. These healing plants can directly connect with the life-giving energies of the earth and channel them within for healing on a spiritual level; additionally, their biochemical makeup also has direct physical impact on the body. This means that these healing plants can connect to us on all three realms: that of the mind, body, and spirit. Let's look at a few key plant allies that can help aid us in our journey of self-care.[41]

Herbalists recognize three kinds of plants that are tremendously helpful for supporting our nervous systems: nervines (short- and long-acting), relaxants, and adaptogens. Nervines provide immediate relief from immediate stressors of life and include Lemon Balm, Catnip, and Chamomile. Some nervine plants have a "tonic" effect that builds up and, if used over time, provides long-term support and healing of the nervous system. They include Oats, Ginseng, Skullcap, and Astragalus. Relaxant herbs are those that can help shut down our minds and promote deep sleep. They include Valerian, Hops, and Borage. Adaptogens help us adapt to the daily stress of life and provide us with resiliency. They include Ashwagandha, Holy Basil, Ginseng, Schisandra, and Reishi mushroom. These herbs can be prepared and grown yourself or purchased commercially. I would suggest connecting with any healing herb on multiple levels and asking that herb for their help: you are working deeply with the land as a land healer, and asking the land for assistance in return is a reasonable request. You might want to talk to an herbalist as well to develop a combination of herbs that will work best for you.

## MOVEMENT AND BODYWORK

Although we live in our bodies each day, sometimes we do not attend to them well. Yet, our body is our vessel in this life—the physical vessel through which all our healing can flow. Focusing on your own body's state through movement, daily check-ins, and body work can really help bring your self-care into focus. Sit with your body. See how your body feels—are you hurting? Do you feel good? Are you exhausted? Consider what you need to do to help the body heal from its current state and build body awareness in general.

There are many accessible options for body work: gentle yoga and other movement-based approaches, massage, or even dancing all can be forms of self-care practices that help us move our bodies, ground, and center ourselves in our practices.

## MOVEMENT MEDITATION

Another physical practice that can help our physical bodies as well as our spirits and emotions is movement meditation. This is a very simple practice. First, find an outdoor place where you can be at peace: a local park, garden, etc. Labyrinths and labyrinth walks are perfect examples of movement meditation spaces. The space doesn't have to be big, but it does have to be quiet if at all possible.

Take a few deep breaths and, as you do, allow worries and concerns to fall away from your mind. Begin walking. You might choose a specific path or simply walk without any direction. As you walk, breathe naturally and gently. Try to keep your mind clear, allowing yourself to simply "be" in the moment, to take in the scenery, and to experience the world with your senses. Do this for any period of time.

**REST IN NATURE**

Sometimes, all that our physical bodies need is a good rest. Allowing ourselves to rest, to not have to do anything, and to simply be. One of my favorite approaches to this (usually combined with the "sacred day approach" later in this chapter) is to simply take a blanket or a tree hammock into a healed natural place and do some forest bathing. I set up the hammock or lay the blanket down and allow myself to rest as long as I feel the need. Other times, I may first open a sacred space and simply lie in the grove, allowing myself to rest or do some light meditation. This is a simple and yet powerful way to work with nature for healing.

# Cultivating Self-Care Practices for the Mind

While all self-care practices benefit different aspects of ourselves, these self-care practices are specifically targeted toward helping ourselves mentally and emotionally and caring for our minds.

# ENERGETIC HEALING WITH PLANTS

One plant suited to clearing our lightbulbs is the Hawthorn tree, with medicine being made from its leaves, flowers/buds, or berries (and the best medicine being made of all three). Hawthorn is superbly good at working with us on the level of the heart and emotions. It has a way of helping us create space and distance from pain, intensity, and so much that is happening in the world and that we engage with. Hawthorn trees are full of thorns on the trunk and branches, the larger thorns looking like miniature trees themselves! When taken within, those thorns energetically help create space and distance for us. If you step into a Hawthorn and get stabbed by a thorn, all you need to do is to step back—the thorns just establish space. Compare this to Blackberry or Rose, which grabs and clings, and the more you try to get out, the more ensnared and entangled you become! Hawthorn's thorns help protect our heart spaces and allow healing to happen. Hawthorn's medicine helps us clean our lightbulb. Hawthorn can be used in many ways—carrying it in a small bag, placing it in a necklace over the heart, drinking it in daily tinctures or teas of Hawthorn consumed in a sacred manner,[42] and rubbing a Hawthorn-infused oil on the heart and temples are a few possibilities.

Three other strong plant allies for this energetic work of clearing and bringing the light back into your life are Sage, Rosemary, and Lavender. Rosemary is wonderfully clearing. You can carry it with you and eat some or smell some if you need a bit of strength. It helps you get through the day, to get through difficult times, and can be generally used as a pick-me-up. I carry Rosemary needles on my key chain in a tiny wooden box that slides open so they are with me when I need them. Lavender clears the mind and offers us focus. I usually use it for this purpose as a sachet or tea. Sage can be taken as a tea or dried and burned as incense, again to help with that clearing and healing effect. You may also find that other plants than these speak to you—use your instincts and see what plant allies reach out. You might go into an herb garden, or into a local herb store—just feel each of the herbs until you find the right one. However, do look it up in an herbal book before using it, since some herbs such as Black Cohosh or Lobelia are extremely strong and can cause side effects if used incorrectly.

## GRIEF RITUALS: ALLOWING MOURNING AND PROCESSING TO TAKE PLACE

In *Coming to Back to Life: Practices to Reconnect Our Lives*, Joanna Macy and Molly Young Brown suggest that in order to participate in what they call the "great turning," or moving from a destructive society to a life-sustaining one, we must acknowledge and allow our own sadness, grief, and any other emotions to flow. From a physiological perspective, when we cry, the cortisol in our bodies is released through tears. Allowing these emotions to flow through us and not get stuck and bottled up within is an important part of healing. Macy and Brown suggest that emotional healing is best done in group settings, rather than alone, and they offer a number of fantastic suggestions in their book of rituals and group activities to help share, release pent-up emotions, and build awareness of the living earth and her needs. One such simple technique you can do is a grief ritual. When you read something, experience something, or have a particularly intense experience with land healing, give yourself time and space to process it. There are several options for how this ritual might take place. In the first ritual, place a stone or bowl of water in the center of your space, then open up a sacred space. While concentrating on the stone or bowl of water, write or speak exactly how you are feeling. As you write or speak, allow the emotions to flow from you, and envision them being absorbed by the stone or water. When you are finished, thank the stone or water and close out your space. Take the stone or water to a healed place; leave the stone there or pour out the water. A second kind of grief ritual can be done in a group setting, where one or more of you do the same ritual as previously described, but center yourselves around the stone or water. This can be a powerful opportunity for emotional healing and processing.

## CLEANSING BATHS

In some American folk magic traditions, a cleansing bath offers healing and clearing on the mental and spiritual levels. One form of cleansing bath is taking a regular bath, using salt and a few tablespoons of vinegar. The other option that works well is to brew up a strong herbal tea (one of my favorite blends is rosemary, sage, and lavender) and add it to the bath. Or you can just throw a sachet of herbs right into the bath. Light some candles and relax. My method for this kind of magical practice is to wash everything off my body and then to sit in the tub as the water drains, imaging that any of the negative gunk that's on me or in me is being pulled out and sent harmlessly down the drain. As I leave the empty tub, I feel clean, whole, and pure. As part of your cleansing bath, consider a healing or purifying drink (an herbal tea, for instance); peppermint-sage tea is a good purifying drink. Use a fresh towel and put on only fresh, clean clothing to avoid picking up any old energies. Jewelry that is worn frequently can also be washed or cleaned at this time.

# MEDITATION

Meditation is one of the best kinds of self-care practices. So many of us live very busy lives, and our brains try to keep up. Meditation gives the mind its own special time to rest and find quietude. Regular meditation does many things, depending on the kind of meditation that you practice: it can help sharpen the mind, it can help clear and ground, and it can help us rest and relax (moving into the parasympathetic nervous system state). Scientific research is now finding evidence for the positive effects of meditation on mental, emotional, and physical health (unsurprising, but reassuring). Simple meditative practices such as the ones that follow can help clear the mind quickly and effectively.

## FOURFOLD BREATH

One of the simplest meditations you can do is called the fourfold breath (this is another practice spiraling out of the AODA druid tradition). After you've settled yourself comfortably in a chair or are lying on the ground, you focus on your breathing. Breathe in to the count of four, hold your breath slightly for the count of four (don't close up your throat entirely; just lightly hold in the breath gently), breathe out for the count of four, and, finally, pause to the count of four. After several rounds, you will find that you will have the pattern of fourfold breath easily enough, and you can do it without counting. This simple exercise helps bring you into the present moment and calm the mind.

## CANDLE MEDIATION

Another technique allowing for quietude and decluttering is a candle meditation. Light a single candle and put it before you—preferably in a comfortable place where you can easily look at it without straining the neck (such as sitting on the floor and having the candle on a small stand at eye level). Use the fourfold breath to find your breathing pattern, then stare at the candle, paying attention only to it. Allow your mind to quiet. Sometimes it's helpful to count slowly to yourself each in breath and out breath as you observe the candle. Even ten breaths in this direction can help you achieve peace and calm you otherwise wouldn't have.

## DISCURSIVE MEDITATION

Discursive meditation can be used effectively to help deal with mental clutter. I have found that discursive meditation can be used to address mental "stuff" that I was holding on to. Discursive meditation is a type of focused thought, where you choose a theme and then explore that theme through meditation, similar to if you were walking on a path through the forest. If you find yourself "off topic," simply retrace your mental steps until you are back on your original path.

For example, as a self-care practice, I would first work to identify the issue at hand that I wanted to explore (one issue at a time). For example, I had feelings of isolation even though I was in a big group. Then, I'd use a series of discursive-meditation practices to focus on those feelings—where did the feelings of isolation come from? Why was I holding on to them? What would my life look like without that unwanted feeling? What did "isolation" even mean to me? Then, if necessary, I would use ritual to let go of those feelings (a simple ritual, such as imbuing a stone with the unwanted feelings and throwing it in moving water or a shore, can work well for this). A series of these discursive-meditation practices really helped me eliminate some of the more problematic clutter I had accumulated over time.

## ELIMINATING MENTAL STAGNATION

In traditional Western herbalism, we recognize that stagnation causes the body tremendous long-term harm. The same is true of our minds; mental stagnation is when things are simply not moving within us or when we are stuck in our own heads. I'm sure you've felt it—when you just feel "blah," when you are uninspired, unmotivated, and unmoving. Sometimes, this is due to adrenal burnout and the body's need to rest, but sometimes it is due to other circumstances, such as the continued experience of everyday life.

Several approaches can help you eliminate mental stagnation. One approach to addressing mental stagnation is to get out to somewhere new. Brain research shows that people learn and create best when they are exposed to new scenery. Traveling to new natural areas, visiting sacred places, and taking a walk around town all are helpful practices. Sometimes blockage can happen because we are wound up too tight: we have such high expectations for ourselves and expect everything we do to be perfect. One of the things I like to do for myself and others is what I call an "ugly" painting day. This is when we go out into the yard with some cheap paints and pieces of board, old canvas shoes, or whatever, and just fling some paint around! It's great fun and helps people return to their creative spirit. You can also do this with finger paints. Other appropriate ways of letting loose include loudly singing your favorite songs, dancing wildly with no one watching (or with good friends), or playing in mud puddles or the rain.

Taking even five or ten minutes per day to write your thoughts down is another way to care for yourself. As a learning researcher, I have seen firsthand the value of reflective activity on the long-term development and well-being of individuals. Even short reflections, such as writing a daily journal entry, can help us process what we've learned, reflect on it, and move forward with deeper integration and enthusiasm.[43] For more information on journaling practices to support self-care and healing, please see *The Sacred Actions Journal* (REDFeather, 2022).

# Cultivating Self-Care Practices for the Spirit

While many of the previously discussed practices have been spiritual in nature, the following practices focus on our spirituality and using that to help us heal and recover.

## FINDING A SOLID FOUNDATION ROOTED IN THE LIVING EARTH

In our world, sometimes it appears that nothing has a solid foundation—friendships, workplaces, political systems, national politics, climate, etc. However, for those engaged in Earth-based spiritual practices, we do have a foundation, and that foundation is our connection to the living earth. One of the best ways to relieve stress and anxiety is remembering that connection and finding our grounding and stability within that connection, even when everything else is out of control. For this practice, it is necessary to connect with a regenerated or healed place: a place where the energy of the land is strong and vitalizing. Go to that place and sit or lie on the earth. Feel the Earth's energy coming up into you, blessing you, healing you, and bringing forth vitality and strength. Allow yourself to bask in this energy as long as you need, resting and relaxing. When you leave, offer this landscape thanks and, with permission, take a small stone, stick, or other object with you. Return when you can, and when you cannot, connect with the object.

## TAKE QUIET MOMENTS WITH PLANTS

Another basic self-care strategy is simply to find some quiet moments to sit with plants. Perhaps these are the same healing plants that are providing your physical or emotional body with support (*see above*), or perhaps these are other plants. Taking quiet moments with plants helps us in two ways: these moments rebuild the ancient bonds between humans and nature, and these moments help us slow down and breathe deeply. A quiet moment with a plant might be sitting with a steaming cup of tea next to a tree, watching the sunrise. It might be sitting in a field of daisies, sitting with the dandelion in a sidewalk, or sitting with a houseplant friend. Even five minutes a day can have meaningful results. I like to take my quiet moments with plants in my gardens—sometimes I'll take a blanket and just lie among my vegetables, or I'll sit with a particular healing herb that I want to develop a deeper relationship with. I might take a blanket and lie in a park and study the bees on the clover, take a sleeping bag out on a cool night and lie under the trees and stars, or sit with the grass that grows up in the crack in the pavement. If you've worked to regenerate or tend physical spaces (chapter 7), these are wonderful places for this work.

## EXCHANGING ENERGY WITH TREES

Energy exchange with trees is another wonderful practice for self-care. Many different druid traditions work with trees in various ways, but one of the most healthful practices you can do with trees is simply sitting with them and exchanging energy. Just as trees and humans form symbiotic relationships with our breath and our waste, so too can we have a similar energetic exchange. Finding the right tree to work with is an important part of this process. You might go up to a tree and use your intuition—does it feel welcoming? Does it invite you in, or do you get the sense that you are not welcome? Once you find the right tree, then the process is quite simple. In *The Celtic Golden Dawn*, John Michael Greer shares insights on a simple tree working based on your needs and connecting with a tree with your body. Since the back of the body is dominated by the central nervous system, those with nervous tension (too much nervous energy or inability to relax) are benefited most by putting their back to the tree. Those who have the opposite problem, those who feel passivity, sluggishness, or burned out, benefit more from putting their front of their body to the tree.

## CULTIVATE A CREATIVE PRACTICE

Another critical self-care practice is cultivating a creative practice. In the druid tradition, we call these the "bardic arts"; these are any of the things we create with our hands, bodies, voices, or minds. When our lightbulbs are dim, the bardic arts can flow through us, healing us, rejuvenating us, and blessing those around us.

In my research[44] on the bardic arts, many of my participants found incredible joy, peace, and self-care through their practices. The bardic arts to them were like breathing; they helped them navigate an increasingly difficult world, process difficult experiences, and create inner peace. The practice of creating something, through words, performance, dance, or one's hands, was what was important for this healing process. Participants were less concerned with how "good" the result itself was, which means that even a beginner could gain much spiritual benefit from engaging in creative practice.

# Sacred Days and Self-Care Retreats

This final section will look at cultivating larger-scale practice, including developing sacred days and creating a spiritual self-care retreat.

## SACRED DAYS OF REST AND REJUVENATION

One of my long-term personal self-care strategies has involved the "wheel of the year" holidays. I arrange to have a day or part of a day, somewhere as close to the eight holidays as possible, entirely to myself. These are the cornerstones of my own long-term self-care strategy. It's on these days that I dedicate time to my creative practices, spend time doing ritual and meditation, and spend time in nature. In other words, I do all the things that fulfill me, rejuvenate me, and make me whole. I turn off electronic devices on these days, let friends/ family know that I am unavailable, arrange pet sitters, and do whatever else I need to ensure that I have my sacred day. These are simply days for me to be with me, not my computer or phone or anything else. It has been hard at points over the years to take these days among work obligations, relationships, family demands, and more, but I work to make it happen.

If you plan on using this technique, I suggest keeping your day or hours you have set aside as "unstructured." That is, rather than packing them full of specific plans of what you want to do, just allow yourself to do whatever it is you want to do in the moment—including nothing at all. Many of the other practices detailed earlier in this chapter, likewise, may be used as part of your sacred day.

## THE HEALING RETREAT

The principle of a retreat is simple: you get away from your everyday life (your home, your family, your work, your other demands) for a period of refreshment, rejuvenation, and seclusion (alone or with select others; see below). Where to take this retreat is a critical thing: I have learned that it's nearly impossible to do this retreat in your everyday living space, because people/pets, stuff, and *patterns* have a way of creeping in. Your home puts particular kinds of demands upon you. For example, your computer is there, beckoning for you to turn it on. Your bathroom is there, in need of a good scrubbing. Your phone is there. Everyone is there: your pets, family, and perhaps kids. These things are necessary, perhaps, and part of your daily rhythms. But they work against us when we need to go on a retreat, because they pull us back into the experiences of everyday living. Likewise, the patterns of everyday living that we establish are critical for our overall "getting things done" and forward momentum, and our spaces are conducive to supporting and encouraging those patterns. Sometimes, we can get stuck in cyclical patterns, especially cyclical patterns associated with being in indoor spaces that harm us. Retreat allows us to detoxify and heal our spirits, emotions, and bodies.

Where to take this retreat is a critical thing: go somewhere you can have peace. This might mean pitching a tent in the woods or taking a camper somewhere, renting a small cabin for a few nights (the absolute best in the winter months), or staying at a friend's secluded and uninhabited guesthouse for a day or two. The important thing is that the healing retreat be secluded, preferably away from other people, certainly away from life's demands. Preferably, it will have no internet service, no cell service, and no television. If you are in good health and have the gear, the cheapest way to do this is to backpack into the woods, get off a path (but know how to get back on it), and pitch a tent for a few days.

I have done healing retreats with others and by myself, and there are benefits to both. A healing retreat with others is as much about strengthening bonds of friendship or love as it is about healing yourself. With that said, there is room for others on this retreat if they are the right kind of others, those who will help heal and rejuvenate rather than drain you. If you are going to take a friend on a healing retreat, make sure you establish in advance what the retreat will be about (for example, making sure each person has a set number of quiet hours a day).

Take at least twenty-four uninterrupted hours for your retreat, although two- or three-day retreats are even better. I would suggest cooking in advance for the retreat or purchasing food you can easily heat up, unless cooking is a particularly healing and nurturing activity for you. Then you can focus your energies only on the retreat and not worry about feeding yourself during it (assuming you are eating; see below).

## HOW TO SET UP THE SACRED SPACE FOR YOUR RETREAT

Setting up the sacred space for healing as part of your retreat is also an important step. For my retreats, I like to set my intentions and open a sacred space. You can use the sacred-space opening shared in chapter 3, or use the following suggestions:

- Start by stating your intention for the retreat: personal healing, rejuvenation, etc.

- Purify yourself with the elements. A simple way of doing this is to have a bowl of incense or a feather, a candle, some clean water, and a bowl of salt or soil from the Earth. For each of the elements, move the bowl of the element around your body, envisioning the element clearing away the unwanted energy. You can also choose to do this just with a smoke-clearing stick, drawing on air and fire.

- Call upon the four directions and four elements for their guidance.

- Place a sphere of protection around the space for the retreat.

## WHAT TO DO ON YOUR RETREAT?

It is generally better if you go into a healing retreat without much of an agenda; that way, you can simply see what flows forth. At the same time, especially for people new to retreat, you might want to include some activities and simple structure if you need them. Any of the following are good retreat activities: rest, reflect, cry, laugh, create, write, read, dance, sleep, nap, do rituals (especially healing rituals, such as cleansing baths), etc. One critical thing to do is to simply be present with yourself: lie by the fire or out in the snow or in the woods, and simply be there for a time. We spend so much time darting from place to place, putting out fire after fire, that we don't just get to sit and collect our thoughts. Spend time in nature simply sitting and observing. If you sit for long enough, wildlife will come around, and you might be offered some powerful signs. Wildlife is most active at dawn and dusk, so finding a spot to sit during those times, in particular, might yield great results.

## TRANSITIONING OUT

As you are nearing the end of your retreat, take some time to write down the insights and conclusions you gained. Maybe that's a set of spiritual practices, maybe that's something you need to do for yourself, maybe it's an actionable list of items. Or maybe it is none of these things, but a sense of tranquility and calm, of completeness. Whatever it is, you want to do your best to preserve that mindset—that state—those feelings and words. I usually give myself at least two or three hours for this kind of work. I am a visual artist and an avid writer, so I will usually do something visual to represent my retreat and also write extensively in my journal. These tactile experiences help start bringing me back into my normal rhythms. Additionally, I always make it a point to express gratitude for the space that I am in, the spirits of land and of place, that have been with me on the journey.

Be careful about how you transition back into your everyday living. Recognize that transitioning back into daily living can be a shocking and intense experience. If at all possible, give yourself some time after you return home to transition back slowly (it is not a good idea, for example, to try to go to work the day after your retreat if you can avoid it).

Finally, recognize that your retreat will continue well beyond the time that you were physically in retreat. Think about the retreat like a rock being thrown into a still pond: the ripples will continue outward for some time. That is, you will continue to gain the benefits of your retreat. Because of this, you may not want to share everything that happened or the wisdom that you gained; sit with it for a time (at least seven days) and allow yourself to process it before offering that energy to anyone else.

# CONCLUSION

**Self-care is a critical part of the larger land-healing work** that we seek to do in the world. If we care for ourselves, we are in a much-better position to do the necessary and sacred action in the world. The key to self-care seems to be getting beyond the cultural challenges surrounding it: fighting against the workaholic culture, allowing oneself to take time off, honoring one's body, and making one's self and one's creative expressions a priority. While this usually is an extended process, it can be a tremendously positive change in the long run. As within, so without.

# *Afterword:*

# A VISION OF A HEALED WORLD

**When I first stepped onto our land in western Pennsylvania**, looking to purchase it, everything seemed perfect. A roof ready for solar, sunny locations for gardening, an old chicken coop ready to be refurbished, a spring-fed stream that provided the house with water and filled a small pond. The house itself was just the right size, a cozy secluded cabin. But when I walked into the woods, my heart was pained. The owners had logged 3 acres of it, leaving behind a hurtful scene. The loggers hadn't only taken down massive trees; they had literally plowed brush into large piles, scraping the forest floor. As I walked on the land, I asked the spirits, "Why?" Why do I keep being drawn to places like this one? My previous land had a similar issue, with a large, logged area that I had to work to heal. I knew this was home for us, but still, it was difficult to walk the land beyond the house and gardens. For the first two years after we moved there, I was overwhelmed with the amount of debris. I was saddened that this would happen, that this destruction would take place, especially just for money.

But then, I started paying attention. First, it was the fungi on the stumps. Many different shelf mushrooms greeted me, including the highly medicinal Turkey Tail mushroom. Mosses and ferns grew forth. I saw the fungi and bugs begin to do their good work and break the many branches down. We designated some areas that we wanted to turn into spaces to practice traditional earth skills and nature spirituality, and our grove and friends came to help us—to clear, to build, to honor. Firewood was hauled off, *hügelkultur* beds with old logs were made, and the land took new shape. As I write this, we are in the process of starting our most ambitious endeavor to date—building an outdoor kitchen and campout area. As we clear, we honor all of those that fell. A grove of Witch Hazels, which has always been a tree that symbolizes a light in the darkness, and the future hope I have for humanity to return to nature, hold sacred space for us there, a new potential grove of renewal. As we engage with this space, we learn so much about healing the land, physical regeneration, but also the power of human hands. This area will eventually be a food forest, a nutrient-rich place where we have orchards and vines and build habitat, ecological diversity, and resiliency.

As I was working on this space, clearing logs and brush and piling it up to turn into *hügelkultur* beds, I was struck with awe. Out of a stump, beautiful mushrooms grew. A pileated woodpecker called in the morning sun. I found a Cucumber Magnolia tree that had been knocked over had sent up four trunks, even stronger than before.

Human hands can certainly destroy, and quite massively when fossil fuels and technology are applied. But those same hands are more effective when they are healing. When we heal the land, we heal within and without. In the words of my favorite author, Wendell Berry, when we can stand on a ruined place, enriching it, healing it—that's how we change this world. That's how we improve things in our lifetime, and that's how we become good ancestors to those who come after us. This is how we live a legacy that focuses on life and earth honoring, and turn the tides so we can envision and enact a brighter future for all life. This is how we can take up our traditional role as caretakers of the land and re-align ourselves with all other life on this planet.

If you are interested in talking about this work and sharing your experiences, please join the Land Healers' Network. More information can be found at www.thedruidsgarden.com/landhealing

# SUGGESTED READING

## UNDERSTANDING TRADITIONAL CARETAKING RELATIONSHIPS WITH NATURE

Anderson, Kat. *Tending the Wild: Native American Knowledge and the Management of California's Natural Resources*. Berkeley: University of California Press, 2005.

Berry, Wendell. *The Unsettling of America: Culture & Agriculture*. Berkeley, CA: Counterpoint, 2015.

Kimmerer, Robin. *Braiding Sweetgrass: Indigenous Wisdom, Scientific Knowledge, and the Teachings of Plants*. Minneapolis: Milkweed Editions, 2013.

Yunkaporta, Tyson. *Sand Talk: How Indigenous Thinking Can Save the World*. Melbourne, Australia: Text, 2019.

## MAGICAL THEORY

Fries, Jan. *Visual Magic: A Practical Guide to Trance, Sigils, and Visualization Techniques*. Oxford: Mandrake, 2007.

Greer, John Michael. *Circles of Power: Ritual Magic in the Western Tradition*. St. Paul, MN: Llewellyn Worldwide, 1997.

Greer, John Michael. *The Druid Magic Handbook: Ritual Magic Rooted in the Living Earth*. San Francisco: Weiser Books, 2008.

Pennick, Nigel, and Paul Devereux. *Lines on the Landscape: Leys and Other Linear Enigmas*. London: Robert Hale, 1989.

Stewart, R. J. *Earth Light: The Ancient Path to Transformation: Rediscovering the Wisdom of Celtic and Fairy Lore*. London: Element Books, 1992.

Wachter, Aidan. *Six Ways: Approaches and Entries for Practical Magic*. Red Temple Press, 2018.

### PHYSICAL LAND REGENERATION

Cotter, Tradd. *Organic Mushroom Farming and Mycoremediation: Simple to Advanced and Experimental Techniques for Indoor and Outdoor Cultivation*. White River Junction, VT: Chelsea Green, 2014.

Fukuoka, Masanobu. *The One-Straw Revolution: An Introduction to Natural Farming*. New York: New York Review of Books, 2009.

Hemenway, Toby. *Gaia's Garden: A Guide to Home-Scale Permaculture*. White River Junction, VT: Chelsea Green, 2009.

Jacke, Dave, and Eric Toensmeier. *Edible Forest Gardens*. Vols. 1 and 2. White River Junction, VT: Chelsea Green, 2005.

### SELF-CARE PRACTICES

Winston, David. *Adaptogens: Herbs for Strength, Stamina, and Stress Relief*. New York: Simon and Schuster, 2019.

Hoffmann, David. *An Herbal Guide to Stress Relief: Gentle Remedies and Techniques for Healing and Calming the Nervous System*. Rochester, VT: Inner Traditions, 1991.

### FOSTERING HOPE AND CHANGE IN THE FUTURE

Macy, Joanna, and Molly Young Brown. *Coming Back to Life: The Guide to the Work That Reconnects*. Gabriola Island, BC: New Society, 2014.

Macy, Joanna, and Chris Johnstone. *Active Hope: How to Face the Mess We're in with Unexpected Resilience and Creative Power*. Rev. ed. Novato, CA: New World Library, 2022.

# ENDNOTES

1. Wendell Berry, *The Unsettling of America: Culture & Agriculture* (Berkeley, CA: Counterpoint, 2015).
2. Damian Carrington, "Earth's Sixth Mass Extinction Event Underway, Scientists Warn," *The Guardian*, July 10, 2017, https://www.theguardian.com/environment/2017/jul/10/earths-sixth-mass-extinction-event-already-underway-scientists-warn.
3. Gerardo Ceballos, Paul R. Ehrlich, and Rodolfo Dirzo, "Biological Annihilation via the Ongoing Sixth Mass Extinction Signaled by Vertebrate Population Losses and Declines," *Proceedings of the National Academy of Sciences* 114, no. 30 (2017): E6089–E6096.
4. Caspar A. Hallmann, Martin Sorg, Eelke Jongejans, Henk Siepel, Nick Hofland, Heinz Schwan, Werner Stenmans, et al., "More Than 75 Percent Decline over 27 Years in Total Flying Insect Biomass in Protected Areas," *PloS One* 12, no. 10 (2017): e0185809.
5. For a discussion of what magic is and why it works, I suggest John Michael Greer's *Druid Magic Handbook* and *Inside a Magical Lodge*, which are sound introductions to magical philosophy. I also recommend Aidan Wachter's, *Six Ways: Approaches and Entries for Practical Magic* which offers a thorough introduction to magic from an animistic and spirit-based perspective that is highly compatible with what I am presenting here. You don't need these magical theories, but I find that they are very helpful for deepening your own understanding.
6. This information was freely available through my Pennsylvania state extension office. Anyone living in the US will have a state extension office, and they will offer many free publications and materials on a wide variety of natural topics. Other countries often have similar offices focused on conservation and public education on natural resources. Field guides and other books on natural ecology will also be useful.
7. Jeffrey Gantz, *Early Irish Myths and Sagas*, vol. 20 (Harmondsworth, UK: Penguin UK, 1981).

8. For much more of this deep-listening work and plant spirit work, see my publication *The Plant Spirit Oracle: Recipes, Meanings, and Journeys*, published by Druid's Garden (www.thedruidsgarden.com).

9. The website www.findaspring.com is a very useful resource.

10. Masanobu Fukuoka, *The One-Straw Revolution: An Introduction to Natural Farming* (New York: New York Review of Books, 2010).

11. Because this book is geared toward more-advanced practitioners, it is assumed that you have some knowledge of inner communication techniques, and thus my treatment of them is brief here. I offer more-in-depth techniques on plant spirit communication in *The Plant Spirit Oracle: Meanings, Recipes, and Journeys.*

12. Bernie Krause, *The Great Animal Orchestra: Finding the Origins of Music in the World's Wild Places* (New York: Little, Brown, 2012).

13. This was a difficult yet critical lesson for me to learn as a land healer. If you carry guilt that is not yours, this can interfere with what you are doing energetically. When lands are suffering, bringing joy and peace into a situation is really important. You cannot bring this joy if you are overwhelmed with sadness and guilt.

14. Cecil Sharp, *The Crystal Spring: English Folk Songs* (Oxford: Oxford University Press, 1975).

15. For this, I'm drawing upon material from the Druid Revival, specifically theories present in the Ancient Order of Druids in America (AODA), with some additions of my own insights and experiences. And although the names and specific principles I'm presenting here are rooted in the Druid Revival, the concepts go much further back—in the final chapter of Pennick and Devereux's *Lines upon the Landscape*, the ways that ancient peoples drew upon the three currents in connection to ancient sites globally are detailed. Specifically, the solar current was often worked and radiated outward through buildings, structures, ley lines, and royalty. In terms of source material for this section, a great source for more information on the three currents can be found John Michael Greer's *The Druidry Handbook* and *Druid Magic Handbook.*

16. William F. Ruddiman, ed., *Tectonic Uplift and Climate Change* (New York: Springer Science & Business Media, 2013).

17. Jeff Lowenfels and Wayne Lewis, *Teaming with Microbes* (New York: Workman, 2010).

18. Fathi Habashi, "Zoroaster and the Theory of Four Elements," *Bulletin for the History of Chemistry* 25, no. 2 (2000): 109–15.

19. John MacNeill, "Notes on the Distribution, History, Grammar, and Import of the Irish Ogham Inscriptions," *Proceedings of the Royal Irish Academy. Section C: Archaeology, Celtic Studies, History, Linguistics, Literature* 27 (1908): 329–70.

20. Pronunciations for ogham vary widely, on the basis of specific dialect. These are based on the pronunciations given by Erynn Rowan Laurie (https://www.seanet.com/~inisglas/).

21. Carl Gustav Jung, *Mandala Symbolism* (from Vol. 9i Collected Works), vol. 42 (Princeton, NJ: Princeton University Press, 2017).

22. For more on how to make sustainable shifts as part of nature spiritual practice, see my book *Sacred Actions: Living the Wheel of the Year through Earth-Centered Sustainable Practice* (Atglen, PA: REDFeather, 2021).

23. In the last decade and with increasing frequency, some traditions and practitioners have decided to work using black magic to influence changes in leadership or leader's perspectives; that is, they are using magic to try to influence and change others' behaviors without their permission or consent. I wholeheartedly reject that approach and believe that it will cause more harm than good. While land healers contend with much in the way of darkness (as is evident in the work of palliative care, of helping spirits pass, and of working with damaged sites), this work should never include trying to unduly influence others magically. And thus, you will not find any such work in this book, and this is why we always start with deep listening. Prayers and putting forth positive energy are appropriate.

24. For more on this concept, I suggest either John Michael Greer's *Inside a Magical Lodge* or Mark Stavish's *Egregores: The Occult Entities That Watch Over Human Destiny*.

25. I am thankful to my friend Elmdea Adams (http://www.elmdeaadams.com/) for sharing the vision board technique with me.

26. The idea of growth at all costs and progress at all costs is the driving narrative of our age. You see this a lot with the clash between conservation of wild places and the desire for profit. Unfortunately, today, profit often wins. For more on this topic, see John Michael Greer's *Not the Future We Ordered: Peak Oil, Psychology, and the Myth of Progress*.

27. My oracle deck and book, *The Plant Spirit Oracle*, offers a number of herbal allies and methods for establishing plant spirit allies and working with plant spirits. Visit www.thedruidsgarden.com for more information.

28. If you boil water, you can be certain that there is nothing microscopic that could damage the waterway that you are offering the sacred water to. Without this step, you might inadvertently introduce new pathogens or issues to the waterway.

29. M. Kat Anderson, *Tending the Wild: Native American Knowledge and the Management of California's Natural Resources* (Berkeley: University of California Press, 2013).

30. John Andrew Eastman, *The Book of Field and Roadside: Open-Country Weeds, Trees, and Wildflowers of Eastern North America* (Mechanicsburg,

PA: Stackpole Books, 2003); John Andrew Eastman, *The Book of Swamp and Bog: Trees, Shrubs, and Wildflowers of the Eastern Freshwater Wetlands* (Mechanicsburg, PA: Stackpole Books, 1995); and John Andrew Eastman, *The Book of Forest and Thicket: Trees, Shrubs, and Wildflowers of Eastern North America* (Mechanicsburg, PA: Stackpole Books, 1992).

31. Chris Arsenalt, "Only 60 Years of Farming Left If Soil Degradation Continues," *Scientific American*, December 5, 2014, https://www.scientificamerican.com/article/only-60-years-of-farming-left-if-soil-degradation-continues/.

32. Simon Dalby, "Biopolitics and Climate Security in the Anthropocene," *Geoforum* 49 (2013): 184–92; and Tomaz Mastnak, Julia Elyachar, and Tom Boellstorff, "Botanical Decolonization: Rethinking Native Plants," *Environment and Planning D: Society and Space* 32, no. 2 (2014): 363–80.

33. James Howard Kunstler, *Geography of Nowhere: The Rise and Decline of America's Man-Made Landscape* (New York: Simon and Schuster, 1994).

34. I recommend checking out any number of permaculture design books or my chapter on sacred gardening in *Sacred Actions: Living the Wheel of the Year through Sustainable Practices* (Atglen, PA: REDFeather, 2021).

35. Evelyn C. Pielou, *After the Ice Age: The Return of Life to Glaciated North America* (Chicago: University of Chicago Press, 2008).

36. I say this with a caveat. A lot of wild animals that I have held space for have had distemper. For these animals, I keep my distance and then bury them several feet down and place rocks over them so the disease does not spread. The burial itself returns them to nature.

37. "Mental Health and Our Changing Climate: Impacts, Implications, and Guidance," American Psychological Association, Climate for Health & ecoAmerica, March 2017, https://www.apa.org/news/press/releases/2017/03/mental-health-climate.pdf.

38. I was given the lightbulb teaching by Michigan folk herbalist Jim McDonald. Jim has deep wisdom and a sacred connection to plants, and his work and classes can be found at www.herbcraft.org.

39. This teaching was conveyed during Jim McDonald's Lindera Herbal Intensive course, of which I was a student in 2014. See www.herbcraft.org.

40. For more on physiological stress, see Pip Waller, *Holistic Anatomy: An Integrated Guide to the Human Body.*

41. For those interested more in healing herbs, the following books are recommended: David Winston and Steven Maimes, *Adaptogens: Herbs for Strength, Stamina, and Stress Relief*; Rosemary Gladstar, *Herbs for Stress and Anxiety*; and David Hoffman, *An Herbal Guide to Stress Relief.* Material for this section came from Jim McDonald's Four-Season Lindera Herbal Intensive Course.

42. Hawthorn is contraindicated for those on heart medications (but feel free to still carry it on your person!)

43. For more on sacred journaling, see my book *The Sacred Actions Journal* (Atglen, PA: REDFeather, 2022).

44. This research was conducted for the Order of Bards, Ovates and Druids' Mount Haemus scholarship series. Dana Driscoll, "Channeling the Awen Within: An Exploration of Learning the Bardic Arts in the Modern Druid Tradition," Order of Bards, Ovates, and Druids, 2018, https://www.druidry.org/events-projects/mount-haemus-award/nineteenth-mount-haemus-lecture.

# Dana O'Driscoll

has been an animist druid for over 15 years and currently serves as Grand Archdruid in the Ancient Order of Druids in America. She is a druid-grade member of the Order of Bards, Ovates, and Druids and is OBOD's 2018 Mount Haemus Scholar. Dana took up the path of land healing because of the deep need in her home region of western Pennsylvania, which is challenged by fracking, acid mine drainage into streams, logging, and mountaintop removal. Dana is a certified permaculture designer and permaculture teacher who teaches sustainable living and wild-food foraging. She lives on a 5-acre homestead with her partner and a host of feathered and furred friends.

She writes at the *Druids Garden* blog and is on Instagram as @druidsgardenart.